FAST AND FLAVORFUL

FAST AND FLAVORFUL

New Food Processor Recipes

VOLUME I

by Abby Mandel

Cuisinart Cooking Club, Inc.
Greenwich, Connecticut

Editor:
Ruth S. McElheny
Art Director:
Christine Goulet
Designer:
Leslie Grann
Photographer:
Jeffrey Weir
Food Stylists:
Michael
di Beneditto,
Marjorie Foster

Library of Congress
Cataloging-in-
Publication Data

Mandel, Abby.
Fast and Flavorful.
Includes index.
1. Food Processor
cookery.
I. McElheny, Ruth S.
II. Cuisinart
Cooking Club.
III. Title
TX840.F6M36
1985   641.5'89
85-20925
ISBN 0-93662-09-3
(pbk.:set)

To my husband,
John Friend,
who is indeed the
best friend I could
ever hope to have.

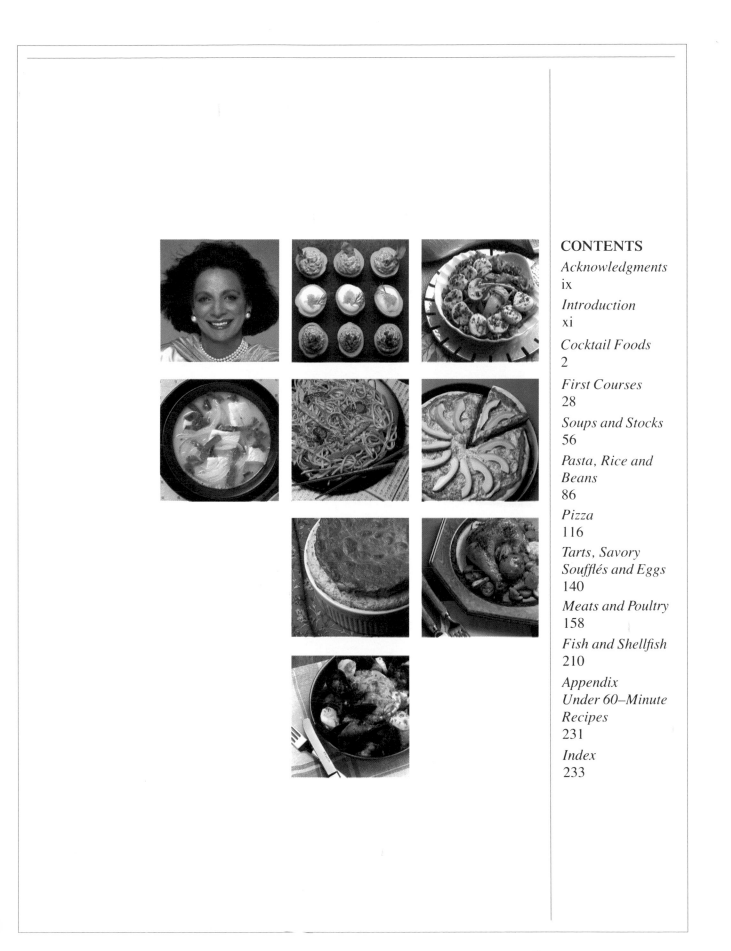

CONTENTS

With deepest appreciation to my associates and good friends: Patricia Dailey, who has worked with me on this book for four and a half years, and Elizabeth Krier, who has been with us this last year. We all share a love of cooking and a commitment to detail.

And special thanks to my editor, Ruth McElheny, for her significant contribution to our second book together, and to Leslie Grann, who is responsible for the beautiful design of this book.

**ACKNOWL-
EDGMENTS**

SKREBNESKI

My instant and unswerving devotion to the food processor almost makes me believe in love at first sight. Thirteen years ago I installed this prodigy in my kitchen, plugged it in and proceeded to make a pizza. It's hardly an overstatement to say that my life hasn't been the same since then. Right beside me in the kitchen is the solution to many of my cooking problems. An uncomplaining work-horse sits on the counter, ready to take on all the humdrum tasks that I don't enjoy.

My interest in cooking began at an early age. Food always fascinated me, and I was drawn to the kitchen where I could revel in its satisfying tastes, textures and aromas. The kitchen was my mother's domain, of course, and I had to follow her rules. Not one bowl left dirty, not a knife out of place, not a speck of flour on the counter. A bit of a problem for an enthusiastic ten-year old! My interest was in cooking and eating, not in cleaning up. So I invented games, to make everything easier and quicker, and to use fewer pans, bowls and spoons. I always looked for shortcuts then and I still do, even when the kitchen is my own.

Imagine my excitement when I discovered the food processor. A new partnership began. Everything I cooked was easier and quicker. I could tackle recipes that I once dismissed as too difficult or time-consuming. The processor brought new skills, new control and a new zest for cooking. Most unexpectedly, it brought a new career. My enthusiasm was so strong that I began to teach, concentrating on a food processor approach. Soon I was writing a cookbook about how to use the food processor as an essential cooking tool. One book led to another and ultimately to this, the most comprehensive I've attempted.

People have asked me, why another food processor cookbook. The answer is that I continue to think "food processor" as I cook and develop new recipes. My enthusiasm for the machine hasn't waned, but increased. I'm convinced that a food processor is indispensable in a functional and well organized kitchen. It makes fast cooking with fresh ingredients so easy that I honestly can't conceive of being without it. Whether I'm eating in restaurants, looking at photographs of food, or reading recipes, I automatically think about how the food processor could uncomplicate the preparation of every dish. So many preparations are streamlined by a food processor. Not to use it is like taking a bus when you could fly.

The underlying philosophy of my cooking is evident throughout this book. The recipes run the gamut from simple, everyday fare to more elaborate and difficult preparations. Cooking for everyday is different from cooking for entertaining, but both have the same purpose. To provide healthy food that tastes good. A concern for health dominates our food choices. Is the food fresh? What are its components, and are they healthy? Is it prepared in a way that doesn't use excess fat and salt? For everyday meals, we look for uncomplicated recipes that accommodate these preferences. And when we cook for friends, we want our food to reflect these concerns as well as to express our own style. We want food that tastes good, that isn't contrived, and that isn't too time-consuming. I've tried to respond to these needs with the recipes in this book.

To help me understand the needs of contemporary cooks, I function as both student and teacher. I learn as I teach and I teach as I learn. Once or twice a year, I work in restaurant kitchens in Europe and the United States. Restaurant chefs are invariably generous and good-natured. Many seem born to teach. They share their recipes, demonstrate their techniques, and bear with me as I badger them with questions. It's like attending an intensive seminar while sampling the restaurant's entire menu. I perform every task assigned to me. At the Crillon in Paris, that meant cleaning and cooking 30 pounds of artichokes. If it sounds like drudgery, it wasn't. How else would I have learned that artichoke bottoms cook to just the right texture if you remove all the leaves before boiling them? That a swivel-bladed vegetable peeler is the best tool for smoothing rough edges, to make a perfect presentation? That artichoke bottoms can be cooked a day or two in advance and refrigerated in their cooking liquid? And — that 30 pounds is a lot of artichokes!

In other kitchens, I've filleted fish, made stock and rolled puff pastry. All these assignments taught valuable lessons. I document the lessons on the spot with scribbles in notebooks, and photographs — hands doing an intricate job, the critical stages of preparation, and finally the finished dish. Transcribed to microcassettes, my notes go on about everything from the size of the kitchen, the type of utensil used, the amount of time spent on a preparation, to the size and design of the china.

Back in my own kitchen, I sift through this mountain of information to extract the essence that will be useful to me and home cooks. The recipes and techniques, both classical and innovative, are a wonderful resource. Each idea generates others, which improve all my cooking — leading to simplified procedures and perfected flavors.

In my teaching role, I write magazine articles and newspaper columns as well as teach classes. This gives me access to cooks at all levels, from novice to professional. In the course of teaching them, I learn — from their questions, conversations and letters. I find out what my students like to cook, what's practical and what's not, what's easy and what's not worth the effort. All this data comes to the kitchen with me every time I cook.

In these pages, I hope you will find recipes that match your tastes, your needs and your life style. In every recipe, I explain the use of the food processor, so it will become a reliable friend. I give equal attention to describing actual cooking techniques, trying to anticipate every question you might have as you follow a recipe. I want you to have success every time you cook from this book — and fun, too!

Happy Cooking!

FAST AND FLAVORFUL

COCKTAIL FOODS

Call them hors d'oeuvre or appetizers, finger food, nibbles or noshes. Whatever their name, they serve as more than just accompaniments to drinks. They break the ice, make guests welcome, and set the pace for a gathering. They can be a prelude, or a party all by themselves. Unlike formal first courses, they're meant to be served away from the table, giving all your guests a chance to meet and build the party spirit, while you get a chance to work on last-minute dinner details.

Part of their appeal lies in their adaptability. You can use them any way that suits your fancy. Serve Crisp Cocktail Chips with sandwiches. Take Chicken Wings Cumberland along on a picnic. Toss a salad with Fresh Herb Dipping Sauce, or bring the flavors of the Mediterranean to your table by serving Pesto Onion Tart for lunch.

When cocktail foods precede a dinner, plan them carefully. Try to complement the menu and to stimulate the appetite without dulling it. Before a large dinner, offer only one or two simple selections, just to set the scene.

COCKTAIL FOODS

Crisp Cocktail Chips
Glazed Pecans
Roquefort Crisps
Cheese Twists

Roquefort and Brie Spread
Herbed Goat Cheese Spread
Hommos bi Tahini
Smoked Salmon Mousse

Stuffed New Potatoes
Glazed Almond Brie
Vegetable Basket with Dipping Sauces
  Pimiento Dipping Sauce
  Watercress Dipping Sauce
  Fresh Herb Dipping Sauce

Chicken Wings Cumberland
Deep Fried Oriental Chicken with Apricot
  Sauce

Pesto Onion Tart with Thick Pesto Sauce
Tomato and Cheese Tart

Chicken Liver Pâté with Apples and
  Walnuts
Country Pâté with Turkey

Middle Eastern Phyllo Pastries
Buckwheat Blini with Caviar and
  Garnishes
Cheese Puff Ring

Rio Grande Cocktail Casserole
Caviar Supreme

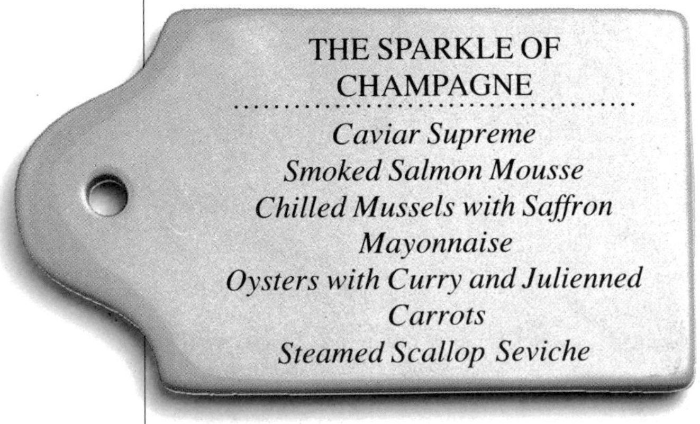

THE SPARKLE OF CHAMPAGNE

Caviar Supreme
Smoked Salmon Mousse
Chilled Mussels with Saffron
Mayonnaise
Oysters with Curry and Julienned
Carrots
Steamed Scallop Seviche

Stuffed New Potatoes
previous pages

3 medium Idaho potatoes or sweet
potatoes, unpeeled; or plantains,
peeled (3 pounds total, 910g), cut
into feed-tube lengths
1 quart (1L) peanut oil
¹/₂ teaspoon salt

*In France, freshly
made potato chips
are served with
drinks at many
luxury hotels. The
French use only
white potatoes;
sweet potatoes or
plantains are
every bit as good.
Try serving a
combination of
three different
chips; it's no more
trouble and
definitely more
interesting.*

Ultra-Thin Slicing Disc (1mm): Stand potatoes or plantains in feed tube and use firm pressure to process potatoes and medium pressure to process plantains. Before frying potato slices, soak them in ice water for at least 2 hours. Drain and pat dry before frying. This is unnecessary with plantains.

Heat oil to 375°F (190°C) in 2-quart (2L) saucepan. Fry slices in small batches until golden brown — about 1¹/₂ minutes. Use slotted spoon to transfer slices to paper towels to drain. Let oil return to 375°F (190°C) before frying another batch. Sprinkle chips with salt and serve warm or at room temperature. They can be fried up to 6 hours in advance.

Makes 8 to 10 servings.

NOTE: Many supermarkets carry plantains, which look like the unripe bananas to which they're related. If you can't locate them, try a Latin-American grocer. Green bananas work very well as a substitute.

*Crisp Cocktail
Chips*

GLAZED PECANS

This simple dish has become my trademark; I serve it with cocktails at all my parties. The glaze doesn't make the pecans sweet; it just covers them with a crackly coating. Almonds, hazelnuts and cashews can be prepared the same way, but I like pecans best. The Maple Pecan variation, a bit sweeter and more strongly flavored, is also delicious.

4 tablespoons unsalted butter
¼ cup (60ml) light corn syrup
2 tablespoons water
1 teaspoon salt
4 cups pecan halves (1 pound total, 455g)

Fifteen minutes before baking, place rack in center of oven and preheat oven to 250°F (120°C). Line jelly-roll pan with heavy-duty aluminum foil.

Put butter, corn syrup, water and salt in 2-quart (2L) saucepan and bring to boil. Remove from heat and add pecans. Toss gently to coat nuts with syrup, then spread in single layer on jelly-roll pan. Bake for 1 hour, stirring every 15 minutes with wooden spoon. Remove from oven and transfer to clean piece of aluminum foil, separating and spreading nuts in single layer. Cool completely.

Can be wrapped airtight and frozen up to 6 months. Bring to room temperature in wrapping. If nuts are not crisp, place them in single layer on jelly-roll pan and bake in preheated 250°F (120°C) oven for 20 minutes. Cool completely before serving.

Makes 1 pound (455g).

MAPLE PECAN VARIATION: Substitute pure maple syrup or maple-flavored syrup for corn syrup.

ROQUEFORT CRISPS

When you want something light and crisp with drinks or a salad, serve these crunchy cheese snacks. I usually use an imported Roquefort but I have also had success with domestic blue cheese, Gorgonzola and Stilton. The key to success with the recipe: don't overprocess the dough.

Glaze
  1 large egg
  1 teaspoon salt

Crisps
  4 ounces (115g) Roquefort cheese
  6 tablespoons unsalted butter, chilled and cut into 6 equal pieces
  3 tablespoons cold water
  1 teaspoon dry mustard
  ½ teaspoon salt
  ¼ teaspoon freshly grated nutmeg
  3 drops Tabasco sauce
  1 cup unbleached all-purpose flour (5 ounces, 140g)
  1 teaspoon baking powder

Preheat oven to 350°F (175°C) and place rack in center 15 minutes before baking. Grease 2 baking sheets and sprinkle them lightly with water.

Metal Blade: Process egg and salt for 2 seconds; remove and reserve. It is not necessary to wash work bowl. Process cheese until smooth. Add butter, water, mustard, salt, nutmeg and Tabasco sauce. Pulse twice, then process for 5 seconds. Add flour and baking powder and process until dough just begins to clump together, but does not form a ball; do not overprocess. Wrap in plastic wrap and refrigerate at least 1 hour.

Divide dough into quarters and work with 1 piece at a time. Leave unworked pieces in refrigerator. On floured board, roll 1 portion to thickness of 1/4 inch (6mm). Cut into rounds with a 1 1/2-inch (4cm) round cookie cutter and place on prepared baking sheets. Use feather brush to brush each round with glaze. Repeat with remaining dough. Bake until lightly browned — about 15 minutes. Carefully transfer with spatula to wire rack to cool. Crisps can be made several days in advance and stored in airtight containers.

Makes 60 crisps.

DILL VARIATION: Substitute 4 ounces (115g) cream cheese for Roquefort. Omit Tabasco sauce and add 1 tablespoon dried dillweed.

ROQUEFORT
CRISPS

5 ounces (140g) imported Parmesan cheese, at room temperature, in 4 pieces

1 recipe Quick Puff Pastry (see Index), well chilled

Fifteen minutes before baking, place rack in center of oven and preheat to 350°F (175°C). Butter large baking sheet.

Metal Blade: Process cheese until very fine.

Roll pastry to 13 by 21-inch (33 by 53cm) rectangle on floured board. Trim to exact 12 by 20-inch (30 by 50cm) rectangle with sharp knife. Spread cheese over entire surface and gently press into pastry with rolling pin. Cut into strips 12 inches (30cm) long and 1/2 inch (12mm) wide. Gently twist each strip, turning it 8 times.

Place on prepared baking sheet and freeze until firm — about 15 minutes. Bake in preheated oven until lightly browned — about 18 to 20 minutes. Transfer to wire rack and cool completely. Store in airtight container up to 3 days.

Makes forty 12-inch (30cm) twists.

**CHEESE
TWISTS**

Be sure to use well aged, imported Parmesan cheese for these pastries, which are a perfect light appetizer to serve with drinks before dinner. To serve them with style, stand them upright in a tall glass, decorative pitcher or basket.

7 ounces (200g) Brie cheese, with rind removed, at room temperature
2 ounces (55g) Roquefort cheese, at room temperature

3 tablespoons unsalted butter, at room temperature
1/4 cup (60ml) whipping cream
Freshly ground white pepper

Metal Blade: Process cheese and butter for 10 seconds. Add cream and pepper and process until smooth, stopping once to scrape work bowl.

Transfer to serving dish and leave at room temperature for 1 hour before serving. Cheese can be prepared up to 3 days in advance, covered and refrigerated. Bring to room temperature before serving.

Makes 1 cup (240ml).

NOTE: For freezing leftover bits of cheese, see page 8 .

**ROQUEFORT
AND BRIE
SPREAD**

This is a savvy way to turn leftover cheese into a flavorful spread. This combination of ingredients is the recommendation of Pierre Wynants, chef-owner of Comme Chez Soi in Brussels. You can substitute any cheeses of equal weight.

HERBED GOAT CHEESE SPREAD

Once I would have specified French cheese. Now I can recommend one from California with equal confidence. Whatever its origin, the cheese should be soft and flavorful. Mixing it with an equal amount of sweet butter extends the cheese while preserving its special flavor.

¹/₂ cup parsley leaves
¹/₂ teaspoon fresh marjoram or ¹/₄ teaspoon dried
1 teaspoon fresh thyme or ¹/₄ teaspoon dried
1 teaspoon fresh oregano or ¹/₄ teaspoon dried
4 ounces (115g) soft goat cheese
1 stick unsalted butter (4 ounces, 115g), at room temperature and cut into 4 pieces

Metal Blade: Process all ingredients until smooth, stopping once to scrape work bowl.

Transfer to 1-cup (240ml) crock or dish, cover airtight and refrigerate at least 2 hours. Soften slightly at room temperature before serving.

Makes 1 cup (240ml).

NOTE: Most cheeses freeze very well when wrapped airtight. You can collect leftover bits of goat cheese in the freezer until you've accumulated the amount specified in the recipe.

HOMMOS BI TAHINI

Everyone has a favorite version of hommos, *and this recipe from the Casbah restaurant in Chicago is mine. Seductively rich in both taste and texture, it is given special flair by the attractive garnish.*

1 small onion (2 ounces, 55g), peeled and quartered
¹/₃ cup parsley leaves
1 large garlic clove, peeled
1 15-ounce can (425g) chickpeas, drained, with liquid reserved
¹/₄ cup (60ml) sesame *tahini*
3 tablespoons fresh lemon juice
Pinch ground cumin
Pinch Hungarian paprika
1 teaspoon olive oil
Warm Pita bread, cut into wedges

Metal Blade: Process onion and parsley until minced; remove and reserve. Turn on machine, drop garlic through feed tube and process until minced. Reserve 6 chickpeas and add remainder to work bowl. Process until a smooth purée — about 20 seconds — stopping once to scrape bowl. Add 3 tablespoons of chickpea liquid, *tahini* and lemon juice; process for 5 seconds to blend.

Can be made to this point one week in advance, covered and refrigerated.

To serve, spoon into shallow 2-cup (480ml) serving dish and sprinkle with cumin and paprika. Arrange onion/parsley mixture around edge of dish, dot surface with reserved whole chickpeas and drizzle oil over all. Serve with warm Pita bread triangles.

Makes 1¹/₂ cups (360ml).

NOTE: *Tahini* is a paste made from ground sesame seeds. You'll find it in Greek and Middle Eastern markets and in many health-food stores. Once opened, *tahini* can be refrigerated, covered airtight, for up to 6 months.

SMOKED SALMON MOUSSE

This is a favorite first course at Restaurant Jacques Cagna in Paris, where it is shaped into ovals on individual plates and sprinkled with fresh chives. It's equally delicious as a spread, mounded in a shallow serving bowl and surrounded by slices of cucumber.

¹/₂ pound (225g) Nova Scotia smoked salmon, cut into 1-inch (2.5cm) pieces
³/₄ cup (180ml) whipping cream, chilled

2 tablespoons sour cream
2 teaspoons fresh lemon juice
Salt to taste
1 tablespoon snipped fresh chives

Metal Blade: Process salmon until smooth, stopping once to scrape work bowl. While machine is running, pour cream through feed tube in thin, steady stream and process until thick. Scrape work bowl. Add sour cream and lemon juice and process for 2 seconds. Add salt to taste.

Cover and refrigerate for 4 hours or overnight.

Makes 1¹/₂ cups (360ml) or 6 servings.

NOTE: To serve as first course, use oval ice cream scoop or 2 soup spoons to shape each portion. (To shape ovals with 2 spoons, scoop a heaping spoonful of mousse with one spoon, then rotate second spoon around it to shape smooth oval.) To prevent mousse from sticking, dip scoop or spoon in warm water and shake to remove excess. Place on salad plate and sprinkle with chives.

STUFFED NEW POTATOES

I first saw tiny stuffed new potatoes served with drinks at the Stanford Court Hotel in San Francisco. They hollowed out cooked potatoes and deep-fried the shells, then stuffed the shells with crème fraîche and topped them with golden caviar and fresh dill. For my variation, I devised two stuffings based on fresh vegetables. If the potatoes are cooked until just tender but still crisp, I don't think they need to be deep-fried.

16 small, uniformly sized red potatoes (1¼ pounds total, 570g)

Mushroom Filling

½ cup loosely packed parsley leaves
1 large shallot (½ ounce, 15g), peeled
12 medium mushrooms (8 ounces total, 225g), cleaned and trimmed
2 tablespoons unsalted butter

4 ounces (115g) cream cheese, at room temperature
1 tablespoon dry sherry
1 teaspoon fresh lemon juice
¼ teaspoon salt
Freshly ground black pepper

Spinach and Anchovy Filling

1 medium garlic clove, peeled
3 flat anchovies, rinsed, patted dry
2½ cups firmly packed spinach leaves with stems (5 ounces total, 140g), washed and dried
Parsley or watercress leaves, for

garnish
4 ounces (115g) cream cheese, at room temperature
1½ teaspoons fresh lemon juice
Freshly ground pepper

Put potatoes in 3 quarts (3L) of salted water and bring to boil. Cook just until potatoes can be pierced with tip of sharp knife — about 10 to 12 minutes. Be careful not to overcook. Drain and hold under cold running water until cool. Refrigerate 4 hours or overnight. Cut 2 small pieces off each potato to form flat top and bottom, then cut in half horizontally. Use melon baller or spoon to scoop out flesh carefully, leaving ¼-inch (6mm) shell. Reserve flesh for thickening soups or vegetable purées or as an ingredient in yeast breads. For crisper shells, deep-fry just before filling in 2 quarts (2L) vegetable oil heated to 350°F (175°C). Fry in several batches until lightly browned — about 3½ minutes. Transfer to paper towels and drain upside down.

Metal Blade: Process parsley until minced; remove and reserve. Turn on machine, drop shallot through feed tube and process until minced. Add mushrooms and process until minced. Melt butter in 10-inch (25cm) skillet and gently cook shallot and mushrooms until all liquid has cooked away — about 55 minutes. Cool completely.

Metal Blade: Process shallot and mushroom mixture with remaining ingredients until smooth, stopping once to scrape work bowl. Fit pastry bag with ½-inch (12mm) round tip and fill with mushroom mixture. Pipe filling into 16 potato halves, mounding it slightly. Garnish with reserved parsley.

Metal Blade: Turn on machine, drop garlic through feed tube and process until minced. Add anchovies and ⅓ of spinach and process until spinach is finely chopped. Transfer to mixing bowl and process remaining spinach in 2 batches. Return all chopped spinach to work bowl. Add cream cheese, lemon juice and pepper and process for 15 seconds, stopping once to scrape bowl.

Fit pastry bag with ½-inch (12mm) round tip and fill with spinach mixture. Pipe filling into remaining potato shells, mounding it slightly. Arrange alternate rows of mushroom and spinach filled potatoes on 12-inch (30cm) square platter. Cover airtight and refrigerate for 2 hours or overnight. Before serving, garnish with parsley or watercress leaves.

Makes 8 to 12 servings.

1 34-ounce (965g) wheel imported
   Brie cheese, well chilled
2 tablespoons confectioners' sugar

½ cup sliced unblanched almonds
   (2 ounces, 55g)
Clusters of red and green seedless
   grapes, for garnish

*The Brie makes a
beautiful
presentation, with
apples and pears,
sliced with the
extra thick (8mm)
slicing disc.
Crackers or
French bread are
also appropriate.*

With small, flexible knife, cut away rind from top of chilled cheese. Be careful not to remove or split rind on sides, which will form wall for melted cheese. Sift 1 tablespoon of confectioners' sugar evenly over surface and arrange almonds on top, pressing gently into place. Cheese can be prepared to this point up to 2 days in advance. Cover loosely with foil and refrigerate. Bring to room temperature before heating.

Fifteen minutes before heating, place rack 6 inches (15cm) from heat source and preheat broiler.

Line large baking sheet with aluminum foil, place cheese on it and sift 1 tablespoon of confectioners' sugar over nuts. Broil cheese until top is evenly browned — about 1 to 2 minutes. Rotate cheese, if necessary, for even browning. Watch carefully so it does not burn.

Use foil to lift cheese and transfer it to serving platter. Tear foil and gently remove it. Garnish with clusters of grapes.

Makes 16 servings.

COCKTAIL SAVOIR FAIRE

Glazed Pecans
Vegetable Basket with Dipping
Sauces
Pesto Onion Tart
Tomato Cheese Tart
Steamed Scallop Seviche
Glazed Almond Brie with
French Bread

VEGETABLE BASKET WITH DIPPING SAUCES

For the most exciting basket, choose the freshest and most beautiful vegetables from the market. The more varieties you use, the more appealing the basket will be. Diversity of color, shape, and texture adds visual interest.

Small vegetables like cherry tomatoes, green beans and asparagus are best left whole. Large ones should be sliced with one of the various slicing discs. Whatever vegetables you choose, mass each variety together for the strongest impact. Strive for contrast in colors and shapes. I use a basket that is just large enough to hold everything snugly, and I arrange several whole vegetables around it, like winter squashes, bouquets of romaine lettuce, large purple eggplants and ears of corn in the husk. Use hollowed-out peppers, squashes, cabbages or eggplants to hold the sauces.

Two lists of suggestions follow: one of vegetables to slice in your food processor and the other of vegetables to leave whole.

Vegetables to slice

Large, fat carrots, peeled and cut in feed-tube widths

Turnips or kohlrabi, scored and cut to fit feed tube

Beets that fit feed tube, well scrubbed

Daikon or Japanese radishes, peeled

Yams, peeled, cut to fit feed tube

Cucumbers, unpeeled, scored and cut in feed-tube lengths

Zucchini or yellow squash, scored and cut in feed-tube lengths

Broccoli, flowerets removed, stems peeled and cut in feed-tube lengths

Red, yellow and green bell peppers, cut into rectangles 2-inches (5cm) wide

Large, firm mushrooms, with opposite sides cut flat

Jicama, peeled, cut to fit feed tube

Vegetables to leave whole

Cherry tomatoes

Brussels sprouts

Scallions

Asparagus spears

Green and waxed beans

Enoki mushrooms

Oyster mushrooms

Small mushrooms

Cauliflowerets

Snow Peas

Pimiento Dipping Sauce (recipe follows)

Watercress Dipping Sauce (recipe follows)

Fresh Herb Dipping Sauce (recipe follows)

Medium Slicing Disc (3mm): Use firm pressure to slice carrots, turnips or kohlrabi, beets, daikon and yams.

All Purpose Slicing Disc (4mm): Use medium pressure to slice cucumbers.

Thick Slicing Disc (6mm) or French Fry Disc: Use medium pressure to slice zucchini or yellow squash.

Thick Slicing Disc (6mm): Use firm pressure to slice broccoli stems.

Extra Thick Slicing Disc (8mm): Stand pepper sections lengthwise in feed tube, fitting them in tightly. Use light pressure to slice. Stand mushrooms in feed tube on flat side and use light pressure to slice.

Make matchstick slices of jicama as follows. Use firm pressure to slice. Stack slices and fit tightly into feed tube, perpendicular to disc. Slice, using medium pressure.

PIMIENTO DIPPING SAUCE

1 1-ounce (30g) jar pimientos, drained and patted dry
3/4 cup (180ml) homemade Mayonnaise (see Index)

1 1/2 teaspoons Hungarian paprika
1/8 teaspoon cayenne pepper
Pinch of sugar

Metal Blade: Process all ingredients until smooth — about 30 seconds.

Can be made up to 3 days in advance, covered and refrigerated. Adjust seasoning before serving.

Makes 1 cup (240ml).

WATERCRESS DIPPING SAUCE

1 large bunch watercress (5 ounces, 140g), with stems removed
3/4 cup parsley leaves
4 medium scallions (2 ounces total, 55g), cut into 1-inch (2.5cm) pieces
2 tablespoons fresh dill or 1 tablespoon dried dillweed
6 flat anchovies, rinsed, patted dry

1 cup (240 ml) sour cream
1/2 cup (120ml) homemade Mayonnaise (see Index)
1 tablespoon fresh lemon juice
1 teaspoon Worcestershire sauce
Freshly ground pepper

Metal Blade: Process watercress, parsley, scallions, dill and anchovies until finely chopped, about 30 seconds. Add remaining ingredients and process for 5 seconds. Adjust seasoning.

Can be made up to 2 days in advance, covered and refrigerated. Adjust seasoning before serving.

Makes 1 2/3 cups (400ml).

FRESH HERB DIPPING SAUCE

1/4 cup mixed fresh herbs
1 small garlic clove, peeled
1 large egg
3 tablespoons white wine vinegar

1 tablespoon Dijon mustard
1/2 teaspoon salt
3/4 cup (180ml) safflower oil

Metal Blade: Put herbs in work bowl and turn machine on. Drop garlic through feed tube and process until minced. Add egg, vinegar, mustard and salt and turn machine on. With machine running, slowly drizzle oil through feed tube.

Can be made up to 2 days in advance, covered and refrigerated. Adjust seasoning before serving.

Makes 1 1/4 cups (300ml).

Chicken Wings
   24 chicken wings (4¹/₂ pounds total, 2kg)

Cumberland Sauce
   Zest of 1 large orange, removed with zester or grater
   3 medium shallots (2 ounces total, 55g), peeled
  1¹/₂ cups (360ml) red-currant jelly
   2 tablespoons red-wine vinegar

  1¹/₂ teaspoons salt
   Freshly ground pepper

   1 tablespoon hot dry mustard
   2 teaspoons ground ginger
   1 teaspoon salt
  ¹/₄ teaspoon cayenne pepper
   Freshly ground pepper

Inexpensive and easy to make ahead, these glazed chicken wings are appealing and practical. Don't restrict them to the cocktail hour; they're tempting on a late-night buffet table and portable for a picnic.

Fifteen minutes before broiling, set rack 5 inches (13cm) from heat source and preheat broiler. Have broiler pan ready.

Snip off wing tips with kitchen shears. Divide wings into 2 batches. Arrange 1 batch, round side down, on broiler pan. Combine salt and pepper and sprinkle ¹/₄ of it on wings. Broil until skin begins to brown lightly — about 5 minutes. Use tongs to turn wings over. Sprinkle with another ¹/₄ of seasoning and broil 5 minutes longer, or until skin begins to brown lightly. Transfer to large bowl. Repeat with remaining wings and seasoning. While wings are broiling, prepare sauce.

Metal blade: Put zest into work bowl and turn on machine. Drop shallots through feed tube and process until minced. Add remaining ingredients and process for 5 seconds.

Pour sauce over hot wings, cover and refrigerate overnight, stirring several times.

Fifteen minutes before baking, place rack in center of oven and preheat to 450°F (230°C). Line 2 jelly-roll pans with heavy-duty aluminum foil.

Divide wings and sauce between pans, placing wings round side down. Bake until well browned but not burned — about 40 minutes. Use tongs to turn wings over, brush with sauce in pan and bake 8 minutes more. Watch carefully so they do not burn. Immediately transfer from pan to serving platter and serve hot or at room temperature.

Makes 8 to 12 servings.

Dipping Sauces for Vegetable Basket

DEEP FRIED ORIENTAL CHICKEN WITH APRICOT SAUCE

It takes less than a minute to prepare these savory nuggets in the food processor. The combination of dark and light chicken meat makes them unusually juicy. The Shrimp Variation will remind you of shrimp toast — without the toast!

2 large garlic cloves, peeled
¹/₂ cup parsley leaves
2 medium scallions (1 ounce total, 30g), including green tops, cut into 1-inch (2.5cm) pieces
1 whole chicken breast, boned, with skin and tendons removed, cut into 1-inch (2.5cm) pieces (6 ounces, 170g meat)
2 chicken thighs, boned, with skin and tendons removed, cut into 1-inch (2.5cm) pieces (6 ounces, 170g meat)

1 large egg white
2 tablespoons cornstarch
1 tablespoon oyster sauce
1 tablespoon dry sherry
1 teaspoon Oriental sesame oil
¹/₂ teaspoon salt
¹/₄ teaspoon sugar
1 8-ounce (225g) can whole water chestnuts, drained
3 cups (720ml) peanut oil
1 tablespoon Oriental sesame oil
Apricot Sauce (recipe follows)

Metal Blade: Turn on machine, drop garlic through feed tube and process until minced. Add parsley, scallions and chicken meat and process until chicken is puréed, stopping once to scrape work bowl. Add egg white, cornstarch, oyster sauce, sherry, sesame oil, salt and sugar and process for 20 seconds, stopping once to scrape work bowl. Add water chestnuts and pulse 10 times to chop coarsely, stopping once to scrape work bowl.

In 2-quart (2L) saucepan, heat peanut and sesame oils to 325°F (160°C). Gently drop five or six 1-inch (2.5cm) balls of chicken mixture into oil and fry until golden brown — about 4 minutes. Use slotted spoon to transfer to paper towels. Let oil return to 325°F (160°C) before frying additional batches.

Can be made 1 day in advance. Cool and refrigerate in airtight container. To reheat, arrange in single layer on baking sheets and place in cold oven. Turn oven to 375°F (190°C) and bake until heated through — about 10 minutes. Serve hot with Apricot Sauce.

Makes 48 appetizers.

SHRIMP VARIATION: Substitute 12 ounces (340g) of frozen shrimp, thawed, for chicken. Mince ¹/₄-inch (6mm) cube of fresh ginger root with garlic.

NOTE: There is no substitute for the sweet pungency of fresh ginger root. To store ginger up to 6 months, peel and cut root in ¹/₂-inch (12mm) pieces and freeze in airtight plastic bag. Remove as needed and process while semi-frozen.

APRICOT SAUCE

8 large dried apricots (1¹/₂ ounces total, 42g)
¹/₂ cup (120ml) apricot preserves

¹/₂ cup (120ml) orange juice
1 teaspoon hot dry mustard
Pinch of salt

Combine apricots, preserves, juice and mustard in small non-aluminum saucepan and simmer, uncovered, for 10 minutes.

Metal Blade: Use slotted spoon to lift apricots from sauce and put in work bowl. Process until puréed — about 30 seconds. There will still be some tiny particles. Add liquid from saucepan and process for 5 seconds.

Add salt to taste and serve warm or at room temperature. Can be made up to 1 week in advance, covered airtight and refrigerated.

Makes ³/₄ cup (180ml).

10 medium onions (2¹/₄ pounds total, 1kg), peeled and cut to fit feed tube
3 tablespoons extra-virgin olive oil
1 tablespoon sugar
¹/₄ cup (60ml) Dijon mustard
1 Prebaked 12 by 18-inch (30 by 46cm) Butter Pastry shell, (see Index)
1 cup (240ml) Thick Pesto Sauce (recipe follows)
27 Nicoise olives, pitted and halved

Fifteen minutes before baking, place rack in center of oven and preheat to 350°F (175°C).

All-Purpose Slicing Disc (4mm): Use firm pressure to slice onions.

Heat oil in 10-inch (25cm) skillet. Add onions and sugar and cook gently until very soft — about 20 minutes; do not let them brown.

Brush mustard evenly over bottom of prebaked pastry shell; spread Pesto Sauce over mustard. Evenly distribute onions over Pesto, bringing to edge of crust. Put 9 olive halves, cut side down, along length of tart and 6 along width; fill in rows of remaining olives.

Bake until edges of pastry are golden — about 30 minutes. Let rest for 5 minutes, then cut into 2-inch (5cm) squares, with olive in center of each.

Tart can be prepared several hours in advance and held at room temperature or reheated. To reheat, put pan into cold oven and turn on to 350°F (175°C). Bake until heated through — about 15 minutes.

Makes fifty-four 2-inch (5cm) squares.

PESTO ONION TART

This tart, and the Tomato Cheese Tart that follows, are perfect for large buffets. They're delicious at room temperature and I serve them together, arranged in alternating rows, on a large wicker serving tray.

| THICK PESTO SAUCE | 2 large garlic cloves, peeled
3 ounces (85g) imported Parmesan cheese, at room temperature, cut into 3 pieces
¹/₄ cup pine nuts or walnuts (1 ounce, 28g) | 2 cups fresh basil leaves, or 2 cups spinach leaves with 2 tablespoons dried basil
¹/₂ teaspoon salt
¹/₄ cup (60ml) extra-virgin olive oil |

Metal Blade: Pulse garlic, cheese, nuts, basil and salt 8 times, then process continuously until cheese is minced. While machine is running, pour oil through feed tube and process until combined.

Can be made 2 weeks in advance and refrigerated.

| TOMATO CHEESE TART | ¹/₂ cup loosely packed parsley
3 large garlic cloves, peeled
1 cup (240ml) olive oil
2 tablespoons fresh basil or 2 teaspoons dried
2 teaspoons salt
1 tablespoon fresh oregano or 1 teaspoon dried
1 tablespoon fresh thyme or 1 teaspoon dried
¹/₈ teaspoon sugar | Freshly ground pepper
16 small Italian-style plum tomatoes (2 pounds total, 910g), cored
1 pound (455g) Emmenthal cheese, at room temperature, cut to fit feed tube
5 tablespoons Dijon mustard
1 Prebaked 12 by 18-inch (30 by 46cm) Butter Pastry shell (see Index) |

Metal Blade: Put parsley in work bowl and turn on machine. While machine is running, drop garlic through feed tube and process until minced. Add oil, basil, salt, oregano, thyme, sugar and pepper and process for 3 seconds. Leave mixture in work bowl.

Medium Slicing Disc (3mm): Stand tomatoes in feed tube, core end down, and use light pressure to process.

Transfer contents of work bowl to large food storage bag and marinate in refrigerator for 6 hours or overnight.

Place rack in center of oven and preheat to 375°F (190°C) 15 minutes before baking.

Shredding Disc: Use light pressure to process cheese.

Brush mustard over bottom of prebaked pastry shell; distribute cheese evenly over mustard. Remove tomatoes from marinade and arrange in slightly overlapping rows along width of tart shell.

Bake until edges of pastry are golden — about 30 minutes. Let rest for 5 minutes, then cut into 2-inch (5cm) squares.

Can be prepared several hours in advance and held at room temperature, or reheated. To reheat, put pan into cold oven and heat to 350°F (175°C). Bake until heated through — about 15 minutes.

Makes fifty-four 2-inch (5cm) squares.

CHICKEN LIVER PATE WITH APPLES AND WALNUTS

This wonderfully rich pâté was inspired by C. Steele & Co., a shop in Scottsdale, Arizona. The tart apple and Calvados provide refreshing counterpoint to the rich chicken livers and cream cheese. Serve as a spread, with crackers or slices of apple.

1 cup walnuts (4 ounces, 115g)
5 medium shallots (2½ ounces total, 70g), peeled
2 large garlic cloves, peeled
1 medium onion (4 ounces, 115g), peeled and quartered
1 stick unsalted butter (4 ounces, 115g)
2 large Granny Smith apples (1 pound total, 455g), peeled, cored and quartered

1 pound (455g) chicken livers, trimmed, with membrane removed
8 ounces (225g) "hot" bulk pork sausage
¼ cup (60ml) Calvados
8 ounces (225g) cream cheese, at room temperature
½ teaspoon salt
½ teaspoon dried tarragon
⅛ teaspoon ground allspice
⅛ teaspoon dried thyme

Lightly oil 6-cup (1.5L) terrine mold or loaf pan.

Metal Blade: Pulse to chop walnuts coarsely; remove and reserve. Turn on machine, drop shallots and garlic through feed tube and process until minced. Add onion and pulse until finely chopped.

Melt 3 tablespoons of butter in 10-inch (25cm) skillet over medium-high heat and add garlic, shallots and onion.

Metal Blade: Add apple and pulse until finely chopped.

Add to skillet and cook gently until ingredients are soft and transparent, about 8 minutes. Return mixture to work bowl. Melt remaining butter in same skillet. Break up sausage with fork and sauté with chicken livers over medium-high heat until cooked through, about 10 minutes. Meanwhile, warm Calvados in small saucepan. When meats are cooked, remove skillet from stove, add Calvados and carefully ignite. Let flame subside.

Metal Blade: Add meats to contents of work bowl and process 30 seconds, stopping once to scrape bowl. Add cream cheese, salt, tarragon, allspice and thyme and process until smooth, stopping once to scrape bowl. Add walnuts and pulse to combine, 3 or 4 times.

Transfer to prepared terrine or loaf pan, cover with plastic wrap and refrigerate for at least 4 hours or as long as 3 days. Serve as spread with French bread, apple slices or crackers.

Makes 12 to 16 servings.

COUNTRY PATE WITH TURKEY

Because it is made primarily of white turkey meat, this pâté is considerably lighter than most, yet it is still juicy and well flavored. It slices paper-thin for easy serving and makes delicious cocktail sandwiches.

Pâté

- 2 large garlic cloves, peeled
- 1 small onion (3 ounces, 85g), peeled and quartered
- 1 pound (455g) uncooked turkey-breast meat, cut into 1-inch (2.5cm) pieces (see NOTE)
- 1/2 pound (225g) slab bacon, rind removed, cut into 1-inch (2.5cm) pieces
- 2 whole chicken livers (3 ounces total, 85g), with membrane removed
- 2 large eggs
- 1/4 cup (60ml) Cognac
- 3/4 teaspoon cinnamon
- 1/2 teaspoon salt
- 1/4 teaspoon ground allspice
- 1/4 teaspoon freshly grated nutmeg
- Freshly ground pepper
- 1/4 pound (115g) imported smoked ham, cut into 1/8 inch (6mm) dice

Garnish

- Baby dill pickles or sour gherkins
- Radish roses
- Parsley sprigs

Fifteen minutes before baking, place rack in center of oven and preheat to 350°F (175°C) degrees. Butter 4-cup (1.5L) terrine or loaf pan and place in shallow baking dish. Bring kettle of water to boil.

Metal Blade: Turn on machine, drop garlic and onion through feed tube and process until minced. Add turkey, bacon and chicken livers and pulse 6 times, then process continuously until smooth. Add eggs, Cognac, cinnamon, salt, allspice, nutmeg and pepper and process for 10 seconds, stopping once to scrape work bowl. Add diced ham and pulse just until mixed in — 3 or 4 times. Do not overprocess.

To check seasoning, form patty with 2 tablespoons of mixture. Sauté in butter, taste and adjust seasoning.

Transfer to prepared terrine, smoothing surface with spatula. Bang pan on counter several times to settle mixture. Cover with piece of buttered aluminum foil. Put on oven rack and pour boiling water in baking dish to come halfway up sides of terrine. Bake until internal temperature is 160°F (70°C) — about 1 1/4 hours. Remove from oven and weight down with small, heavy object (foil-wrapped brick works well). Bring to room temperature, then refrigerate until well chilled.

Can be refrigerated up to 5 days or wrapped airtight and frozen up to 3 months. Wipe out work bowl with paper towel.

Thin Slicing Disc (2mm): Lay pickles in feed tube and use light pressure to slice them. Loosen pâté from pan with small flexible spatula and invert onto serving platter. Surround with radish roses and parsley sprigs and decorate surface with fans of sliced pickles. Serve in thin slices with variety of spicy mustards.

Makes 10 to 12 servings.

NOTE: 1 pound (455g) of uncooked white chicken meat can be substituted for turkey.

½ cup parsley leaves
4 medium scallions (3 ounces total, 85g), including green tops, cut into 1-inch (2.5cm) pieces
12 ounces (340g) Muenster cheese, cut into 1-inch (2.5cm) cubes
1 large egg
12 sheets phyllo dough, defrosted if frozen
4 tablespoons unsalted butter, melted

MIDDLE EASTERN PHYLLO PASTRIES

When warm from the oven, these triangles of paper-thin dough ooze delicious melted cheese. This version is authentically Middle Eastern. The Jalapeño Cheese variation is only one of many possible alternate versions. You can improvise your own by substituting any leftover cheese for the Muenster, and by adding herbs, garlic, onions, or bits of pepperoni.

Fifteen minutes before baking, place rack in center of oven and preheat to 400°F (205°C). Have large baking sheet ready.

Metal Blade: Process parsley until minced. Add scallions, cheese and egg and pulse 7 times to chop cheese coarsely.

Sheets of phyllo dough are paper-thin; they are very easy to handle when moist, but they crack if allowed to dry out. Be sure to keep all sheets except those you are actually working with closely covered with plastic wrap.

Lay 1 sheet of dough on flat surface. Lightly brush entire top surface of dough with melted butter and fold lengthwise into thirds. Fill pastries according to picture below, and fold like a flag from left to right. After last complete turn, use sharp knife to trim any excess dough. Prepare all remaining sheets in same way. Place on baking sheet and brush tops lightly with melted butter. Bake until golden brown — about 10 minutes. Serve immediately.

To freeze unbaked pastries, place on baking sheets lined with waxed paper. Freeze, then transfer to airtight plastic bags. At serving time, place frozen pastries on baking sheets and brush with melted butter. Bake as directed above, allowing 8 to 10 minutes additional time. Serve hot.

Makes 12 pastries.

JALAPENO CHEESE VARIATION: Substitute ¼ cup of cilantro for parsley. Halve, stem, and discard veins from 1 or 2 jalapeño peppers and add them to scallions. Substitute 6 ounces (170g) each of Monterey Jack and Longhorn Colby cheese for the Muenster.

NOTE: Fresh phyllo dough is available at many Middle Eastern bakeries. Unless you're very experienced, I recommend using it or frozen phyllo dough instead of making the dough yourself. Leftover dough can be wrapped airtight and frozen.

1. *Pastry filling in work bowl*   2. *Spooning filling onto dough*   3. *Folding triangle*   4. *Middle Eastern Phyllo Pastry*

BUCKWHEAT BLINI WITH CAVIAR AND GARNISHES

The perfect showcase for caviar — elegant, yet simple to serve. These pancakes, with the bland, slightly nutty flavor of buckwheat, are the classic complement for caviar. For impromptu celebrations, use buttered thin slices of white toast instead of blini.

Blini

1 cup (240ml) milk
2 teaspoons sugar
1 teaspoon active dry yeast
6 tablespoons bread flour
2 tablespoons buckwheat flour

2 teaspoons dried dillweed
1/4 teaspoon salt
2 large eggs
4 teaspoons unsalted butter
Additional butter for frying blini

Garnishes

2 hard cooked large eggs, peeled and quartered, whites separated
1 medium onion (5 ounces, 140g) peeled and quartered

1 7-ounce (200g) jar golden caviar or caviar of your choice
1 cup Crème Fraîche (see Index) or sour cream

In small saucepan, gently heat milk to lukewarm (105 to 115°F, 40 to 46°C). Stir in sugar and yeast and let stand until foamy — about 10 minutes.

Metal Blade: Put both flours in work bowl with dill, salt, eggs and butter and turn machine on. Pour yeast mixture through feed tube and process for 30 seconds, stopping once to scrape work bowl. The batter should be the consistency of heavy cream.

Transfer batter to 1-quart (1L) bowl and cover with plastic wrap. Place in warm spot (75 to 80°F, 24 to 26°C) and let rise until doubled — about 1 hour.

In 9-inch (23cm) griddle or skillet, heat 1 tablespoon of butter until sizzling. Stir batter. Spoon 2 teaspoons of batter into pan for each blini, making rounds 2 1/2 inches (6cm) in diameter. Cook over medium heat until top is bubbly and sides are set. Turn and cook until golden brown. Set aside in single layer. Repeat with remaining batter, adding more butter to pan as needed.

Blini can be made in advance and refrigerated or frozen. Stack them, separated by sheets of waxed paper, and wrap airtight in plastic bag. Bring to room temperature while still sealed. Remove from plastic and rewrap in aluminum foil. Reheat for 8 minutes in preheated 325°F (160°C) oven.

Metal Blade: Use 6 pulses to chop egg whites coarsely; remove and reserve. Process yolks until finely chopped; remove and reserve. Wipe work bowl with paper towel. Turn on machine and drop onion through feed tube; process until minced.

Just before serving, spread blini with Crème Fraîche or sour cream and top with egg white, egg yolk, onion and caviar. Or serve garnishes in separate dishes.

Makes 36 blini, 2 1/2 inches (6cm) in diameter.

NOTE: American golden caviar, from whitefish, represents the best price-to-quality ratio of caviars. The eggs are firm and less salty than in many varieties.

Though you may think it unlikely, there may come a time when you have leftover caviar. Even if it has been frozen once, as is the case with most American golden caviar, it can be refrozen. Wrap it airtight and freeze it as soon as possible after opening; there will be little or no perceptible loss in quality.

Glaze

1 large egg

Dough

6 ounces (170g) Gruyère, Monterey
    Jack or Parmesan cheese, well
    chilled
6 tablespoons unsalted butter
1¹/₂ cups (360ml) water
1¹/₄ teaspoons salt

¹/₂ teaspoon salt

Freshly ground pepper
1¹/₂ cups unbleached all-purpose flour
    (7¹/₂ ounces, 215g)
6 large eggs
2 teaspoons crushed red chiles
    (optional)

This is actually a Gougère, a classic Burgundian recipe created to accompany the wines of the region. It is a spectacular companion to wine or any cocktail. The authentic recipe calls for Gruyère cheese, but others can be substituted. Made with Monterey Jack cheese and chiles, it becomes a perfect companion to the Rio Grande Cocktail Casserole.

Fifteen minutes before baking, place oven rack in lower third and preheat oven to 425°F (220°C). Grease large baking sheet and sprinkle it lightly with water. Use your finger to draw 10-inch (25cm) circle on baking sheet to use as guide for shaping ring.

Metal Blade: Process egg and salt for 5 seconds; remove and reserve.

Shredding Disc: Use light pressure to shred cheese; remove and reserve.

Put butter, water, salt, and pepper in 2-quart (2L) saucepan and bring to boil, stirring to melt butter. Remove pan from heat and add flour. Beat with wooden spoon until mixture is well combined and leaves sides of pan, about 1 minute. Cook over moderate heat for 2 minutes, stirring constantly.

Metal Blade: Put hot flour mixture into work bowl. Add eggs and process for 30 seconds, stopping once to scrape bowl. Add chiles, if using them, and half of reserved cheese and process for 5 seconds.

Use 2 large spoons to place dough on prepared cookie sheet, using circle as guide. Each spoonful of dough should touch the one beside it. Use feather brush to brush glaze carefully over ring, covering entire surface. Sprinkle remaining cheese over dough. Bake for 10 minutes, then reduce oven temperature to 400°F (205°C) and continue baking until ring is golden brown, about 32 to 35 minutes more. Use spatula to remove from cookie sheet, place on wire rack and let rest for 5 minutes. Place Cheese Ring on round plate and serve while still warm.

Makes one 15-inch (38cm) ring.

INDIVIDUAL CHEESE PUFF VARIATION: Decrease water to 1 cup (240ml) and use ¹/₂ cup (120ml) of milk. Grease 3 baking sheets and sprinkle lightly with water. Spoon dough into 16-inch (40cm) pastry bag fitted with ³/₄-inch (2cm) round tube. Pipe in 1¹/₄-inch (3cm) rounds onto prepared baking sheets, leaving 1¹/₂ inches (4cm) between rounds. Brush with reserved egg glaze and bake in 400°F (205°C) oven until golden — about 23 minutes. Makes about 60 puffs.

NOTE: Cheese Puffs freeze well. Cool completely on wire rack, then freeze on baking sheet. When frozen, wrap airtight in food storage bag and freeze up to 4 months. To reheat, place on cookie sheet while still frozen and put into preheated 300°F (150°C) oven. Bake until hot — about 10 minutes for individual puffs and 20 minutes for ring.

RIO GRANDE COCKTAIL CASSEROLE

The enduring popularity of Caviar Supreme suggested another layered creation, this one with my favorite ingredients from the Southwest. It's an appetizer for casual entertaining. It's so delicious that it's addictive, especially when served with the Cheese Puff Ring made with Monterey Jack cheese, or with warm, fried corn tortillas.

1 package unflavored gelatin
¹/₄ cup (60ml) cold water
6 ounces (170g) Longhorn Colby cheese
6 ounces (170g) Chihuahua or Monterey Jack cheese, chilled
12 large scallions (8 ounces total, 225g) including green tops, with root ends trimmed, cut into thirds
¹/₂ large head iceberg lettuce (8 ounces, 225g)
3 medium tomatoes (1 pound total, 455g), cored

Avocado Mixture
¹/₄ cup cilantro leaves
1 small onion (1 ounce, 30g), peeled
2 ripe avocados (1 pound total, 455g), peeled and quartered
1 tablespoon fresh lemon juice
6 drops Tabasco sauce
¹/₄ cup (60ml) Mayonnaise (see Index)
¹/₂ teaspoon salt

Refried Bean Mixture
1 15-ounce (425g) can refried beans
2 tablespoons red-wine vinegar
3 tablespoons Mayonnaise (see Index)
3 teaspoons chili powder
1 3-ounce (85g) can chopped green chiles, drained and patted dry
1¹/₂ cups (360ml) sour cream
1 teaspoon dried chiles

Cheese Puff Ring (see Index), made with Monterey Jack cheese

Have ready 10-cup (2.5L) straight-sided glass bowl or soufflé dish.

Sprinkle gelatin over water in measuring cup. When water is absorbed, set cup in pan of hot water to dissolve gelatin or leave for 50 seconds in microwave oven set at medium. All granules should be completely dissolved. Cool slightly. (Gelatin will be divided between avocado and sour cream layers.)

Shredding Disc: Use light pressure to shred each cheese separately; remove and reserve each.

Medium Slicing Disc: Stand scallions in feed tube and use light pressure to slice; remove and reserve. Use light pressure to slice lettuce; wrap in airtight bag and refrigerate.

French Fry Disc: Use light pressure to process tomatoes and transfer to colander to drain. (If you do not have French Fry Disc, see page 229 for coarse chopping of tomatoes.)

Metal Blade: Put cilantro in work bowl and turn machine on. With machine running, drop onion through feed tube and process until minced. Add avocado, lemon juice, Tabasco, Mayonnaise and salt and process for 30 seconds, stopping once to scrape work bowl. Add 2 tablespoons dissolved gelatin and process 3 seconds; reserve. Wipe out work bowl with paper towel.

Process refried beans, vinegar, Mayonnaise and 1 teaspoon of chili powder for 30 seconds, stopping once to scrape work bowl.

Spoon bean mixture into bottom of 10-cup (2.5L) bowl and smooth surface. Use paper towel to wipe any smears from inside of dish. Spread chopped green chiles evenly over beans. Reserve 2 tablespoons of sliced scallions and sprinkle remainder over chiles. Sprinkle Colby cheese evenly over scallions and sprinkle with 1 teaspoon of chili powder. Carefully spread avocado mixture over cheese with rubber spatula. Wipe off inside of dish as necessary. Top avocado layer with Chihuahua cheese and 1 teaspoon of chili powder.

Distribute drained tomatoes over cheese. Stir remaining 2 tablespoons gelatin into sour cream then carefully smooth sour cream over tomatoes. Sprinkle reserved scallions and dried chiles over sour cream.

Cover bowl with plastic wrap and refrigerate 4 hours or overnight. Remove from refrigerator 30 minutes before serving. Center bowl in Cheese-Puff Ring and serve shredded lettuce in separate dish. Can also be served with warm flour tortillas, fried corn tortillas or crackers.

Makes 12 to 16 servings.

NOTE: For correct handling of gelatin, see note following Caviar Supreme.

RIO GRANDE COCKTAIL CASSEROLE

Rio Grande Cocktail Casserole

CAVIAR SUPREME

Even those who steadfastly maintain that caviar is an acquired taste concede the wide appeal of this delicious appetizer. The gelatin is needed to maintain the stunning layering of egg, avocado and sour cream mixtures; it is not detectable.

1 package unflavored gelatin

¹/₄ cup (60ml) cold water

Egg Layer
¹/₄ cup parsley leaves
1 large scallion (1 ounce, 28g), including green top, cut into 1-inch (2.5cm) pieces
¹/₂ cup (120ml) Mayonnaise (see Index)

Dash Tabasco sauce
¹/₂ teaspoon salt
Freshly ground black pepper
4 large eggs, hard-cooked, peeled and halved

Avocado Layer
1 large shallot (¹/₂ ounce, 15g), peeled
2 large ripe avocados (1 pound total, 455g), peeled and halved
2 tablespoons fresh lemon juice

2 tablespoons Mayonnaise (see Index)
Dash Tabasco sauce
¹/₂ teaspoon salt
Freshly ground pepper

Sour Cream Layer
¹/₂ small onion (1 ounce, 28g), peeled
1 cup (240ml) sour cream
1 3¹/₂-ounce (100g) jar black, red or golden caviar

Thin slices rye or pumpernickel bread
Cucumber slices

Line 1-quart (1L) soufflé dish with aluminum foil, extending it 4 inches (10cm) on 2 sides. Smooth out any wrinkles in foil and oil lightly.

Sprinkle gelatin over water in measuring cup. When water is absorbed, dissolve gelatin by setting cup in pan of hot water or heating it for 50 seconds in microwave oven set at medium. All granules should be completely dissolved. Cool slightly. (Gelatin will be divided among layers.)

Metal Blade: Process parsley until minced. Add scallion and process for 10 seconds. Add Mayonnaise, Tabasco sauce, salt, pepper and 1 tablespoon of dissolved gelatin and process for 3 seconds. Add eggs and pulse to chop coarsely. Do not overprocess; eggs should retain some texture.

Spread egg mixture in smooth layer in prepared dish. Clean any smears on inside of dish with paper towel. Refrigerate while preparing next layer.

Metal Blade: With machine running, drop shallot through feed tube and process until minced. Add 1 avocado and process until smooth, stopping once to scrape work bowl. Add lemon juice, Mayonnaise, Tabasco sauce, salt and pepper and 1 tablespoon of dissolved gelatin and process for 3 seconds. Leave mixture in bowl and remove metal blade.

French Fry Disc: Use light pressure to cut remaining avocado. (If you do not have French Fry Disc, cut avocado into strips 2 by ¹/₄ inches (5cm by 6mm) and add to puréed avocado.)

Spread avocado mixture in neat, even layer over egg mixture. Clean any smears on inside of dish with paper towel. Refrigerate while preparing next layer.

Metal Blade: With machine running, drop onion through feed tube and process until minced. Add sour cream and remaining 2 tablespoons of dissolved gelatin. Pulse 2 or 3 times to mix.

Spread sour cream mixture over avocado layer. Cover airtight with plastic wrap and refrigerate 6 hours or overnight.

At serving time, use foil extensions to lift Caviar Supreme out of dish. Carefully transfer to serving platter. To remove foil, split it down center and remove each piece. Drain caviar and spread over top, smoothing it to edge with table knife. Refrigerate until serving time. Serve surrounded with crackers, thin slices of rye or pumpernickel bread and cucumber slices.

Makes 12 to 16 servings.

NOTES: For large buffets, double recipe and use oiled 8-inch (20cm) springform pan. Cover bottom of pan with piece of plastic wrap that extends beyond edge. Attach side of pan, leaving plastic wrap outside. Oil plastic. To serve, remove side of pan and use plastic wrap to lift Caviar Supreme carefully. Center on serving platter and trim away excess plastic wrap.

It's not difficult to use gelatin if you handle it correctly. First, pour cold water or other liquid into dish and sprinkle 1 package of gelatin evenly over entire surface. Let rest until all gelatin is moistened and translucent — about 5 minutes. If any dry granules remain, stir mixture until they disappear. Next, gelatin must be dissolved completely. Set dish in simmering water, or heat for 50 seconds in microwave oven set at medium. Stir any granules from side of dish. When all granules are completely dissolved, gelatin is ready to use. If gelatin thickens and sets, reheat in simmering water or microwave oven until it melts.

FIRST COURSES

Not every dinner starts with the fanfare of a first course. When I include one, I like to offer something special, even a bit extravagant. These recipes are strongly influenced by my training in European restaurant kitchens. More than half were inspired by the genius of three-star chefs. Despite their impressive heritage, none is extremely difficult to prepare and each adds special dazzle to an important dinner.

Many can appear beyond the first course. Chicken Livers with Zucchini and Capers are good for brunch. So are Spinach Rolls with Mushroom Cream Sauce. Any of the salads could serve as the centerpiece of a light lunch or supper. And a main course of Shrimp Wrapped in Cabbage Leaves with Caviar Butter would delight any lover of caviar.

The first course sets the tone and should fit with those that follow. Try to achieve harmony, with each course complementing and balancing the others. An elaborate first course, like Vegetable Terrine with Liver Pâté, should precede lighter courses, while a more simple dish like Broiled Scallops can lead to a substantial main offering.

FIRST COURSES

Scotch Salmon Salad
Sliced Artichoke Bottoms with Walnut
  Vinaigrette
Lobster Salad with Port Vinaigrette
Chilled Mussels with Saffron Mayonnaise
Salad of Scallops and Julienned
  Vegetables with Raspberry Vinaigrette

Oysters with Curry and Julienned Carrot
Broiled Scallops on Shells
Steamed Scallop Seviche
Shrimp Wrapped in Cabbage Leaves with
  Caviar Butter

Leek and Ham Timbales
Fish and Leek Mousseline with Red-Wine
  Sauce
Snails with Garlic and Celery Root

Seafood Sausage with Tomato Butter
  Sauce
Spinach Rolls with Mushroom Cream
  Sauce
Open Ravioli with Woodland Mushrooms
Café Provençal Vegetable Tarts
Chicken Livers with Zucchini and Capers

Fish Terrine with Cucumber Sauce
Vegetable Terrine with Liver Pâté
Leek and Vegetable Terrine with Walnut
  Vinaigrette
Chicken Liver Mousse with Tomato Sauce

For additional recipes, see these chapters

FISH AND SHELLFISH
Steamed Mussels in Basil Butter

SALADS AND SALAD DRESSINGS
Chiffonade of Lettuce with Goat Cheese
  Fritters
Provençal Salad
Goat Cheese with Julienned Beets

*Salad of Scallops and
Julienned Vegetables
with Raspberry
Vinaigrette
previous pages*

SPRING GARDEN
LUNCHEON
....
Salad of Scallops and
Julienned Vegetables with
Raspberry Vinaigrette
Whole-Grain Country
Bread
Goat Cheese
Strawberries Romanoff
Walnut Wafers

Salad
- 1 lime, scored and cut flat at bottom
- 1 small cucumber (8 ounces, 225g), peeled
- 4 small scallions (2 ounces total, 55g), including green tops, cut into feed-tube widths
- 2 medium heads Boston lettuce (12 ounces total, 340g), cored, crisped and cut to fit feed tube
- 12 ounces (340g) thinly sliced Scotch salmon

Creamy Lime Dressing
- ³/₄ cup (180ml) whipping cream
- ¹/₃ cup (80ml) fresh lime juice
- 1¹/₂ tablespoons fresh dill or 1 teaspoon dried dillweed
- ¹/₄ teaspoon salt, or to taste
- Freshly ground white pepper
- Fresh dill, snipped, for garnish

Medium Slicing Disc (3mm): Stand lime in feed tube and use firm pressure to slice; remove and reserve slices and any juice.

Split cucumber lengthwise and remove seeds with a spoon. Cut in feed-tube lengths.

Thin Slicing Disc (2mm): Stand cucumber in feed tube and use medium pressure to slice. Stand scallions in feed tube and use light pressure to slice.

Extra Thick Slicing Disc (8mm) or Thick Slicing Disc (6mm): Stand lettuce in feed tube and use light pressure to slice.

Transfer to mixing bowl.

Metal Blade: Process cream, 3¹/₂ tablespoons of lime juice, dill, salt and pepper for 3 seconds.

Add to salad and toss gently. Adjust seasoning.

To serve, divide all ingredients among 6 salad plates. Place dressed greens in center of each plate. Lay salmon slices over top, overlapping slightly to cover lettuce completely. Tuck in any ends of lettuce. Drizzle salmon with remaining lime juice and season with freshly ground white pepper. Garnish with dill and place lime slice in center. Serve immediately.

Makes 6 servings.

Smoked Salmon

★ Smoked salmon is an expensive delicacy, and it's definitely worth the splurge. Many people maintain that the smoked salmon imported from Scotland and Ireland is the best in quality. Both of these are very good, and our own state of Washington also produces an excellent variety. (Smoked salmon is not the same as lox, which is salmon that is cured in brine, then soaked in fresh water to remove the salt.) Be sure your fishmonger slices the salmon very thin.

SCOTCH SALMON SALAD

Christiane Massia served this delicious salad when I worked at L'Aquitaine, her restaurant in Paris. It's a simple first-course salad that's always sensational. It can also be served as a light luncheon.

SLICED ARTICHOKE BOTTOMS WITH WALNUT VINAIGRETTE

Tender artichoke bottoms, sliced paper-thin with a 1mm slicing disc or a slicing machine, are shaped into rosettes for this extravagant salad from the Crillon Hotel in Paris. It involves a lot of work but every step can be done in advance. The artichokes must be the large size specified. If you can't bear to discard the artichoke leaves, try the variation that uses the whole artichoke — or steam the leaves for family fare.

Salad

12 large artichokes, each 13 to 14 ounces (370 to 400g)	4 white radishes (3 ounces total, 85g), peeled
3 tablespoons fresh lemon juice	1 large carrot (7 ounces, 200g), peeled and cut into feed-tube widths
2 tablespoons flour	
1 tablespoon salt	

Vinaigrette

1/4 cup (60ml) walnut oil	3/4 teaspoon salt
1/4 cup (60ml) safflower oil	Freshly ground pepper
1 tablespoon beef broth	1 medium bunch watercress (4 ounces, 115g), with stems removed, for garnish
1 tablespoon sherry vinegar	
3/4 teaspoon fresh lemon juice	

Cut off top two thirds of artichokes, then cut stem flush with base. Remove all leaves around base, trimming as close as possible without removing any flesh from bottom. Leave choke intact.

Put artichokes in 5-quart (5L) pot with 3 quarts (3L) of water, lemon juice, flour and salt. Bring to boil and cook, uncovered, until artichokes are just tender when pierced with sharp knife — about 18 minutes. Do not overcook. Remove artichokes from pot and reserve liquid. When artichokes are cool enough to handle, remove their fuzzy chokes with a spoon; they should slip out easily.(Can be prepared to this point up to 3 days in advance. Return them to their cooking liquid and refrigerate. Drain before using.)

Ultra Thin Slicing Disc: Put artichokes in feed tube, stem side down, and use light pressure to slice; remove and reserve. Reserve any broken slices for soups.

Fine Shredding Disc: Lay radishes in feed tube and use medium pressure to shred; remove and reserve. Lay carrot in feed tube and use medium pressure to shred; remove and reserve.

Metal Blade: Process both oils, beef broth, vinegar, lemon juice, salt and pepper until mixed — about 3 seconds.

On each of 6 large individual salad plates, arrange sliced artichokes in rosette design and spoon 1 tablespoon of vinaigrette over them. The salad can be prepared to this point 6 hours in advance. Cover each plate with plastic wrap and refrigerate.

Just before serving, divide remaining vinaigrette between radishes and carrots and toss lightly. Arrange 3 small clusters of carrots at equal intervals around outer edge of each artichoke and cluster of radishes in center. Garnish outer edge of plate with watercress leaves.

Makes 6 servings.

WHOLE ARTICHOKE VARIATION: Substitute 6 medium artichokes, about 10 ounces (285g) each, for 12 large artichokes and make 1 1/2 times the amount of Walnut Vinaigrette. Cut 1/2 inch (12mm) from tip of each leaf and immediately put in 8-quart

(8L) pot with 5 quarts (5L) of water, lemon juice, flour and salt. To keep artichokes immersed in water, hold them down with plate that is slightly smaller than diameter of pot. Wrap plate in aluminum foil, bunching excess foil on top to form handle for lifting plate from pot. Place wrapped plate on top of artichokes, handle facing up, and bring liquid to boil. Cook, uncovered, until artichokes are tender — about 35 to 40 minutes. Drain artichokes and rest them upside down until cool enough to handle. Quarter them lengthwise and completely remove fuzzy chokes with small, sharp knife. While they are still warm, toss artichokes with all but 3 tablespoons of vinaigrette. Cover and refrigerate for at least 2 hours or up to 4 days before serving.

To serve, arrange 4 artichoke quarters on salad plate, cut side down, with stems meeting in center. Toss remaining 3 tablespoons of vinaigrette with radishes and carrots and garnish each plate with 3 small clusters of carrots and one of radishes. Adjust seasoning.

Makes 6 servings.

SLICED ARTICHOKE BOTTOMS WITH WALNUT VINAIGRETTE

Sliced Artichoke Bottoms with Walnut Vinaigrette

LOBSTER SALAD WITH PORT VINAIGRETTE

Chef Pierre Wynants serves this salad as a first course at his restaurant, Comme Chez Soi, in Brussels. He lets it rest for about 8 minutes after tossing it with vinaigrette, to allow the flavors to mellow. If you're in an especially extravagant mood, garnish the salad with thinly sliced truffles, as Wynants does, and add 2 teaspoons of truffle juice to the vinaigrette.

Salad

2 large lobster tails in shell (1 1/2 pounds total, 680g), thawed if frozen

3 large artichokes (2 1/4 pounds total 1kg)

3 tablespoons fresh lemon juice

2 tablespoons flour

1 tablespoon salt

1 large head Boston lettuce (8 ounces, 225g), washed, chilled and torn into bite-size pieces

1 large bunch watercress (5 ounces, 140g), washed, chilled and trimmed of stems

3/4 cup loosely packed parsley leaves

2 large hard-cooked egg whites

1 medium celery rib (4 ounces, 115g), strings removed with vegetable peeler and cut into 1-inch (2.5cm) pieces

2/3 cup walnut halves (2 2/3 ounces, 75g)

12 medium asparagus spears (6 ounces total, 170g), cooked until tender but crisp and cut into 4-inch (10cm) lengths

6 ounces green beans, cooked until tender but crisp

Port Vinaigrette

1/3 cup (80ml) walnut oil

3 1/2 tablespoons Ruby Port

3 tablespoons red-wine vinegar

2 teaspoons Dijon mustard

1/2 to 3/4 teaspoon salt

Freshly ground white pepper

Bring 4 quarts (4L) of water to rolling boil. Add lobster tails, reduce heat and cook gently for 12 minutes. Drain lobster and let it cool. Split shells and carefully remove meat in one piece. Refrigerate meat until well chilled, then cut it into 1/3-inch (8mm) slices.

Cut off top two-thirds of artichokes, then cut stem flush with base. Remove all leaves around base, trimming as close as possible without removing any flesh from bottom. Leave choke intact.

Put artichokes in 3-quart (3L) pot with 1 1/2 quarts (1.5L) of water, lemon juice, flour and salt. Bring to boil and cook, uncovered, until artichokes are just tender when pierced with sharp knife — about 18 minutes. Do not overcook. Remove from pot, drain and reserve liquid. When artichokes are cool enough to handle, remove their fuzzy chokes with spoon; they should slip out easily. (The artichokes can be prepared to this point up to 3 days in advance. Return them to their cooking liquid and refrigerate them. Drain and dry before using.) Cut artichokes into sixths.

Put lettuce and watercress in large mixing bowl.

Metal Blade: Process parsley until minced; remove and reserve. Pulse egg whites 3 or 4 times to chop them coarsely; remove and reserve. Pulse celery to mince it; add to mixing bowl.

Medium Shredding Disc: Use light pressure to shred walnuts.

Add to lettuce along with artichokes, asparagus and green beans and toss gently. Recipe can be prepared to this point several hours in advance. Wrap salad and lobster separately and refrigerate. Leave vinaigrette at room temperature and let lobster come to room temperature before serving.

Metal Blade: Process vinaigrette ingredients until mixed —about 3 seconds.

Toss sliced lobster with ¹/₄ cup (60ml) of vinaigrette. Just before serving, toss chilled salad greens with remaining vinaigrette.

Divide greens among 6 to 8 individual serving plates. Arrange lobster on top and sprinkle with chopped egg whites, pepper and reserved parsley. Let stand 8 minutes before serving.

Makes 6 to 8 servings.

LOBSTER SALAD WITH PORT VINAIGRETTE

48 small mussels (1³/₄ pounds total, 795g)	1 cup loosely packed parsley leaves
¹/₈ teaspoon saffron threads	³/₄ cup (180ml) Mayonnaise (see Index)
1 medium head Romaine lettuce (1 pound total, 455g), trimmed and cut into feed-tube lengths	1 tablespoon fresh lemon juice Pinch cayenne pepper

CHILLED MUSSELS WITH SAFFRON MAYONNAISE

This unusual salad pairs the Prince and the Pauper. Just a pinch of saffron, the costliest spice in the world, adds a sublime flavor to our greatest shellfish bargain.

Scrub mussels and remove their beards. Discard any open mussels that do not close when tapped on counter. Transfer them to 4-quart (4L) pot, cover with cold water and add 1 teaspoon of salt. Soak for 30 minutes. Wash several times to remove grit, then drain well. Return to pot with only water clinging to them. Cover and cook over high heat just until shells open - about 6 or 7 minutes. Discard any that do not open. Drain them and reserve liquid.

Stir saffron threads into 1 tablespoon of hot mussel liquid; reserve.

All-Purpose Slicing Disc (4mm): Stand lettuce in feed tube and use light pressure to slice.

Wrap airtight and refrigerate until serving time.

Metal Blade: Process parsley until minced. Reserve 1 tablespoon for garnish. To remainder, add Mayonnaise, lemon juice, pepper and saffron mixture and process for 3 seconds.

Transfer to large mixing bowl.

When mussels are just cool enough to handle, but still warm, remove them from shells and fold into Mayonnaise. Cover and refrigerate for 2 to 4 hours. Adjust seasoning.

At serving time, divide lettuce among 6 large salad plates. Center portion of mussels on lettuce and garnish with reserved parsley. Serve immediately.

Makes 6 servings.

SALAD OF SCALLOPS AND JULIENNED VEGETABLES WITH RASPBERRY VINAIGRETTE

For the original version of this outstanding salad, chef Gérard Boyer of the Restaurant Boyer in Reims, France used a base of mixed dark green French lettuces and a garnish of thinly sliced truffles. I have substituted curly endive, which is more readily available than French lettuce.

Vinaigrette
- 1/3 cup loosely packed parsley leaves
- 2/3 cup (160ml) safflower oil
- 1/4 cup (60ml) extra-virgin olive oil
- 1/4 cup (60ml) raspberry vinegar
- 4 tablespoons snipped fresh chives
- 1 teaspoon fresh tarragon or 1/2 teaspoon dried
- 1 teaspoon salt
- Freshly ground white pepper

Salad
- 1 large leek (8 ounces, 225g), with coarse greens trimmed away, cut into feed-tube lengths
- 2 cups (480ml) clam juice
- 1 pound (455g) sea scallops, halved horizontally
- 1 large red pepper (8 ounces, 225g)
- 12 medium mushrooms (1/2 pound total, 225g), with 2 opposite sides cut flat
- 1 large celery root (14 ounces, 395g), peeled and cut to fit feed tube
- 1 10-ounce (285g) package frozen artichoke hearts, thawed, drained and halved
- 2 tablespoons fresh lemon juice
- 1/2 pound (225g) curly endive, washed, chilled and snipped into bite-size pieces

Metal Blade: Process parsley until minced. Add both oils, vinegar, 3 tablespoons of chives, tarragon, salt and pepper and process until mixed — about 3 seconds; remove and reserve vinaigrette. Wipe work bowl with paper towel.

All-Purpose Slicing Disc (4mm): Stand leek in feed tube; use medium pressure to slice.

Transfer to 1-quart (1L) saucepan and add clam juice. Bring to boil, reduce heat and simmer for 10 minutes. Strain, return liquid to pan and reserve leeks (see NOTE). Cook scallops, in 3 batches, just until opaque — about 25 seconds; do not overcook. While they are still warm, toss scallops with 1/4 cup (60ml) of vinaigrette. Cover loosely with foil and reserve. (Scallops can be cooked and marinated 1 day in advance. Let them cool, wrap airtight and refrigerate. Bring to room temperature before serving.)

Stand pepper on cutting board. Use sharp knife to cut off sides in 3 or 4 vertical slices, leaving only core and stem. Remove any membrane from slices.

Medium Slicing Disc (3mm): Stand red pepper slices in feed tube lengthwise with cut sides down. Wedge them in tightly and use light pressure to slice. Put mushrooms in feed tube with flat side down and use light pressure to slice.

Transfer to 2-quart (2L) mixing bowl.

3mm Julienne Disc or Medium Slicing Disc (3mm): Cut celery root into matchsticks by using firm pressure to cut with julienne disc. Or, use double-slicing technique to cut it into matchsticks with slicing disc as follows. Use firm pressure to slice. Stack slices and fit them tightly into feed tube, with slices perpendicular to slicing disc. Slice again, using medium pressure.

Add to mixing bowl along with artichokes and lemon juice, and toss gently.

At serving time, toss vegetables with 1/2 cup (120ml) of vinaigrette. Adjust seasoning.

Arrange base of endive on 12-inch (30cm) round serving platter or individual salad plates. Spoon remaining vinaigrette over greens and arrange vegetables on top. Garnish border with scallops and sprinkle with remaining 1 tablespoon of chives.

Makes 6 to 8 servings.

NOTE: Leeks used to flavor clam broth are delicious as a vegetable course. Reheat them with butter, salt and freshly ground pepper.

16 oysters, opened, on half-shell	Pinch of salt (oysters vary in
1 small carrot (2 ounces, 55g),	saltiness — little additional salt is
cooked until tender but crisp and	required)
cut into thirds	6 tablespoons unsalted butter,
1 cup (240ml) Crème Fraîche (see	chilled and quartered
Index)	Freshly ground white pepper
1 teaspoon curry powder or to taste	

OYSTERS WITH CURRY AND JULIENNED CARROT

A masterful presentation of oysters, created by Gilbert Le Coze of Le Bernardin in Paris. When making the sauce, add enough curry to give a well defined flavor, but not so much as to overpower the oysters.

Fifteen minutes before baking, place rack in center of oven and preheat to 500°F (260°C). Arrange oysters on jelly-roll pan and refrigerate.

3mm Julienne Disc: Lay carrot horizontally in feed tube and use medium pressure to julienne; remove and reserve.

Put Crème Fraîche, curry and salt in 1 1/2-quart (1.5L) saucepan and boil until reduced to 1/2 cup (120ml) — about 7 minutes. This can be done 1 day in advance; reheat mixture before continuing. Remove from heat and whisk in butter, one piece at a time; wait until each piece is incorporated before adding another. Fold in carrots, add pepper, adjust seasoning and keep mixture warm.

Bake oysters only until shells are very hot — about 2 minutes. Oysters will not be cooked.

Remove from oven and quickly transfer oysters, in their shells, to serving platter or individual plates. Top each with 2 teaspoons of sauce and serve immediately.

Makes 4 servings.

To Shuck an Oyster

★ Place a fine mesh sieve over a bowl to catch the oyster liquor. Put a folded dish towel in the palm of your hand to cushion it. Grasp an oyster in your protected hand, holding it with the hinged side down in your palm. Working over the bowl, insert the point of an oyster knife between the shells, next to the hinge. Work the knife along the seam between the shells, moving it away from the hinge, to sever the muscle. If the shell crumbles, insert the knife on the other side of the hinge and try again.

BROILED SCALLOPS ON SHELLS

A recipe couldn't possibly be more simple than this, yet in Frédy Girardet's able hands, it's masterful. Made with fresh, sweet scallops and fresh thyme, it's a delicious first-course.

1 cup (240ml) Vegetable Stock (see Index)
9 large sea scallops (14 ounces total, 395g), halved horizontally
1¼ cups (300ml) whipping cream
2 teaspoons fresh thyme or ½ teaspoon dried
⅛ teaspoon salt
Freshly ground white pepper

Fifteen minutes before broiling, place rack 6 inches (15cm) from heat source and preheat broiler. Lightly butter 6 large scallop shells or 4-inch (10cm) gratin dishes. Have baking sheet ready.

Bring stock to boil in 1-quart (1L) saucepan. In 2 batches, poach scallops just until opaque — about 25 seconds. Remove each with slotted spoon as soon as it is cooked; drain well and reserve.

Boil stock until reduced to 1 tablespoon — about 25 minutes. Add cream and cook over medium-high heat until reduced to ¾ cup (180ml). Add thyme. Taste and season with salt and pepper.

Arrange 3 scallop halves on each shell and add 2 tablespoons of sauce to each. Recipe can be prepared to this point several hours in advance, covered and refrigerated. Bring to room temperature before broiling.

Place shells on baking sheet and broil until lightly browned — about 4 to 5 minutes. Serve immediately.

Makes 6 servings.

Steamed Scallop Seviche

1 1/2 pounds (680g) bay scallops
3 tablespoons fresh lime juice
3 tablespoons Mayonnaise (see
   Index)
2 1/2 tablespoons raspberry vinegar
3/4 teaspoon salt
   Freshly ground pepper

1 small red onion (4 ounces, 115g),
   peeled and halved
2 medium tomatoes (12 ounces total,
   340g), cored and halved
1/4 cup finely julienned fresh basil
   leaves
   Whole basil leaves for garnish

STEAMED SCALLOP SEVICHE

I love scallops, but prefer not to eat them raw. Steaming them just until they barely turn opaque preserves their natural texture and sweetness. When you make this dish in the summer, use firm, ripe tomatoes and fresh basil. At other times of year, substitute red peppers and parsley (see NOTE). Either combination is delicious with the fruity raspberry vinegar.

Fill bottom of steamer with water. Water should not touch steamer insert. Cover and bring water to boil. Add half of scallops, cover and cook, stirring twice, just until they become opaque — about 30 seconds. Do not overcook. Transfer scallops to 6-cup (1.5L) bowl. Steam remaining scallops. Add to bowl and immediately toss with lime juice while scallops are warm. Cover and refrigerate from 4 to 12 hours, stirring several times.

Drain scallops. Mix Mayonnaise with raspberry vinegar, salt and pepper and add to scallops.

French Fry Disc: Use firm pressure to cut onion and add to scallops. Stand tomato halves in feed tube and use light pressure to cut. (If you do not have a French Fry Disc, see page 229 for coarse chopping.)

Use slotted spoon to lift tomato pieces from seeds and juice. Add pieces to scallops; discard seeds and juice. Add basil strips and adjust seasoning.

Can be made several hours in advance and refrigerated. To serve, drain any liquid and adjust seasoning. Divide scallops among shells or small serving plates and garnish with basil leaves.

Makes 6 to 8 servings.

NOTE: Substitute 2 medium red peppers (10 ounces total, 285g) for tomatoes and 2 tablespoons of minced parsley for basil. Stand peppers on cutting board and cut off 3 or 4 vertical slices, leaving only core and stem. Remove any membrane from slices.

Medium Slicing Disc (3mm): Stand slices lengthwise in feed tube, fitting them in tightly to hold. Use medium pressure to slice.

SHRIMP WRAPPED IN CABBAGE LEAVES, WITH CAVIAR BUTTER

This elegant and beautiful creation, in which the lowly cabbage is combined with shrimp and caviar, has become one of Frédy Girardet's signature dishes. You can serve this as a first course for eight people or as a main course for four.

Shrimp and Cabbage

2 tablespoons safflower oil
16 extra-jumbo shrimp (1½ pounds total, 680g), in the shell, thawed and patted dry
8 large outer leaves cabbage, preferably Savoy
Salt
Freshly ground pepper
1 tablespoon unsalted butter

Caviar Butter

2 large shallots (1 ounce total, 30g), peeled
2 tablespoons white-wine vinegar
2 tablespoons Fish Stock (see Index) or clam juice
2 sticks unsalted butter (8 ounces total, 225g), chilled and cut into 8 pieces
1 tablespoon black caviar
Pinch of cayenne pepper
½ teaspoon salt
Freshly ground pepper
2 teaspoons finely diced pimiento

Fifteen minutes before baking, place rack in center of oven and preheat to 475°F (245°C). Butter 8-inch (20cm) baking dish.

Heat oil over medium-high heat in 10-inch (25cm) sauté pan. Cook shrimp just until opaque, removing each one as cooked; do not overcook. When shrimp are cool enough to handle, peel them and remove black vein.

Add 1 teaspoon of salt to 2 quarts (2L) of water and bring to boil. Cook cabbage leaves in 2 batches until tender and pliable, but not soft — about 8 minutes. Remove with slotted spoon and put in bowl of ice water to cool completely. Drain and pat dry with paper towels. Cut away any thick central ribs.

Arrange leaves on cutting board with outside down and season lightly with salt and pepper. Nest 2 shrimp on upper third of each leaf. Fold up bottom to cover shrimp, then fold sides and top, making a neat packet. Place packets, seam side down, in prepared baking dish. The packets can be prepared to this point 1 day in advance, covered airtight and refrigerated. Bring to room temperature before baking.

Dot with butter and bake uncovered until heated through — about 10 minutes. While packets bake, prepare Caviar Butter.

Metal Blade: Turn on machine, drop shallot through feed tube and process until minced.

In 1-quart (1L) saucepan, cook shallots, vinegar and Fish Stock or clam juice over medium-high heat until reduced to 1 tablespoon. Whisk in butter, one piece at a time; wait until each piece is incorporated before adding another. When all butter has been added, add caviar, cayenne pepper, pepper and salt. Keep warm in pan of warm water or on warm stove for up to 10 minutes.

To serve, place 1 shrimp packet on each of 8 warm salad plates. Spoon 1 tablespoon of Caviar Butter over each and garnish with diced pimiento. Serve immediately.

Makes 8 servings.

1/4 cup pine nuts (1 ounce, 30g)
1 large garlic clove, peeled
2 small leeks (8 ounces total, 225g), white part only, split and cleaned
2 tablespoons extra-virgin olive oil
3 ounces (85g) imported smoked ham, like Westphalian, cut into 1/4-inch (6mm) dice
3 large egg whites
2 teaspoons white vinegar

4 large egg yolks
1/2 cup (120ml) whipping cream
3/4 teaspoon finely snipped fresh tarragon or 1/4 teaspoon dried
1/4 teaspoon salt
Freshly ground pepper
1 small tomato (4 ounces, 115g), peeled, seeded and diced (to peel tomatoes, see page 217)
6 sprigs fresh tarragon

see page 217

LEEK AND HAM TIMBALES

A light and inviting first course that lies somewhere between a soufflé and a custard. Use young, tender leeks if you can find them; they are more delicate in flavor than larger ones.

Fifteen minutes before baking, place rack in center of oven and preheat to 400°F (205°C). Butter 6 timbale molds of 1/3-cup (80ml) capacity. Have ready kettle of boiling water and baking dish large enough to hold molds.

Put pine nuts in single layer on jelly-roll pan and bake until golden — about 7 minutes. Reserve them and reduce oven temperature to 350°F (175°C).

Metal Blade: Turn on machine, drop garlic through feed tube and process until minced.

Medium Slicing Disc (3mm): Stand leeks in feed tube; use medium pressure to slice.

Heat oil in 10-inch (25cm) skillet. Add garlic, leeks and ham and cook gently, stirring often, until leeks are limp — about 20 minutes. Wipe out work bowl with paper towel.

Metal Blade: Process egg whites for 15 seconds. With machine running, pour vinegar through feed tube and process until egg whites are whipped and hold their shape — about 1 minute. Gently transfer to mixing bowl. Process egg yolks, cream, tarragon, salt and pepper for 3 seconds. Add reserved pine nuts and contents of skillet and pulse twice. Spoon egg whites onto mixture in circle and pulse 2 or 3 times to combine. Do not overprocess; some streaks of egg white will still be visible.

Divide custard and vegetables evenly among prepared molds. Put molds in baking dish and place dish on oven rack. Pour in boiling water to come halfway up sides of molds. Bake until set — about 25 minutes. Remove from water bath and let rest for 5 minutes. Invert onto individual plates and garnish with diced tomato and sprig of tarragon.

Can be made up to 2 days in advance. Let cool completely in molds, then cover airtight and refrigerate. Uncover, leave in molds and reheat in water bath on top of stove for 25 to 30 minutes.

Makes 6 servings.

FISH AND LEEK MOUSSELINE WITH RED-WINE SAUCE

A red-wine sauce with fish may strike you as unusual, but Frédy Girardet uses this delicious dish to show how well they complement each other. Instead of using fish stock, he cooks the fish in vegetable stock, which lends a delicate flavor.

1 small leek (4 ounces, 115g), with coarse greens trimmed away, cut into thirds
12 ounces (340g) fresh sea bass or halibut fillets, chilled
4 tablespoons unsalted butter, softened, in 2 pieces
2 large eggs
$1/2$ teaspoon salt
$1/4$ teaspoon freshly grated nutmeg

$1/8$ teaspoon cayenne pepper
$1/3$ cup (80ml) whipping cream, softly whipped
2 cups (480ml) Vegetable Stock (see Index)
1 small scallion ($1/2$ ounce, 15g), including green top, sliced into thin rings
Red-Wine Sauce (recipe follows)

Fifteen minutes before baking, place rack in center of oven and preheat to 375°F (190°C). Generously butter 6 timbale molds of $1/2$-cup (120ml) capacity. Have ready kettle of boiling water and pan large enough to hold molds.

Add 1 teaspoon of salt to 2 quarts (2L) of water and bring to boil. Cook leek until soft — about 8 to 12 minutes. Immediately hold under cold running water until cool. Wrap in towel and squeeze gently to remove as much moisture as possible.

Metal Blade: Process leek and 2 ounces (55g) of fish until smooth, stopping once to scrape work bowl. Add butter, eggs, salt, nutmeg and cayenne and process for 2 minutes, stopping once to scrape work bowl.

Transfer to mixing bowl and gently fold in whipped cream. Divide mixture among prepared molds, filling each to within $1/2$ inch (12mm) of top. Tap lightly on counter to remove any air pockets. Put molds in baking dish and place dish on oven rack. Pour boiling water into dish to halfway up sides of molds. Bake until lightly colored and firm in center — about 20 minutes. Carefully remove molds from pan and let them rest for 5 minutes.

While mousselines bake, cut remaining 10 ounces (285g) of fish on diagonal into 18 triangular strips of uniform size. Heat Vegetable Stock in 8-inch (20cm) skillet. Cook fish in 2 batches just until opaque — about 1 minute. Use slotted spoon to transfer them to warm platter and cover with tent of aluminum foil to keep them warm.

To serve, spread about $2 1/2$ tablespoons of Red-Wine Sauce on each of 6 warm serving plates. Loosen timbales and invert them onto plates. Arrange 3 pieces of fish on each plate. Sprinkle lightly with scallions and serve immediately.

Makes 6 servings.

NOTE: Vegetable Stock can be strained and frozen for reuse.

2 large shallots (1 ounce total, 30g),
  peeled
³/₄ cup (180ml) dry red wine
¹/₄ cup (60ml) Fish Stock (see Index)
  or clam juice
¹/₂ cup (120ml) Vegetable Stock (see
  Index)

1 stick plus 1 tablespoon unsalted
  butter (4¹/₂ ounces, 130g), chilled
  and cut into 9 pieces
Pinch of sugar
Pinch of cayenne pepper
Pinch of salt
Freshly ground pepper

RED-WINE SAUCE

Metal Blade: Turn on machine, drop shallots through feed tube and process until minced.

In 1-quart (1L) non-aluminum saucepan, cook shallots, wine, Fish Stock or clam juice and Vegetable Stock until reduced to ¹/₄ cup (60ml). Strain and return liquid to saucepan. Continue cooking until reduced to 3 tablespoons. Sauce can be prepared to this point 1 day in advance. Reheat gently before proceeding. Whisk in butter, one piece at a time; wait until each piece is incorporated before adding another. Add remaining ingredients. Sauce can be placed over gently simmering water and kept warm for up to 15 minutes.

Makes ³/₄ cup (180ml).

¹/₄ cup loosely packed parsley leaves
¹/₄ cup whole blanched almonds (1
  ounce, 30g)
4 large shallots (2 ounces total, 55g),
  peeled
5 large garlic cloves, peeled
1 small piece celery root (1 ounce,
  30g), peeled

1¹/₂ sticks unsalted butter (6 ounces,
  170g), softened, cut into 6 pieces
1 tablespoon Cognac
1 teaspoon salt
¹/₂ teaspoon freshly grated nutmeg
Freshly ground pepper
24 canned snails, rinsed, patted dry
French bread

SNAILS WITH GARLIC AND CELERY ROOT

This recipe, derived from my work with Jean Delaveyne, chef-owner of Le Camélia in the Paris suburb of Bougival, is typical of the subtle sophistication of his cooking. A garlicky butter sauce with the slight crunch of almonds and celery root is irresistible fare for snail lovers. If celery root isn't available, double the amount of almonds — you'll have the crunch of the celery root, if not the taste.

Fifteen minutes before baking, place rack in center of oven and preheat to 400°F (205°C). Have ready 4 soufflé dishes of ¹/₂-cup (120ml) capacity or 24 natural or ceramic snail shells and shallow baking pan large enough to hold them.

Metal Blade: Process parsley, almonds, shallots, garlic and celery root until minced. Add butter, Cognac, salt, nutmeg and pepper and process for 30 seconds, stopping once to scrape work bowl.

If using soufflé dishes, place 6 snails in each and divide butter mixture among dishes, spreading it evenly over snails. If using individual snail shells, put scant teaspoon of butter mixture in bottom of each shell, top with snail and press gently. Dot tops with remaining butter. Can be prepared 1 day in advance, covered airtight and refrigerated. Before baking, bring to room temperature. Place dishes or shells in baking dish and bake until bubbling — about 10 minutes. Serve immediately with slices of warm French bread.

Makes 4 servings.

SEAFOOD SAUSAGE WITH TOMATO BUTTER SAUCE

Known in France as Boudin Blanc, *these are elegant, delicately flavored sausages of shrimp and scallops. Traditionally, they are stuffed with a sausage stuffer into natural hog casings. Since most cooks don't have a sausage stuffer, I've given instructions for wrapping them in Saran plastic wrap.*

1¼ pounds (570g) medium shrimp, in shells
1 large shallot (½ ounce, 15g), peeled
6 large mushrooms (4 ounces total, 115g)
2 tablespoons unsalted butter
1 slice white bread (1 ounce, 30g), with crust trimmed
1 tablespoon safflower oil
1 pound (455g) sea scallops
1½ teaspoons salt
½ teaspoon Tabasco sauce
½ teaspoon freshly grated nutmeg
Freshly ground white pepper
2 large egg whites
1 cup (240ml) whipping cream, chilled
Tomato Butter Sauce (recipe follows)

Peel shrimp and reserve shells for Tomato Butter Sauce. Hold shrimp under running water and remove black vein; pat dry.

Metal Blade: Turn on machine, drop shallot through feed tube and process until minced. Add mushrooms and process until minced.

Melt butter over medium-high heat in 10-inch (25cm) skillet. Add shallots and mushrooms and cook gently until they are very soft — about 8 to 10 minutes. Transfer to mixing bowl.

Metal Blade: Process bread into fine crumbs and add to mixing bowl.

Gently heat oil in same skillet. Sauté all but 8 ounces (225g) of shrimp, removing each one as it becomes opaque; do not overcook.

Metal Blade: Add cooked shrimp in 2 batches and pulse to chop them coarsely; place them in separate mixing bowl. Process scallops until smooth, stopping once to scrape work bowl; remove and reserve. Process uncooked shrimp, shallots, mushrooms, bread crumbs, salt, Tabasco, nutmeg and pepper until smooth, stopping once to scrape work bowl. Return scallops to work bowl, turn machine on and pour egg whites through feed tube; process for 15 seconds. With machine running, slowly pour cream through feed tube and process for 15 seconds more.

Add mixture to minced shrimp and combine thoroughly.

Spoon about ¾ cup (180ml) of mixture onto 10-inch (25cm) length of Saran brand plastic wrap (see NOTE). Fold wrap over and work through plastic to shape seafood mixture into 8-inch (20cm) cylinder of uniform thickness. Do not taper ends. Roll up and seal ends tightly with wire twist-ties.

Sausages can be made several hours in advance and refrigerated. Before cooking, bring them to room temperature.

Place sausages in large pot with water. Let simmer gently until internal temperature of sausages is 160°F (70°C); make sure water temperature never goes above 200°F (95°C). This will take about 25 to 30 minutes.

Remove sausages from water, carefully remove plastic and cut each sausage into 8 slices. To serve, spoon 3 tablespoons of Tomato Butter Sauce onto individual warm plates. Arrange overlapping slices of sausage in a circle over sauce and pass remaining sauce.

Makes 6 to 8 servings.

NOTE: For information about cooking with Saran wrap, see page 105

1. *Spooning mixture onto Saran wrap*

2. *Rolling in Saran wrap*

3. *Twisting ends*

4. *Sealing with twist-ties*

TOMATO BUTTER SAUCE

2 large shallots (1 ounce total, 30g), peeled
1 cup (240ml) dry white wine or dry vermouth
  Shrimp shells reserved from Seafood Sausage, rinsed and dried
1 tablespoon tomato paste
1 teaspoon sugar
2 large tomatoes (14 ounces total, 395g), peeled, quartered and seeded (to peel tomatoes, see page 217)
$^1/_2$ cup (120ml) whipping cream
$^1/_2$ teaspoon salt
  Freshly grated nutmeg
  Freshly ground pepper
4 tablespoons unsalted butter, chilled and quartered

Metal Blade: Turn on machine, drop shallots through feed tube and process until minced.

Transfer to 1-quart (1L) non-aluminum saucepan and add wine and shrimp shells. Bring to boil, then let simmer, uncovered, for 15 minutes. Strain and return liquid to saucepan. Add tomato paste and sugar.

Metal Blade: Add tomatoes and pulse to chop them coarsely; add to saucepan.

Cook gently, stirring occasionally, until reduced to 1$^1/_4$ cups (300ml). Add cream, salt, nutmeg and pepper and let simmer for 5 minutes. Transfer to work bowl.

Metal Blade: Process until smooth, stopping once to scrape work bowl.

Can be prepared to this point 1 day in advance. Let cool, then refrigerate.

Return to saucepan and bring to simmer. Whisk in butter, 1 piece at a time; wait until each melts before adding another. Adjust seasoning and serve immediately.

Makes 1$^1/_2$ cups (360ml).

SPINACH ROLLS WITH MUSHROOM CREAM SAUCE

Egg-roll wrappers can be used for more than egg rolls. Here they function as a crêpe, encasing a flavorful spinach and cheese filling. The wrappers are much crisper than crêpes and nicely chewy. The Spinach Rolls are perfect for a midday meal or light supper as well as a first course. If you have any filling left, it's delicious in an omelette.

2 large scallions (3 ounces total, 85g), including green tops, trimmed and cut into 1-inch (2.5cm) pieces
1 slice white bread (1 ounce, 30g), quartered
8 ounces (225g) fresh spinach with stems, washed and dried
8 ounces (225g) cream cheese, quartered

2 ounces (55g) blue cheese
1 large egg
1/4 teaspoon freshly grated nutmeg
1/4 teaspoon salt
Freshly ground pepper
8 egg-roll wrappers
3 tablespoons unsalted butter
Mushroom Cream Sauce (recipe follows)

Metal Blade: Process scallions, bread and 1/4 of spinach until minced. Transfer to mixing bowl. Process remaining spinach in 3 batches. Return all 4 batches to work bowl and add both cheeses, egg, nutmeg, salt and pepper. Pulse about 6 times to blend, stopping once to scrape work bowl.

Place egg-roll wrapper on flat surface. Spoon about 4 1/2 tablespoons of spinach mixture along length of wrapper, leaving 1/2-inch (12mm) border. Fold border onto spinach mixture, press lightly, then roll into compact cylinder. Brush 1/2 inch (12mm) of outside flap with water and press gently to seal.

Melt butter in 12-inch (30cm) skillet. Gently cook spinach rolls, seam side down, until golden — about 4 minutes. Turn and cook other side for about 4 more minutes.

Spoon 2 1/2 tablespoons of sauce over each roll and serve immediately.

Makes 8 servings.

MUSHROOM CREAM SAUCE

20 small mushrooms (8 ounces total, 225g), with stems trimmed and 2 opposite sides cut flat
6 tablespoons unsalted butter
1/2 teaspoon salt

1/4 teaspoon freshly grated nutmeg
Freshly ground pepper
1/4 cup (60ml) ruby Port
1 cup (240ml) whipping cream

Medium Slicing Disc (3mm): Stand mushrooms in feed tube on flat side and use light pressure to slice.

Melt butter in 8-inch (20cm) skillet, add mushrooms, salt, nutmeg and pepper and cook gently for 5 minutes. Add Port, bring to simmer and cook for 3 minutes. Add cream and cook over high heat until cream has thickened sufficiently to coat mushrooms — about 15 minutes. Keep sauce warm over gently simmering water while preparing spinach rolls.

Sauce can be made 2 days in advance and refrigerated. Reheat gently before serving.

Makes about 1 1/3 cups (320ml).

1 ounce (30g) European dried
  mushrooms
¼ cup (60ml) hot water
24 large mushrooms (1 pound total,
  455g), with 2 opposite sides cut flat
7 tablespoons unsalted butter
½ cup (120ml) Port
½ cup (120ml) whipping cream
¼ cup (60ml) beef broth
¼ teaspoon salt

¼ teaspoon freshly grated nutmeg
  Freshly ground pepper
½ recipe freshly cooked Semolina
  Pasta Circles (see Index), cooked al
  dente
½ cup (120ml) Crème Fraîche (see
  Index) or sour cream
1 tablespoon snipped fresh chives
  Watercress leaves

Soak mushrooms in hot water until soft. Remove them and squeeze out excess liquid.
Line strainer with paper towel or coffee filter, place over bowl and strain liquid;
reserve.

Medium Slicing Disc (3mm): Stand fresh mushrooms in feed tube on flat side and use
light pressure to slice.

Melt 3 tablespoons of butter over medium-high heat in 12-inch (30cm) skillet. Cook
mushrooms until they begin to soften — about 4 minutes. Add soaked mushrooms and
their liquid, Port, cream, beef broth, salt, nutmeg and pepper and cook, uncovered,
over medium heat until liquid is consistency of whipping cream — about 10 minutes.
Whisk in remaining 4 tablespoons of butter, 1 tablespoon at a time, waiting until each
is melted before adding another.

Place 2 pasta circles on each of 8 individual salad plates and spoon 2 tablespoons of
mushroom mixture onto each. Cut 2 additional pasta circles in half and overlap them
across bottom half of mushrooms. Spoon ½ tablespoon of Crème Fraîche or sour
cream in center and sprinkle with chives. Garnish with watercress and serve
immediately.

Makes 8 servings.

OPEN RAVIOLI WITH WOODLAND MUSHROOMS

*The pasta must be
freshly cooked
because it must be
hot when the dish
is assembled. The
last-minute work
is definitely
worthwhile! If you
have a microwave
oven, you can
assemble the dish
completely in
advance and
reheat it at serving
time. Arrange the
ravioli and
mushrooms on
serving plates and
hold at room
temperature for up
to 3 hours. Just
before serving,
cover and cook
them for 30 to 40
seconds at the
medium setting.*

*Open Ravioli with
Woodland
Mushrooms*

CAFE PROVENCAL VEGETABLE TARTS

Leslee Reis, chef and owner of Café Provençal in Evanston, Illinois, created this fantastic recipe. It makes an elegant first course that can be prepared in advance. Fill the tarts just before serving so the buttery pastries stay crisp.

½ cup loosely packed parsley leaves
3 medium onions (14 ounces total, 395g), peeled and halved lengthwise
6 fresh artichokes
5 tablespoons unsalted butter
15 garlic cloves (1½ ounces total, 45g), peeled
1 tablespoon finely snipped fresh basil or ¾ teaspoon dried
1 teaspoon freshly snipped fresh thyme or ¾ teaspoon dried

2 whole bay leaves
½ teaspoon salt
Freshly ground pepper
1 large head Boston lettuce (6 ounces, 170g), cut to fit feed tube
2 large red peppers (12 ounces total, 340g)
¼ cup sugar (1¾ ounces, 50g)
¼ cup (60ml) red-wine vinegar
¼ cup (60ml) white wine
6 prebaked 4-inch (10cm) Flaky Pastry tart shells (see Index)

Metal Blade: Process parsley until minced; remove and reserve.

Thin (2mm) or Medium Slicing Disc (3mm): Stand onions in feed tube and use firm pressure to slice.

Remove top two thirds of artichokes, then cut stem flush with base. Remove all leaves around base, trimming them as close as possible without removing any flesh from bottom. Spoon out fuzzy choke and cut bottoms into sixths.

Melt 3 tablespoons of butter in 10-inch (25cm) sauté pan and add onions, artichoke bottoms, garlic, basil, thyme, bay leaves, salt and pepper. Cover and cook gently for 5 minutes.

All-Purpose Slicing Disc (4mm): Use light pressure to slice lettuce.

Place lettuce over vegetables in pan. Cover and cook gently until artichokes are tender — about 35 to 40 minutes. Meanwhile, prepare peppers.

Stand peppers on cutting board. Use sharp knife to cut 3 or 4 vertical slices, leaving only core and stem. Remove any membrane from slices.

Medium Slicing Disc (3mm): Stack slices and stand them lengthwise in feed tube, fitting them in tightly to hold. Use light pressure to slice.

Melt remaining 2 tablespoons of butter in 8-inch (20cm) skillet. Add peppers and cook over medium heat just until they begin to soften — about 5 minutes. Add sugar, vinegar and wine and cook, stirring often, until liquid becomes syrupy and coats peppers.

Add peppers and parsley to vegetables and adjust seasoning. Vegetables can be cooked 2 days in advance and reheated gently at serving time.

Place prebaked tarts on baking sheet and bake in preheated 300°F (150°C) oven until warm — about 10 minutes. Spoon warm vegetable mixture into tart shells and serve immediately.

Makes 6 individual tarts.

12 large chicken livers (12 ounces
    total, 340g)
1 cup (240ml) milk
¼ cup unbleached all purpose flour
    (1¼ ounces, 35g)
1 teaspoon salt
    Freshly ground pepper
1 small zucchini (3 ounces, 85g)

2 to 3 tablespoons safflower oil
2 to 3 tablespoons unsalted butter
2 tablespoons walnut oil
2 tablespoons red-wine vinegar
2 tablespoons Port wine
¼ teaspoon sugar
1½ tablespoons drained capers
2 tablespoons snipped fresh chives

Trim membrane from livers and separate each into 2 pieces. Put them in small dish with milk and soak for 30 minutes. Drain and pat dry.

Season flour with ¾ teaspoon of salt, and pepper to taste. Dip each liver in flour, turn to coat it evenly and shake off excess flour.

All-Purpose Slicing Disc (4mm): Stand zucchini in feed tube and use medium pressure to slice.

Heat 1 tablespoon each of safflower oil and butter in 10-inch (25cm) skillet. When very hot, add zucchini and ⅛ teaspoon of salt and cook just until zucchini turns bright green — about 1½ minutes. Remove with slotted spoon and reserve. Add ½ of livers to skillet and cook over medium-high heat, turning only once, until brown and crusty on both sides — about 3 minutes. Do not overcook; they should be crisp outside, but still soft and slightly pink inside. Transfer to platter and cover with tent of aluminum foil to keep them warm. Cook remaining livers, adding more butter and oil to skillet if necessary.

Put walnut oil, vinegar, Port, sugar and remaining ⅛ teaspoon of salt in small saucepan and bring to boil. Stir in capers and remove from heat.

Arrange 3 or 4 zucchini slices and 3 pieces of chicken liver on individual plates. Spoon about 2 teaspoons of vinegar and caper mixture over livers and sprinkle with fresh chives. Serve immediately.

Makes 8 servings.

CHICKEN LIVERS WITH ZUCCHINI AND CAPERS

Many chefs cook fresh foie gras *by quickly sautéeing it over high heat. This method produces perfectly cooked livers with a crisp exterior and a juicy, pink inside.*

Café Provençal Vegetable Tarts

FISH TERRINE WITH CUCUMBER SAUCE

This delicate and vibrantly beautiful terrine is representative of the Provençal cooking of Roger Vergé, owner and chef of Le Moulin de Mougins restaurant in the south of France. Strips of fish, pistachio nuts and bits of crisply cooked carrots are interspersed in silken mousse, which is bordered with sliced lemons and pimientos.

1 small leek (4 ounces, 115g), with coarse greens trimmed away, cut into feed-tube lengths
1 cup (240ml) clam juice
9 ounces (255g) gray sole or ocean catfish fillets, cut diagonally along grain into strips 1/2 inch (12mm) wide
2 medium carrots (6 ounces total, 170g), peeled, cooked until tender but crisp and cut into feed-tube widths
1 lemon, scored and cut flat at bottom
3 large shallots (2 ounces total, 55g), peeled
8 ounces (225g) sea scallops, chilled

8 ounces (225g) scrod, cut into 2-inch (5cm) cubes and chilled
1 1/4 teaspoons salt
Freshly ground white pepper
Freshly grated nutmeg
Dash of Tabasco sauce
1 1/3 cups (320ml) whipping cream, chilled
3 large eggs
8 ounces (225g) natural pistachio nuts, shelled and skinned (see NOTE)
2 3 3/4-ounce (105g) jars whole pimientos, drained and patted dry
Watercress leaves
Cucumber Sauce (recipe follows)

Fifteen minutes before baking, place rack in center of oven and preheat to 300°F (150°C). Line 7-cup (1.7L) terrine or loaf pan with aluminum foil, extending it 3 inches (8cm) over ends of terrine. Smooth out wrinkles.

Have ready kettle of boiling water and baking dish large enough to hold terrine.

All-Purpose Slicing Disc (4mm): Stand leek in feed tube and use medium pressure to slice.

Let clam juice and leeks simmer for 10 minutes in 6-inch (15cm) skillet. Strain leeks, reserving liquid. In same liquid, cook fish strips in batches just until opaque — about 30 seconds. Do not overcook. Remove fish with slotted spoon and drain on paper towels. Refrigerate until ready to assemble terrine.

French Fry Disc: Lay carrots horizontally in feed tube and use medium pressure to cut; remove and reserve. (If you do not have a French Fry Disc, see page 229.)

All-Purpose Slicing Disc (4mm): Use firm pressure to slice lemon; remove and reserve. Wipe out work bowl with paper towel.

Metal Blade: Turn on machine, drop shallots through feed tube and process until minced. Add scallops, scrod, salt, pepper, nutmeg and Tabasco and process for 1 minute, stopping once to scrape work bowl. With machine running, drizzle cream through feed tube, adding it only as fast as purée can absorb it; this may take as long as 1 minute. Add eggs and process for 15 seconds.

Arrange row of lemon slices along bottom of terrine; do not overlap them. Reserve remaining slices for garnish. Use spatula to spread 1/2-inch (12mm) layer of mousse over lemons. Sprinkle with pistachios. Carefully spread 1-inch (2.5cm) layer of mousse over nuts. Arrange 2 evenly spaced rows of fish strips down length of terrine. Fill in spaces between fish strips with mousse, then cover with 1/4-inch (6mm) layer of mousse. Lay carrots lengthwise in terrine and use remaining mousse to "cement" them in place. Cut pimientos to lie flat and arrange over terrine. Bang terrine on counter several times to remove any air bubbles. Fold foil over top, pressing pimientos lightly into mousse. Cover with piece of foil. Put terrine in baking dish. Place on oven rack and pour boiling water in baking dish to depth of 1 1/2 inches (4cm). Bake until firm — about 1 hour. Uncover and cool completely, then refrigerate.

To serve, invert onto serving platter. Garnish platter with watercress sprigs and reserved lemon slices. Pass Cucumber Sauce separately.

Makes 12 servings.

NOTE: To skin pistachio nuts, submerge them in boiling water for 30 seconds. Drain and immediately rub between 2 towels to remove skins.

**CUCUMBER
SAUCE**

2 medium cucumbers (1 1/2 pounds total, 680g), peeled, halved lengthwise, seeded and cut into feed-tube lengths
3/4 teaspoon salt
1/4 cup loosely packed parsley leaves

1 large shallot (1/2 ounce, 15g), peeled
1 cup (240ml) whipping cream
1 tablespoon white-wine vinegar
Freshly ground pepper

Medium Slicing Disc (3mm): Stand cucumber in feed tube and use medium pressure to slice.

Transfer to colander and toss with 1/4 teaspoon of salt. Let drain for 30 minutes, then pat dry. Wipe out work bowl with paper towel.

Metal Blade: Put parsley in work bowl, turn on machine and drop shallot through feed tube. Process until minced. With machine running, pour cream through feed tube and process until thick — about 1 minute. Add vinegar, remaining 1/2 teaspoon of salt and pepper and process for 5 seconds.

Gently combine sauce with cucumbers. Can be prepared up to 1 day in advance. Drain excess liquid before serving.

Makes about 3 cups (720ml).

VEGETABLE TERRINE WITH LIVER PATE

The original version of this fabulous terrine was on the menu at Frédy Girardet's restaurant in Crissier, Switzerland, when I worked there several years ago; it still is. It's a lovely interplay of rich, mild flavored pâté with crisp vegetables. Girardet uses fresh foie gras; I've worked out a satisfactory substitute with chicken, chicken livers, butter and egg. The terrine involves more steps than most recipes in this book, but it can all be done in advance.

Terrine

1 juice carrot (6 ounces, 170g), peeled (see NOTE)
2 medium turnips (6 ounces total, 170g), peeled
4 ounces (115g) green beans of uniform size, trimmed
3¹/₂ cups, (6 ounces, 170g) broccoli flowerets
2 cups loosely packed parsley leaves
7 ounces (200g) uncooked chicken-breast meat, cut into 1-inch (2.5cm) pieces

¹/₂ cup (120ml) whipping cream, chilled
1 large egg white
1 teaspoon salt
¹/₂ teaspoon freshly grated nutmeg
Freshly ground pepper
4 large chicken livers (4 ounces total, 115g), trimmed, with membrane removed
3 tablespoons unsalted butter, softened
1 large egg

Garnish

¹/₃ cup walnuts (1¹/₃ ounces, 40g)
1 4-ounce (115g) wedge red cabbage, cored

6 small red radishes (3 ounces, 85g), trimmed
Walnut Vinaigrette (recipe follows)

Fifteen minutes before baking, place rack in center of oven and preheat to 250°F (120°C). Generously butter 4-cup (1L) terrine or loaf pan and fit bottom with parchment paper. Butter paper and season lightly with salt and pepper. Refrigerate prepared terrine for at least 30 minutes.

At baking time, have ready kettle of boiling water and baking dish large enough to hold terrine.

Add 1 teaspoon of salt to 3 quarts (3L) of water and bring to boil. (Water will be used to cook vegetables in separate batches; bring to full boil before adding each batch.) Add carrot and cook until just tender but not soft — about 6 minutes. Use slotted spoon to remove from pan; hold under cold running water until cool and blot dry with paper towels. Use same procedure to cook and cool each vegetable as follows: cook turnips for 12 minutes, green beans for 6 minutes and 1 cup of broccoli flowerets for 3 minutes. Cook remaining 2¹/₂ cups of broccoli flowerets until very soft — about 10 minutes. Put parsley in strainer and immerse in boiling water for 10 seconds. Drain each vegetable well and pat dry with paper towels; it is essential to remove all excess moisture.

Cut carrots, turnips and green beans into ¹/₄-inch (6mm) dice with sharp knife. Transfer to mixing bowl and combine with crisp-cooked broccoli flowerets. Vegetables can be prepared to this point 1 day in advance; cover airtight and refrigerate. Combine soft-cooked broccoli and parsley; wrap airtight and refrigerate.

Metal Blade: Process 3 ounces (85g) of chicken for 10 seconds, stopping once to scrape work bowl. Add broccoli and parsley mixture and process for 10 seconds. With machine running, slowly pour cream through feed tube. Add egg white, ¹/₂ teaspoon of salt, ¹/₄ teaspoon of nutmeg and pepper and process for 5 seconds.

Transfer purée to mixing bowl and refrigerate.

Metal Blade: For pâté, process remaining 4 ounces (115g) of chicken for 5 seconds. Add livers, butter, egg, remaining ¹/₂ teaspoon of salt, remaining ¹/₄ teaspoon of nutmeg and pepper and process for 10 seconds, stopping once to scrape work bowl.

With back of spoon, coat sides and bottom of prepared pan with ¹/₈-inch (3mm) layer of broccoli purée. Stir remaining purée into mixed vegetables and spread ¹/₂ of mixture over bottom of mold, being careful not to displace coating on sides. Spread liver pâté evenly on top and finish with remaining vegetable mixture. Cover with buttered parchment paper and use your hands to press terrine gently into compact form. Cover with close-fitting lid or lightly oiled aluminum foil and place terrine in baking dish. Place dish on oven rack and pour in boiling water to come within ¹/₂ inch (12mm) of top of terrine. Bake until firm — about 1 hour and 15 minutes. Remove from water bath, let cool, then refrigerate overnight or up to 2 days.

Metal Blade: Pulse to chop walnuts coarsely.

Ultra Thin Slicing Disc (1mm): Use firm pressure to slice cabbage and medium pressure to slice radishes.

Transfer to mixing bowl and toss with 5 tablespoons of Walnut Vinaigrette. To serve, carefully loosen mousse from pan with small flexible spatula and invert onto platter. Slice into 8 servings and carefully transfer each to serving plate. Mixture will not be solid; it may be necessary to reshape slice. Garnish plate with cabbage mixture.

Makes 8 servings.

NOTE: Juice carrots are much larger than ordinary cello-packed carrots, and they have less fiber. If they are not available, use only thick end of carrots.

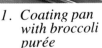

1. *Coating pan with broccoli purée*

2. *Spreading mixed vegetables*

3. *Spreading liver pâté*

4. *Finishing with mixed vegetables*

¹/₂ cup (120ml) safflower oil
1 tablespoon walnut oil
3¹/₂ tablespoons red-wine vinegar

¹/₂ teaspoon salt
¹/₂ teaspoon freshly grated nutmeg
Freshly ground pepper

Metal Blade: Process all ingredients until mixed — about 3 seconds.

Use immediately or refrigerate up to 1 week.

Makes ³/₄ cup (180ml).

LEEK AND VEGETABLE TERRINE WITH WALNUT VINAIGRETTE

My interest in less rich foods, especially as openers, inspired this exceptionally light vegetable terrine. The vegetables are lightly bound with gelatin instead of butter, cream and eggs, then compressed into a dense mass.

3 medium leeks (1¼ pounds total, 570g), including green tops
1 cup loosely packed parsley leaves
1 medium onion (6 ounces, 170g), peeled and quartered
2 medium celery stalks (4 ounces total, 115g), strings removed with vegetable peeler, cut into feed-tube lengths
2 tablespoons safflower oil
8 large carrots (2 pounds total, 910g), peeled and cut into feed-tube widths
4 large parsnips (1 pound total, 455g), peeled and cut into feed-tube widths
1½ teaspoons salt
Freshly ground pepper
4 teaspoons unflavored gelatin (2 packages)
3 tablespoons water
Red leaf lettuce
Walnut Vinaigrette (see Index)
2 tablespoons snipped fresh chives

Line terrine or loaf pan of at least 5¾-cup (1.4L) capacity with heavy-duty aluminum foil. Leave root end of leeks intact and trim away coarse greens. Split lengthwise to within 1 inch (2.5cm) of root and clean well under cold running water. Trim all green from one leek. Add 2 teaspoons of salt to 6 quarts (6L) of water and bring to boil. Add two whole leeks and cook until very tender — about 12 to 14 minutes. Hold under cold running water until cool. Drain well, wrap in towel and squeeze to remove as much moisture as possible. Trim root ends and cut cooked leeks to exact length of terrine. Lay leeks in pan with white ends opposite each other; fan leaves to cover bottom.

Metal Blade: Process parsley until minced; remove and reserve. Pulse to mince onion; leave in work bowl.

Thin Slicing Disc (2mm): Stand celery in feed tube and use medium pressure to slice. Lay uncooked leek horizontally in feed tube and use medium pressure to slice.

Heat oil in 12-inch (30cm) sauté pan. Add contents of work bowl and cook gently until soft — about 5 minutes.

3mm Julienne Disc or Medium Shredding Disc: Lay carrots and parsnips in feed tube and use firm pressure to process.

Add to pan along with salt and pepper and stir well. Cover and cook gently, stirring occasionally, until very soft — about 35 minutes. Blot vegetables with paper towels to remove as much liquid as possible. Stir in reserved parsley.

Sprinkle gelatin over water in measuring cup. When water is absorbed, dissolve gelatin by setting cup in pan of hot water, or leave for 50 seconds in microwave oven set at medium. All granules should be completely dissolved. Cool slightly.

Pour dissolved gelatin over hot vegetables and mix thoroughly. Transfer to terrine and press evenly and firmly into place. Cover and refrigerate overnight or up to 3 days.

To serve, carefully invert terrine onto platter. Use serrated knife to cut into 1-inch (2.5cm) slices. Arrange lettuce on plates and top with slice of terrine. Spoon Walnut Vinaigrette over and sprinkle with chives.

Makes 10 to 12 servings.

1/4 cup loosely packed parsley leaves
1/2 small garlic clove, peeled
   4 large chicken livers (3 1/2 ounces total, 100g), with membrane removed
1/2 cup beef marrow (1 3/4 ounces, 50g) (see NOTE)
   1 large egg

2 large egg yolks
1 cup (240ml) milk
1 teaspoon salt
1/4 teaspoon freshly grated nutmeg
   Pinch of cayenne pepper
1 1/2 cups (360ml) Tomato Cream Sauce (see Index)

Fifteen minutes before baking, place rack in center of oven and preheat to 350°F (175°C). Butter 6 ovenproof dishes of 1/3-cup (80ml) capacity. Have ready kettle of boiling water and baking dish large enough to hold 6 dishes.

Metal Blade: Process parsley until minced; remove and reserve. Turn on machine, drop garlic through feed tube and process until minced. Add chicken livers and process until smooth, stopping once to scrape work bowl. Add marrow and process for 1 minute, stopping once to scrape work bowl. Add egg and egg yolks and turn on machine. With machine running, slowly pour milk through feed tube. Add salt, nutmeg and pepper and process for 2 seconds.

Divide mixture among 6 prepared dishes and place dishes in baking dish. Place baking dish on oven rack and pour in boiling water to come halfway up sides of small dishes. Bake until mousse feels firm — about 20 minutes. Remove from water bath and let stand for 10 minutes.

Gently separate mousse from dishes with small, flexible knife and invert onto individual serving plates. Surround each with 1/4 cup (60ml) of Tomato Cream Sauce and garnish with reserved parsley.

Makes 6 servings.

NOTE: Many beef bones contain some marrow but chuck and leg bones have more than most. They are also easy to get and it's easy to extract the marrow from them. For 1/2 cup of marrow, you will need about 4 pounds (1.8kg) of bones.

CHICKEN LIVER MOUSSE WITH TOMATO SAUCE

Beef bone marrow is the unexpected ingredient in this terrine from Alain Chapel's restaurant in Mionnay, France. It gives depth and a rich, succulent flavor. The terrine is baked in individual dishes which make especially attractive servings. Little soufflé dishes work very well.

SOUPS & STOCKS

Soup has always had an honored place in the repertoire of most cooks, but my love for it developed slowly. To make up for lost time, I've lately gone soup-happy, experimenting with all types. I now have the greatest respect for soup in its infinite variety: hearty or delicate; down-to-earth or subtle; warm and comforting; cold and refreshing. Whatever its nature, soup is always fun to cook. A kettle of soup simmering on the back burner seems to take the chill off a winter night, while an uncooked soup is a godsend in a summer kitchen. Make a soup of substance like Mulligatawny and call it a meal, or introduce a multi-course meal with a light soup like Essence of Celery.

Homemade stock, vastly superior to canned, is one of a cook's best friends. If you're not in the habit of making stock, give it a try. It's easy on the cook, requiring little attention most of the time. It enriches soups, sauces and casseroles. To intensify the flavor, reduce it by boiling it down. It's easy to freeze in 1 or 2-cup containers, which are just as convenient as cans!

SOUPS AND STOCKS

SOUPS

Curried Carrot Soup
Corn and Parsnip Chowder
Spinach and Coconut Soup
Butternut Velvet Soup
Essence of Celery Soup
Cream of Cabbage Soup
Autumn Root Soup
Hearty Mushroom Soup
Cream of Garden Vegetable Soup
Italian Vegetable Soup with Pesto
Split Pea Soup
Tomato Soup with Allspice and Honey
Clear Broth with Vegetables and Tofu

Cold Tomato Soup with Fennel Mousse
Fresh Beet Sherbet
Tomato and Basil Sherbet
Spicy Gazpacho
Sorrel and Pear Soup
Spiced Avocado Soup

Mulligatawny Soup
Hearty Beef and Vegetable Soup
Sweet and Sour Cabbage Soup

Fish and Vegetables in Broth with
  Cilantro
New England Style Clam Chowder
Mussels in Their Own Broth
Smoked Oyster Soup with Spinach and
  Watercress

STOCKS

Chicken Stock
Beef or Veal Stock
Lamb Stock
Meat Glaze
Quick Fish Stock
Fish Stock
Court Bouillon
Vegetable Stock

Fish and Vegetables in Broth with Cilantro previous pages

TEMPURA TASTING
....
Clear Broth with Vegetables and Tofu
Shrimp and Vegetable Tempura with Dipping Sauce
Fluffy White Rice
Lemon Sherbet
Rich Butter Cookies

6 large carrots (1¹/₂ pounds total,
  680g), peeled and cut into
  feed-tube widths
1 large Granny Smith or other tart
  apple (8 ounces, 225g), peeled,
  halved, and cored
2 medium onions (6 ounces total,
  170g), peeled and cut to

fit feed tube
5 cups (1.2L) Chicken Stock (see
  Index) or chicken broth
¹/₂ teaspoon salt
¹/₄ teaspoon curry powder
¹/₈ teaspoon cinnamon
¹/₈ teaspoon turmeric
1 cup (240ml) whipping cream

Medium Shredding Disc: Use firm pressure to shred carrots and medium pressure to shred apple and onions.

Put them in 3-quart (3L) saucepan, add stock or broth, and bring to boil. Cover, reduce heat, and simmer gently until vegetables are soft — about 45 minutes. Strain liquid into large bowl; reserve liquid and solids.

Metal Blade: Process solids until smooth, stopping once to scrape work bowl. Add ¹/₂ cup (120 ml) of reserved liquid, salt, curry powder, cinnamon, and turmeric, and process for 5 seconds.

Stir purée and cream into remaining liquid and heat gently until simmering. Adjust seasoning and serve hot or cold. The soup can be made up to 3 days in advance.

Makes 7¹/₂ cups (1.8L).

2 medium parsnips (8 ounces total,
  225g), peeled and cut into 1-inch
  (2.5cm) pieces
2 large shallots (1 ounce total, 30g),
  peeled
2³/₄ to 3¹/₂ cups (660 to 840ml) milk
¹/₂ cup (120ml) water
2¹/₂ cups cooked corn (15 ounces total,
  425g)

1¹/₄ teaspoons salt
1¹/₂ teaspoon snipped fresh thyme, or
  ¹/₂ teaspoon dried
¹/₂ teaspoon freshly grated nutmeg
  Freshly ground white pepper
1¹/₂ teaspoons very finely snipped
  fresh chives

Metal Blade: Process parsnips and shallots until minced.

Put them in 2-quart (2L) saucepan with 1¹/₂ cups (360ml) of milk and water and bring to boil. Cover, reduce heat and simmer gently until very soft — about 35 minutes. Strain liquid into large bowl; reserve liquid and solids.

Metal Blade: Process solids until smooth, stopping once to scrape work bowl. Add 1 cup (240ml) of reserved cooking liquid and process to combine — 20 seconds.

Transfer mixture to saucepan; and add corn, salt, thyme, nutmeg, pepper, remaining 1¹/₄ cups (300ml) of milk and remaining cooking liquid. Heat and serve, garnished with chives. Can be prepared up to 2 days in advance and refrigerated. Heat before serving; thin with up to ³/₄ cup milk and adjust seasoning, if necessary.

Makes 6 cups (1.5L)

CURRIED CARROT SOUP

All the vitamins of carrots delivered in a particularly palatable way, sparked by a touch of curry. I prefer this soup hot, but it's good cold, too. Omitting the cream will reduce the calorie and cholesterol count. The soup will be a little less smooth in texture, but every bit as flavorful.

CORN AND PARSNIP CHOWDER

The seductively rich finish of this soup suggests a generous amount of cream, but there's not a drop! The parsnip contributes body and vitamins while keeping the calorie count down.

SPINACH AND COCONUT SOUP

A memorable soup typical of the elegant style of Roger Vergé, owner-chef of the Moulin de Mougins restaurant in the south of France. It's refreshingly delicious cold, but its unusual flavor is even more pronounced when served hot. Vergé strains it, but I prefer not to, as the flecks of coconut and spinach add interesting textural contrast.

1 pound (455g) fresh, young spinach leaves, including stems
1 medium lemon (about 3 ounces, 85g), scored, with bottom cut flat
2 medium onions (8 ounces total, 225g), peeled
2 tablespoons unsalted butter

3 1-inch (2.5cm) squares fresh coconut (2 ounces total, 55g) see NOTE
5 to 6 cups (1.2 to 1.4L) Chicken Stock (see Index), or chicken broth
1/2 teaspoon freshly grated nutmeg
Salt to taste
Freshly ground pepper

Wash spinach thoroughly. Cook it over high heat with only the water clinging to its leaves, until just wilted. Immediately transfer it to colander and hold under cold running water until completely cool. Wrap in towel and squeeze firmly to release as much moisture as possible; reserve.

Thin Slicing Disc (2mm): Use firm pressure to slice lemon; remove and reserve.

All-Purpose Slicing Disc (4mm): Use firm pressure to slice onions.

Cook them gently with butter in 3-quart (3L) saucepan until soft, but not brown — about 10 minutes.

Medium Shredding Disc: Use firm pressure to shred coconut.

Add it and 5 cups (1.2L) of stock or broth to onions and bring to boil. Cover, reduce heat and simmer gently until vegetables are soft — about 20 minutes. Strain liquid into large bowl; reserve liquid and solids.

Metal Blade: Process solids until smooth. Add reserved spinach and process for 1 minute, stopping once to scrape work bowl. Add 1/2 cup (120ml) of reserved liquid and process for 15 seconds.

Return this mixture to saucepan and add seasoning. If soup is too thick, add remaining stock or broth. Adjust seasoning, and serve hot, garnished with reserved lemon slices.

Makes 6 cups (1.4L).

NOTES: This is one of the few soups that cannot be made entirely in advance; if it were, the spinach flavor would be overpowering. You can blanch the spinach in advance, however, and refrigerate it. Just before serving, purée it with the cooked onions and coconut. Reheat the broth, add the vegetables, heat through, and adjust the seasoning.

To prepare fresh coconut: Use hammer and nail to punch out three eyes of coconut. Drain and discard liquid. Place coconut in 400°F (205°C) oven for 20 minutes. Remove it from oven, wrap in towel and hit with hammer until it cracks open. Separate white meat from shell and remove dark skin with vegetable peeler. (You can shred leftover coconut and freeze it in air-tight plastic bag for another use; it will thaw in minutes at room temperature.)

1 large butternut squash (about 1³/₄ pounds, 795g), peeled and cut to fit feed tube
1 large Granny Smith or other tart apple (6 ounces, 170g), peeled, halved, and cored
1 medium onion (5 ounces, 140g), peeled and cut to fit feed tube

2 cups (480 ml) Chicken Stock (see Index), or chicken broth
2 cups (480ml) Beef Stock (see Index), or beef broth
¹/₂ teaspoon salt
Freshly grated nutmeg
Freshly ground pepper

All-Purpose Slicing Disc (4mm): Use firm pressure to slice squash and medium pressure to slice apple and onion.

Put them in 3-quart (3L) saucepan, add Chicken and Beef Stock or broth and bring to boil. Cover, reduce heat and simmer gently until vegetables are very soft — about 25 minutes. Strain liquid into large bowl; reserve liquid and solids.

Metal Blade: Process solids until smooth, stopping once to scrape work bowl. Add ¹/₂ cup (120ml) of reserved liquid and remaining ingredients and process for 10 seconds.

Return this mixture to saucepan, stir in remaining reserved liquid, adjust seasoning and serve hot.

Makes 7 cups (1.6L).

BUTTERNUT VELVET SOUP

A snap of tart apple strengthens the flavor of butternut squash and imparts an illusion of richness. The soup is quite low in calories and high in Vitamin A.

Butternut Velvet Soup

61   *Soups*

ESSENCE OF CELERY SOUP

Using fruits to enhance the flavor of vegetables is a technique used brilliantly by Michel Guérard, owner-chef of the acclaimed restaurant Les Sources et Les Près d'Eugénie in Eugénie-les-Bains in southwest France. In his innovative cuisine minceur, he sought to achieve complex depths of flavor without using rich and fattening ingredients like flour, butter, eggs and cream. Celery and pears may seem an unlikely combination, but this soup will convince you that it works.

¹/₄ cup loosely packed parsley leaves
1 large garlic clove, peeled
1 small bunch celery (1 pound total, 455g), including leaves, trimmed, strings removed with vegetable peeler, cut into 2-inch (5cm) pieces
3 tablespoons unsalted butter
3 medium onions (12 ounces total, 340g), peeled and quartered
1 large ripe pear (8 ounces, 225g) peeled, cored and quartered
3¹/₂ to 4 cups (840 to 960ml) Chicken Stock (see Index), or chicken broth
Salt to taste
Freshly ground pepper

Metal Blade: Process parsley until minced; remove and reserve. Turn on machine, drop garlic through feed tube and process until minced. Add celery, pulse about 6 times, then process continuously until mixture is finely chopped — about 30 seconds.

Melt butter in 3-quart (3L) saucepan and add contents of work bowl.

Metal Blade: Process onions and pear until finely chopped and add to saucepan. Cover and cook gently for 10 minutes. Add 3¹/₂ cups (840ml) of stock or broth and bring to boil. Cover, reduce heat and simmer gently until vegetables are very soft — about 35 minutes. Strain liquid into large bowl; reserve liquid and solids.

Metal Blade: Process solids until smooth, stopping once to scrape work bowl.

Combine with reserved liquid in pan, add salt and pepper and reheat. If too thick, add remaining broth. Adjust seasoning and garnish with parsley. Serve hot or chilled.

Makes 6 cups (1.4L).

CREAM OF CABBAGE SOUP

Hearty and warming, but not at all heavy. To draw out their smoky flavor and tenderize the meat, ham hocks are cooked slowly in a simmering broth. The vegetables, by contrast, are cooked quickly, just enough to soften them and blend the flavors.

2 ham hocks (1¹/₂ pounds total, 680g)
4 cups (960ml) Chicken Stock (see Index), or chicken broth
³/₄ cup loosely packed parsley leaves (³/₄ ounce, 21g)
4 large garlic cloves, peeled
3 medium onions (15 ounces total, 425g), peeled
¹/₂ small head green cabbage (³/₄ pound, 340g), cored and cut to fit feed tube
3¹/₂ tablespoons unsalted butter
2 bay leaves
5 cups (1.2L) milk
1 cup (240ml) whipping cream
¹/₂ teaspoon dried thyme
¹/₂ teaspoon salt
Freshly ground pepper
1¹/₂ tablespoons flour

Put ham hocks and stock or broth into 4-quart (4L) saucepan and bring to boil. Cover, reduce heat and cook gently for 1¹/₂ hours. When ham hocks are cool enough to handle, remove from liquid and cut meat from them. Reserve meat and broth in mixing bowl.

Metal Blade: Process parsley until minced; remove and reserve. With machine running, drop garlic through feed tube and process until finely chopped.

Thin Slicing Disc (2mm): Use firm pressure to slice onions.

All-Purpose Slicing Disc (4mm): Use firm pressure to slice cabbage.

Melt 2 tablespoons of butter in 4-quart (4L) saucepan used to simmer ham hocks. Add contents of work bowl and bay leaves. Cover and cook until vegetables are soft — about 15 minutes. Add reserved meat and broth, milk, cream, thyme, salt and pepper and bring to simmer; do not allow to boil.

Melt remaining 1 1/2 tablespoons of butter in small saucepan and stir in flour. Cook over low heat for 1 minute, stirring constantly; do not let mixture brown. Whisk in 3/4 cup (180ml) of hot soup and cook for 1 minute. Add to soup and stir well to combine. Adjust seasoning and serve soup hot, garnished with reserved parsley.

Makes about 10 cups (2.4L).

NOTE: If you wish, substitute meaty ham bone of same weight as hocks. Trim off all fat, cook it gently in chicken broth for 30 minutes, and proceed with recipe.

Four root vegetables, easily sliced in your food processor, cook quickly and are then puréed to silken smoothness. Another rich, sumptuous soup quickly made from a base of puréed vegetables.

1 medium onion (4 ounces, 115g), peeled
1 medium celery root (12 ounces, 340g), peeled and cut to fit feed tube
2 small parsnips (6 ounces total, 170g), peeled and cut to fit feed tube
3 medium carrots (8 ounces total, 225g), peeled and cut into

feed-tube lengths
5 to 6 cups (1.2 to 1.4L) Chicken Stock (see Index), or chicken broth
1/2 teaspoon freshly grated nutmeg
Salt to taste
Freshly ground pepper
1/2 cup (120ml) sour cream
2 tablespoons snipped fresh dill or 2 teaspoons dried dillweed

All-Purpose Slicing Disc (4mm): Use firm pressure to slice onion, celery root, parsnips and carrots.

Put vegetables and 5 cups (1.2L) of stock or broth into 4-quart (4L) saucepan and bring to boil. Cover, reduce heat and simmer gently until vegetables are very soft — about 30 minutes. Strain liquid into large bowl; reserve liquid and solids.

Metal Blade: Process solids until smooth, stopping once to scrape work bowl. Add 1/2 cup (120ml) of reserved liquid and process for 10 seconds more.

Return this mixture to saucepan and stir in reserved liquid, nutmeg, salt and pepper. If soup is too thick, add remaining stock or broth and adjust seasoning. Serve hot, garnishing each serving with dollop of sour cream sprinkled with dill.

Makes 10 cups (2.4L).

HEARTY MUSHROOM SOUP

I developed this recipe for a class that featured a meatless meal. Instead of using beef stock to enrich the soup, I cooked the onions and garlic until their natural sugar caramelized. This procedure gives the soup an intensity of flavor that will surprise you.

1 large onion (8 ounces, 225g), peeled and cut to fit feed tube
1 medium garlic clove, peeled and split
2 tablespoons unsalted butter
12 large mushrooms (8 ounces total, 225g), cleaned, trimmed, cut flat at opposite sides

1 ounce (30g) European dried mushrooms, rinsed in cold water
4 cups (960ml) water
1¼ teaspoons salt
¼ teaspoon freshly grated nutmeg
Freshly ground pepper
1 tablespoon Ruby Port
½ cup (120ml) whipping cream

All-Purpose Slicing Disc (4mm): Use firm pressure to slice onion.

Put into 2-quart (2L) saucepan with garlic and butter and cook gently over low heat, stirring occasionally, until vegetables are deep, caramel brown — about 45 minutes. Do not let them burn.

Thin Slicing Disc (2mm): Stand mushrooms in feed tube flat side down and use light pressure to slice.

Reserve 8 slices and add remainder to saucepan with dried mushrooms, water, salt, nutmeg and pepper. Bring to boil. Cover, reduce heat and simmer gently until mushrooms are soft — about 25 minutes. Strain liquid into large bowl; reserve liquid and solids.

Metal Blade: Process solids until smooth, stopping once to scrape work bowl. Add ½ cup (120ml) of reserved liquid and process for 20 seconds more.

Return to saucepan and stir in remaining liquid and Port. Bring to boil; remove from heat and add cream. Adjust seasoning and garnish with mushrooms. Serve hot.

Makes 4½ cups (1L).

VEGETARIAN TONIGHT
....
Hearty Mushroom Soup
Vegetable Cassoulet
Onion Triticale Bread
Herbed Goat Cheese
Spread
Mixed Greens with
Balsamic Vinaigrette
Mixed Fruit Crisp

2 large garlic cloves, peeled
1 medium onion (5 ounces, 140g),
   peeled and quartered
2 medium parsnips (9 ounces total,
   255g), peeled and cut into 1-inch
   (2.5cm) pieces
2 medium celery stalks (4 ounces
   total, 115g), including leaves,
   strings removed with vegetable
   peeler, cut into 1-inch (2.5cm)
   pieces
5³/₄ cups (1.4L) Chicken Stock (see
   Index), or chicken broth
1 cup tightly packed fresh spinach

leaves (2 ounces, 55g), including
   stems
¹/₄ cup (60ml) whipping cream
¹/₂ teaspoon dried dillweed
   Salt to taste
   Freshly ground pepper
2 ounces (55g) fresh green beans,
   trimmed and cut into feed-tube
   lengths
1 small zucchini (4 ounces, 115g)
   unpeeled and trimmed
6 small mushrooms (2 ounces total,
   55g), cleaned, trimmed, cut flat at
   opposite sides

*This is an
all-seasons garden
soup — a fresh
tasting purée
made entirely of
vegetables that are
available all year
round. For crisp
contrast, the soup
is finished with
vegetables that are
just cooked briefly.*

Metal Blade: Process garlic, onion, parsnips and celery until very finely chopped.

Put them into 4-quart (4L) saucepan with 1 cup (240ml) of stock or broth and bring to boil. Cover, reduce heat and simmer gently until vegetables are very soft — about 20 minutes.

Metal Blade: Process contents of saucepan until smooth, stopping once to scrape work bowl. Add spinach and process for 20 seconds more. Put mixture in saucepan with remaining broth, cream, dillweed, salt and pepper and bring to simmer; do not allow to boil.

Thick Slicing Disc (6mm): Stand green beans in small feed tube and use light pressure to slice.

Add to soup and cook gently for 4 minutes.

French Fry Disc: Stand zucchini in small feed tube and use medium pressure to cut. (If you do not have French Fry Disc, see page 229.)

Add to soup and cook for 2 minutes more or just until vegetables are tender but still crisp; remove from heat.

Thin Slicing Disc (2mm): Stand mushrooms in feed tube on flat side and use light pressure to slice.

Stir slices into hot soup and adjust seasoning. Serve soup hot or cold.

Makes about 6¹/₂ cups (1.5L).

ITALIAN VEGETABLE SOUP WITH PESTO

In this fresh and appealing version of Minestrone, some vegetables are puréed to thicken the broth while others are cooked until tender but still crisp, providing an interesting contrast in textures.

½ cup navy beans (4 ounces, 115g), rinsed and sorted
4 large garlic cloves, peeled
4 medium onions (1 pound total, 455g), peeled and quartered
3 medium celery stalks (6 ounces total, 170g) strings removed with vegetable peeler and cut into 1-inch (2.5cm) pieces
1 medium turnip (4 ounces, 115g), peeled and quartered
2 tablespoons olive oil
5½ cups (1.3L) Beef Stock (see Index) or beef broth
6 tablespoons tomato paste
2 medium tomatoes (12 ounces total, 340g), peeled, seeded and quartered
3 medium carrots (9 ounces total, 255g), peeled and cut into 2-inch (5cm) lengths
½ pound (225g) fresh green beans, trimmed and cut into 2-inch (5cm) lengths
2 small zucchini (8 ounces total, 225g), unpeeled and cut into feed-tube lengths
2 teaspoons salt
Freshly ground pepper
¾ cup (180ml) Thick Pesto Sauce (see Index)

Cover beans with water and soak overnight. Drain and reserve.

Metal Blade: Turn on machine, drop garlic through feed tube and process until minced. Process onion, celery and turnip until finely chopped.

Put chopped vegetables in 4-quart (4L) saucepan with oil. Cover with circle of waxed paper and cook very gently for 15 minutes. Remove paper and stir occasionally to prevent browning. Remove waxed paper, add 1½ cups (360ml) of stock or broth and bring to boil. Cover, reduce heat and simmer gently until all vegetables are soft — about 30 minutes.

Metal Blade: Process contents of saucepan until smooth, stopping once to scrape work bowl. Return purée to saucepan with reserved navy beans, remaining 4 cups (960ml) of broth, tomato paste and tomatoes.

Medium Slicing Disc (3mm): Stand carrots in feed tube and use firm pressure to slice. Add to saucepan, cover and cook gently for 30 minutes. Lay green beans in feed tube and use light pressure to slice; remove and reserve.

French Fry Disc: Stand zucchini in feed tube and use medium pressure to cut. (If you do not have French Fry Disc, see page 229.)

Add green beans, zucchini, salt and pepper to saucepan and simmer until vegetables are tender but still crisp — about 10 minutes. Adjust seasoning and serve hot, garnishing each serving with dollop of Thick Pesto Sauce.

Makes 12 cups (3L).

NOTE: This recipe uses a valuable cooking technique. When waxed paper is placed directly on vegetables as they cook, condensation collects on paper and continually moistens vegetables. This allows them to cook in less oil. The procedure is called "sweating." You'll encounter it throughout the book.

2 large garlic cloves, peeled
2 large celery stalks (6 ounces total, 170g), including leaves, strings removed with vegetable peeler, cut into 1-inch (2.5cm) pieces
2 medium carrots (6 ounces total, 170g) peeled and cut into 1-inch (2.5cm) pieces
1 medium onion (5 ounces, 140g), peeled and quartered
1½ cups green split peas (11 ounces, 310g), rinsed and sorted

1 4-ounce piece salt pork (115g), with rind removed
6 cups (1.5L) water
1 whole bay leaf
4 ounces (115g) imported smoked ham, cut into ⅛-inch (3mm) dice
1 teaspoon salt
  Freshly ground pepper
  Milk, if necessary

SPLIT PEA SOUP

This recipe calls for salt pork and diced ham because they're easily available. But if you have a good, meaty ham bone on hand, by all means use it instead. Simmer it with the peas, then remove it. Dice the meat and return the pieces to the saucepan with the garlic and celery. Omit the salt pork and diced ham.

Metal Blade: Turn on machine, drop garlic through feed tube and process until finely chopped. Add celery to work bowl and process until finely chopped; remove and reserve.

Process carrots and onion until finely chopped.

Put them in 3-quart (3L) saucepan with peas, salt pork, water and bay leaf and bring to boil. Cover, reduce heat and simmer gently for 1½ hours. Remove bay leaf and salt pork and cut lean part of pork into ⅛-inch (3mm) dice. Strain liquid into large bowl; reserve liquid and solids.

Metal Blade: Process solids until smooth, stopping once to scrape work bowl. Add ½ cup (120ml) of reserved liquid and process for 10 seconds more.

Return mixture to saucepan with remaining liquid, lean salt pork, ham, salt, pepper and reserved garlic and celery. If soup is too thick, add milk to reach desired consistency. Adjust seasoning and serve hot.

Makes 6 cups (1.5L).

★ Edible Extras to Garnish Soups

Fine-shredded cheese or radishes
Julienned (2x2mm) Parmesan cheese , radishes, carrots or zucchini
Sliced (2mm) lemon or lime
Sliced (2mm) cucumbers or mushrooms
Diced red, green or yellow peppers
Hard-cooked eggs, chopped fine with metal blade

Sliced (3mm) scallions
Fresh parsley minced with fresh or dried herbs
Shredded carrots
Shredded zucchini
Garlic croutons (see Index)
Sour cream
Plain yogurt
Swirl of sweet butter

TOMATO SOUP WITH ALLSPICE AND HONEY

I'm particularly fond of this rosy tomato soup because of the subtle flavors of allspice and honey. Both garlic and onions have a natural sweetness that can be coaxed out with long, slow cooking. Together with honey, they counterbalance the acidity of the tomatoes.

3 medium onions (12 ounces total, 340g), peeled and cut to fit feed tube
2 large garlic cloves, peeled and halved
3½ to 4 cups (840 to 960ml) tomato juice
5 large tomatoes (2½ pounds total, 1kg), cored
¼ cup (60ml) honey
1 teaspoon salt
½ teaspoon ground allspice
Freshly ground pepper
½ cup (120ml) sour cream or plain yogurt, for garnish

All-Purpose Slicing Disc (4mm): Use firm pressure to slice onions.

Put them in 3-quart (3L) saucepan with garlic and 3½ cups (840ml) of tomato juice and bring to boil. Cover, reduce heat and simmer gently until onions are completely soft — about 40 minutes.

French Fry Disc: Put tomatoes in feed tube, cut side down, and use light pressure to process. Use slotted spoon to remove tomato pieces carefully, leaving seeds and juice in bottom of work bowl. Discard seeds and juice. (If you do not have French Fry Disc, see page 229 for coarse chopping of tomatoes.)

Put tomato pieces, honey, salt, allspice and pepper in saucepan, cover and cook gently for 15 minutes. Strain liquid into large bowl; reserve both liquid and solids.

Metal Blade: Process solids until smooth, stopping once to scrape work bowl. Add ½ cup (120ml) of reserved liquid and process for 10 seconds.

Return this mixture to saucepan, stir in remaining liquid and adjust seasoning. If soup is too thick, add remaining tomato juice. Serve hot or cold, garnishing each serving with dollop of sour cream or yogurt.

Makes 8 cups (1.9L).

CLEAR BROTH WITH VEGETABLES AND TOFU

This make-ahead soup sets the mood for an Oriental meal and leaves you free to cook the stir-fry dishes at the last minute. You can put the vegetables, tofu and lemon juice into soup bowls ahead of time.

3 cups (720ml) Chicken Stock (see Index), or chicken broth
3 cups (720ml) Beef Stock (see Index), or beef broth
½ cup (120ml) sake (Japanese rice wine)
1 teaspoon soy sauce
1 large carrot (5 ounces, 140g), peeled and cut into 2-inch (5cm) pieces
3 large scallions (2 ounces total, 55g), including green tops, root ends trimmed, cut into 2-inch (5cm) pieces
6 medium spinach leaves, trimmed of stems
Zest of ½ lemon, removed with vegetable peeler, cut into 1/16-inch (1.5mm) wide strips
6 ounces (170g) tofu, drained, cut into ½-inch (12mm) cubes

Put the Chicken and Beef Stock or broth, sake and soy sauce in 2½-quart (2.5L) saucepan. Bring to boil.

2mm Julienne Disc or Fine Shredding Disc: Lay carrot in feed tube and use firm pressure to process.

Thin Slicing Disc (2mm): Lay scallions in feed tube and use light pressure to sliver.

Stack spinach leaves and roll them into tight cylinder, starting at stem end. Use sharp knife to slice cylinders at $1/10$-inch (2mm) intervals.

Divide vegetables, lemon zest and tofu evenly among six individual soup bowls. Add broth and serve immediately.

Makes 7 cups (1.7L).

NOTE: Leftover tofu will keep in refrigerator for 5 to 7 days when treated as follows: Drain it, place it in container and add cold water to cover. Cover tightly and change the water daily.

Tomato Soup with Allspice and Honey

COLD TOMATO SOUP WITH FENNEL MOUSSE

This specialty of the Crillon Hotel in Paris makes a most dramatic presentation. An individual fennel mousse is surrounded by tomato soup flecked with red and green peppers and black olives.

Tomato Soup

- 6 ripe medium tomatoes (2¼ pounds total, 1kg), cored and quartered
- ¼ cup (60ml) tomato paste
- 2 tablespoons olive oil
- 1 tablespoon celery salt
- ½ teaspoon sugar
- ½ teaspoon salt
  Freshly ground white pepper
- ½ cup (120ml) Beef Stock (see Index), or beef broth
- 1 small red pepper (3 ounces, 85g), cored and cut into 1-inch (2.5cm) squares
- 1 small green pepper (3 ounces, 85g), cored and cut into 1-inch (2.5cm) squares
- 4 pitted jumbo black olives
- 1 recipe Fennel Mousse (recipe follows)
- 6 sprigs fennel greens

Metal Blade: Process half the tomatoes with tomato paste, olive oil, celery salt, sugar, salt and pepper until tomatoes are puréed. Transfer mixture to strainer set over 2-quart (2L) bowl. Process remaining tomatoes, add to strainer and press through.

Stir in stock or broth and adjust seasoning. Refrigerate until well chilled. Can be prepared up to 3 days in advance and refrigerated. Just before serving, add more stock or broth if soup is too thick. Adjust seasoning and prepare garnish of peppers and olives.

Metal Blade: Pulse peppers until finely chopped; remove and reserve. Process olives until finely chopped and reserve in separate dish.

Remove fennel mousse from molds by running small knife around inside edge of molds. Invert each mousse into center of shallow soup bowl and spoon about ¾ cup (180ml) of soup around each. Sprinkle chopped peppers and olives on soup and put sprig of fennel green on each mousse.

Makes 4½ cups (1L) soup.

Fennel Mousse

- 1 medium fennel bulb (14 ounces, 395g), with feathery greens and stems removed, peeled with vegetable peeler and cut into 1-inch (2.5cm) cubes (see NOTE)
- ¾ teaspoon salt
  Freshly ground pepper
- 1 tablespoon olive oil
- 7 tablespoons milk
- 1 large egg yolk
- 1 teaspoon unflavored gelatin
- ½ cup (120ml) whipping cream, whipped

Metal Blade: Process fennel until minced.

Cook fennel, salt and pepper in oil over high heat in 10-inch (25cm) skillet, stirring often, until fennel is just hot — about 2 minutes. Transfer to 1-quart (1L) mixing bowl; refrigerate until cool.

Lightly oil six ⅓-cup (80ml) timbale molds.

Metal Blade: Process milk, egg yolk and gelatin for 5 seconds.

Pour mixture into 1-quart (1L) saucepan and cook gently, stirring constantly, until thick enough to coat back of spoon. It will register about 180°F (80°C). Do not allow it to boil! Immediately strain into small dish and refrigerate until it begins to set around edges. (If it becomes too firm, return it to work bowl and process until smooth.)

Wrap cool fennel in towel and squeeze gently, but firmly, to remove as much moisture as possible. Return to mixing bowl, stir in gelatin mixture and gently fold in whipped cream. Adjust seasoning. Divide mousse among prepared molds, cover with plastic wrap and refrigerate until firm. Mousse can be made up to 2 days in advance and refrigerated.

NOTES: If fennel is not available, substitute an equal weight of celery and 1 teaspoon of fennel seeds.

Mousse is simple to make if you treat gelatin correctly. Processing gelatin with milk and egg yolk before cooking it ensures that it dissolves completely.

FRESH BEET SHERBET

Beets are distinguished by many attributes, perhaps the most notable being their vibrant color. Here the color shines in a cool, refreshing sherbet.

8 medium beets (2¼ pounds total, 1kg)	1 teaspoon salt
1 cup (240ml) orange juice concentrate	2 large egg whites
¼ cup (60ml) cider vinegar	1 cup (240ml) sour cream or plain yogurt
	Fresh dill or watercress leaves

Cook beets in boiling water to cover until very tender — about 45 minutes. Drain them. When they are completely cool, peel and quarter them.

Metal Blade: Process beets in 2 batches until smooth. Leave second batch in work bowl and add orange juice concentrate, vinegar and salt; process for 20 seconds.

Transfer contents of work bowl and remaining beet purée to 1½-quart (1.5L) freezer container and stir well to combine. Freeze until semi-frozen. (It should be sufficiently frozen so there is no liquid, but not frozen solid. If solid, thaw until it can be spooned into work bowl.)

Metal Blade: Spoon semi-frozen mixture into work bowl and process until smooth. With machine running, pour egg whites through feed tube and process until fluffy — about 1 minute.

Sherbet can be served immediately or frozen. If frozen, let thaw slightly before serving. If crystals form during extended storage, sherbet can be reprocessed. Let thaw until it can be spooned into work bowl. Process with metal blade until smooth.

Serve in scoops and garnish with dollop of sour cream or yogurt and dill or watercress leaves.

Makes about 5 cups (1.2L).

TOMATO AND BASIL SHERBET

When tomatoes are vine-ripened to perfection, this sherbet can be their most glorious statement. Rosy colored and intensely flavored with fresh basil, it is a pleasing alternative to chilled soup.

6 medium tomatoes (2¼ pounds total, 1kg), peeled, halved and seeded
2 or 3 tablespoons sugar (1 to 1¼ ounces, 30 to 40g)
⅓ cup (80ml) tomato paste
¼ cup (60ml) cider vinegar
3 drops Tabasco sauce
½ teaspoon salt
2 large egg whites
3 tablespoons finely snipped fresh basil
Fresh basil leaves, for garnish

Drain tomato halves on paper towels for 30 minutes. Cut halves into quarters.

Metal Blade: Process tomatoes in 2 batches until smooth. Leave second batch in work bowl and add sugar, tomato paste, vinegar, Tabasco sauce and salt; process for 1 minute.

Transfer contents of work bowl and remaining tomato purée to 1½-quart (1.5L) freezer container and stir to combine. Freeze until semi-frozen. (It should be sufficiently frozen so there is no liquid, but not frozen solid. If solid, let thaw until it can be spooned into work bowl.)

Metal Blade: Spoon semi-frozen mixture into work bowl. Process until smooth. With machine running, pour egg white through feed tube and process until fluffy — about 1 minute. Add basil and process for 3 seconds.

Sherbet can be served immediately or frozen. If frozen, let thaw slightly before serving. If crystals form during extended storage, sherbet can be reprocessed. Let thaw until it can be spooned into work bowl Process with metal blade until smooth.

Serve in scoops, garnished with basil leaves.

Makes about 5 cups (1.2L).

NOTE: If tomatoes are not sufficiently flavorful, use additional 1 to 2 tablespoons of tomato paste to strengthen their flavor.

Fresh Beet Sherbet and Tomato Basil Sherbet

4 cups (960ml) tomato juice
1/2 cup (120ml) catsup (see NOTE)
2 tablespoons fresh lemon juice
1 tablespoon prepared horseradish, or to taste
1 tablespoon Worcestershire sauce
Freshly ground pepper
1 medium cucumber (1 pound, 455g), unpeeled, split lengthwise, seeded and cut into 1-inch (2.5cm) pieces
1 medium red or green pepper (5 ounces, 140g), cored and cut into

1-inch (2.5cm) pieces
6 large scallions (4 ounces total, 115g), trimmed and cut into 1-inch (2.5cm) pieces
4 medium celery stalks (6 ounces total, 170g), including leaves, strings removed with vegetable peeler, cut into 1-inch (2.5cm) pieces
5 large tomatoes (2 pounds total, 910g), cored and cut in half crosswise

Garnish
1 firm, ripe avocado (8 ounces, 225g), peeled, pitted and quartered

1 teaspoon fresh lemon juice

SPICY
GAZPACHO

Low-calorie, delicious and filling. Always have a container in the refrigerator to ensure that a diet succeeds! Although the classic Gazpacho is always served cold, this soup is surprisingly good when hot.

Put tomato juice, catsup, lemon juice, horseradish, Worcestershire sauce and pepper in 3-quart (3L) mixing bowl and stir to combine.

Metal Blade: Divide cucumber, pepper, scallions and celery into 2 batches. Pulse until chopped medium-fine, about 7 times. Do not overprocess; you want to retain some texture. Transfer each batch to mixing bowl.

French Fry Disc: Put tomatoes in feed tube cut side down and use light pressure to cut. Use slotted spoon to remove tomato pieces, leaving seeds and juice in work bowl. Add tomato pieces to soup and stir to combine. Discard seeds and juice. Cover soup and chill it. (If you do not have French Fry Disc, see page 229 for coarse chopping of tomatoes.)

Stand avocado pieces in feed tube cut side down and use light pressure to cut. Toss chunks in lemon juice. Before serving soup, adjust seasoning and garnish each serving with diced avocado.

Makes 11 cups (2.5L).

TEX-MEX VARIATION: Omit horseradish and Worcestershire sauce. Add 1/2 cup loosely packed cilantro leaves, 1 large peeled garlic clove and 2 split jalapeño peppers, with seeds removed. Process these with cucumber, pepper, scallions and celery.

NOTES: You can replace catsup with 6 tablespoons of tomato paste, 1 1/2 tablespoons of light brown sugar and 1 1/2 tablespoons of cider vinegar.

You'll probably be most tempted to make Gazpacho in the summer when tomatoes are at their best, but you needn't save the recipe for that short season. The flavor of tomatoes that are less than perfect can be improved with several tablespoons of tomato paste to taste and a pinch of sugar.

SORREL AND PEAR SOUP

This light fruit soup requires no cooking at all. The slightly sour flavor of sorrel sets off the sweetness of the pears. Don't be deterred from making the soup if sorrel isn't available; replace it with spinach and lemon juice. The soup will be fresh and delicious, although it will not have the unique flavor of sorrel.

2 29-ounce (820g) cans pear halves in light syrup, well chilled and drained
2 cups sorrel leaves (4 ounces total, 115g) with veins and stems removed (see NOTE)
1 1/2 cups (360ml) plain yogurt
1/4 teaspoon grated nutmeg
Freshly ground white pepper
4 1/2 to 5 cups (1 to 1.2L) Chicken Stock (see Index) or chicken broth, chilled
Salt to taste

Metal Blade: Process pears and sorrel until smooth. Add yogurt, nutmeg and pepper and process for 5 seconds more.

Transfer to large bowl and stir in 4 1/2 cups (IL) of stock or broth. If soup is too thick, add remaining stock or broth. Adjust seasoning and serve well chilled.

Makes 9 cups (2L).

NOTE: If sorrel is not available, substitute an equal amount of spinach with 1 tablespoon of fresh lemon juice.

SPICED AVOCADO SOUP

Refreshing on the hottest days and easy on the cook — it takes just minutes to assemble. For best results, use dark-skinned California avocados that are on the point of being overripe.

1 small onion (1 1/2 ounces, 45g), peeled
2 large ripe avocados (14 ounces total, 395g), peeled, pitted and halved
1/2 teaspoon ground cardamom
1/2 teaspoon red pepper flakes
1 1/2 teaspoons salt
2 cups (480ml) buttermilk
2 cups (480ml) milk

Metal Blade: Turn on machine, drop onion through feed tube and process until minced. Cut 3 avocado halves in thirds, add to onion in work bowl and process until smooth, stopping once to scrape work bowl. Add cardamom, pepper flakes and salt and turn on machine. With machine running, pour buttermilk and milk through feed tube and process for 5 seconds. Transfer to mixing bowl.

French Fry Disc: Use light pressure to cut remaining avocado half and fold it into liquid. (If you do not have French Fry disc, see page 229.)

Can be made up to 2 hours in advance and refrigerated, covered airtight. Before serving, stir well and adjust seasoning. Serve cold.

Makes about 5 cups (1.2L).

1 cup loosely packed parsley leaves
  (1 ounce, 30g)
2 large garlic cloves, peeled
3 medium onions (12 ounces total,
  340g), peeled and quartered
1 1/2 pounds (680g) lean beef chuck, cut
  into 1-inch (2.5cm) cubes
1 14 1/2-ounce can (410g) whole
  tomatoes, drained, with liquid
  reserved
1 large Idaho potato (12 ounces,
  340g), quartered
3 medium carrots (10 ounces total,
  285g), peeled and cut into

feed-tube lengths
4 medium celery stalks (8 ounces
  total, 225g), including leaves,
  strings removed with vegetable
  peeler and cut into feed-tube
  lengths
1 46-ounce (1.3kg) can tomato juice
1/2 cup pearl barley (3 1/4 ounces, 92g)
1 bay leaf
1 teaspoon dried marjoram
1 teaspoon dried thyme
1 1/2 teaspoon salt
  Freshly ground pepper

HEARTY BEEF AND VEGETABLE SOUP

Chock-full of meat and vegetables, this is almost more of a stew than a soup. Like many stews, it tastes even better reheated a day or two later.

Metal Blade: Process parsley until finely chopped and reserve. Turn on machine, drop garlic through feed tube and process until finely chopped. Add onions and pulse to chop coarsely. Put in 4-quart (4L) saucepot. Process meat in 2 batches until coarsely chopped.

Add to saucepot and cook for 10 minutes, stirring often.

Metal Blade: Pulse to chop tomatoes coarsely and add to pot with their reserved liquid.

French Fry Disc: Use firm pressure to cut potato; remove and reserve. (If you do not have French Fry Disc, see page 229.)

All-Purpose Slicing Disc (4mm): Stand carrots in feed tube and use firm pressure to slice. Stand celery in feed tube and use medium pressure to slice.

Add potato, carrots and celery to pot with remaining ingredients. Bring to boil, reduce heat and simmer gently, uncovered, until vegetables are soft — about 50 minutes. Stir occasionally. Add reserved parsley, adjust seasoning and serve hot.

Makes 11 cups (2.5L).

BEAT THE HEAT
....
(A no-cook menu for summer)
Spiced Avocado Soup
Southwestern Corn, Millet and
Vegetable Salad
Sherbet with Frozen Fresh Fruit

MULLIGATAWNY SOUP

This Anglo-Indian soup is perfectly suited for serving as a main course. It is elegant in its subtlety, yet hearty and sustaining. Cooking whole chicken pieces in the vegetable-filled broth gives the soup tremendous depth of flavor.

2 tablespoons unsalted butter
2 tablespoons safflower oil
1 whole frying chicken (3¼ pounds, 1.5kg), cut in serving pieces
2 medium Granny Smith apples (12 ounces total, 340g), peeled, cored, and cut into eighths
2 medium leeks (10 ounces total, 285g), white part only, cut into 1-inch (1.25cm) pieces
2 medium carrots (7 ounces total, 200g), peeled and cut into 1-inch (2.5cm) pieces
3 stalks celery (6 ounces total, 170g), strings removed with vegetable peeler, cut into 1-inch (2.5cm) pieces
¼ cup long-grain white rice (1¾ ounces, 50g)
3½ to 4½ cups 840ml to 1L) Chicken Stock (see Index) or chicken broth
¼ cup (60ml) dry white wine
1¼ teaspoons curry powder, or to taste
⅛ teaspoon ground cloves
⅛ teaspoon ground mace
1 tablespoon tomato paste
1 medium tomato (6 ounces, 170g), peeled, seeded and quartered
¼ cup cilantro leaves
Salt to taste

Heat butter and oil in 6-quart (6L) pot. When hot, add chicken pieces, including neck and back, and cook gently until lightly browned on all sides — about 15 minutes.

Metal Blade: Process apples until minced and add to chicken. Process leeks, carrots and celery until minced.

Add to chicken along with rice, 3 cups (720ml) of stock or broth, wine, curry powder, cloves and mace. Cook, covered, until vegetables are very soft — about 18 minutes.

Remove chicken pieces. Place strainer over bowl and strain cooking liquid. Wrap chicken, rice, and vegetables separately and refrigerate. Refrigerate cooking liquid until fat solidifies on top.

Skim fat and particles from surface of cooking liquid and discard. Return liquid to pot. Remove and discard chicken skin; cut meat into ¾-inch (2cm) cubes and add it to pot.

Metal Blade: Process rice and vegetables with tomato paste until smooth, stopping once to scrape work bowl. Add 1 cup (240ml) of cooking liquid and process for 10 seconds. Add to pot and bring to simmer.

Metal Blade: Pulse tomato to chop it coarsely.

Add to pot with cilantro and ½ to 1½ cups (120 to 360ml) of remaining stock or broth to reach desired consistency. Adjust seasoning and serve hot.

Can be made up to 3 days in advance and refrigerated. Reheat, add stock or broth if soup is too thick and adjust seasoning.

Makes 7 cups.

4 pounds (1.8kg) beef short ribs
1 medium onion (5 ounces, 140g),
  unpeeled, halved and stuck with 2
  whole cloves
1 large carrot (4 ounces, 115g),
  trimmed and cut into thirds
1 large celery stalk (3 ounces, 85g),
  including leaves, trimmed and cut
  into thirds
1 large parsley sprig
12 cups (3L) water
2 medium onions (10 ounces total,
  285g), peeled, quartered
1 14$^1/_2$-ounce (410g) can whole

tomatoes, drained, with liquid
  reserved
1 medium head green cabbage (1$^1/_2$
  pounds, 680g), core removed, cut
  in wedges to fit feed tube
$^1/_2$ cup (120ml) tomato paste
$^1/_2$ cup light brown sugar (4 ounces,
  115g)
$^1/_3$ cup (80ml) fresh lemon juice
1$^1/_2$ teaspoons salt
$^1/_2$ teaspoon ground allspice
$^1/_4$ teaspoon paprika
  Freshly ground pepper

SWEET AND SOUR CABBAGE SOUP

Served with freshly made bread and a tossed green salad, this soup is one of my family's favorite warming winter meals. Preparation is so quick with the food processor that I often make an extra batch to keep in the freezer.

Put short ribs, onion with cloves, carrot, celery, parsley and water in 6-quart (6L) pot. Bring to boil, reduce heat and simmer, uncovered, for 1 hour. Take ribs from liquid, remove meat from bones and cut into $^1/_2$-inch (12mm) cubes. Reserve meat; discard bones and vegetables. Skim fat from broth. (See NOTE.)

Metal Blade: Process onions until finely chopped and add to broth. Pulse tomatoes to chop coarsely and add to broth with their reserved liquid.

All-Purpose Slicing Disc (4mm): Use firm pressure to slice cabbage. Add to broth with reserved meat and remaining ingredients and bring to boil. Cover, reduce heat and simmer gently — about 40 minutes. Adjust seasoning and serve hot.

Makes 12 cups (3L).

NOTE: You can skim fat off top of broth with large spoon while it is still hot, but the degreasing will be easier and more complete if you refrigerate broth until chilled. All fat will rise to surface and congeal; it can then be easily removed.

OPEN-HOUSE SOUP
SUPPER
....
Mulligatawny Soup
Italian Vegetable Soup
with Pesto
Millet Crunch Bread
Herbed Goat Cheese
Spread
Frozen Fudge Brownie Pie

MUSSELS IN THEIR OWN BROTH

Genius is a word that comes easily when I speak of Frédy Girardet, owner-chef of a remarkable restaurant in the tiny village of Crissier, Switzerland. When I first worked with him in 1979, he was just beginning to be the talk of culinary circles. It was already evident that this was a unique talent. When I returned to his kitchen a year later, he was serving this marvelously simple soup. As with many of his recipes, Girardet here transforms ordinary ingredients into a dish that is truly extraordinary.

64 small mussels (3 pounds total, 1.4kg)
1 tablespoon salt
4 cups (960ml) Vegetable Stock (See Index)
3 small red potatoes (8 ounces total, 225g), unpeeled
½ leek, including green top (2½ ounces, 70g), cut lengthwise, with tough green edges trimmed, cut into feed-tube lengths
1 stick unsalted butter (4 ounces, 115g), chilled, cut into tablespoon-size pieces
Salt
Freshly ground pepper

Scrub mussels with wire brush and remove beards. Discard any that are open and do not close when tapped on counter. Transfer to 4-quart (4L) pot, cover with cold water and salt and soak for 30 minutes. Wash several times to remove grit, then drain well.

In 4-quart (4L) pot, bring Vegetable Stock to boil. Add mussels, cover, and cook until all have opened — about 3 minutes. Discard any that don't open. With slotted spoon, carefully remove mussels in their shells and reserve.

Boil liquid, uncovered, until reduced to 3¾ cups (900ml). Pour through strainer lined with coffee filter or double thickness of cheesecloth. Rinse out pot.

Meanwhile, cook potatoes until very soft. When just cool enough to handle, peel.

Medium Shredding Disc: Use light pressure to shred warm potatoes. Leave in work bowl.

Metal Blade: Add ½ cup (120ml) of reduced mussel cooking liquid and process until smooth, stopping once to scrape work bowl.

Add to pot with remaining liquid. Can be prepared to this point up to 4 hours in advance. Refrigerate mussels and liquid separately.

Thin Slicing Disc (2mm): Stand leek in small feed tube and use medium pressure to slice.

Just before serving, bring soup to simmer; whisk in butter, 1 tablespoon at a time, waiting until each piece is melted before adding another. Add mussels in their shells and season to taste. Cook only until mussels are heated through; do not overcook.

Divide mussels among 4 deep soup bowls for main-course servings or 8 shallow soup bowls for soup course. Divide broth evenly among bowls. Garnish with reserved leeks and serve immediately.

Makes 8 soup or 4 main-course servings.

NOTE: When they are available, I prefer small or medium mussels to larger ones. The smaller ones are sweeter and more tender and they make a more attractive presentation. Now that more mussels are being cultivated, smaller mussels are more consistently available.

2½ cups firmly packed fresh spinach leaves (5 ounces total, 140g), with stems removed
1 large bunch watercress (5 ounces, 140g), with stems removed
2 medium garlic cloves, peeled
1 medium onion (4 ounces, 115g), peeled and quartered
1 medium leek (6 ounces, 170g), with coarse greens removed, cut into 1-inch (2.5cm) pieces
2 tablespoons unsalted butter

3⅔ ounce (105g) can smoked oysters, well drained
3 cups (720ml) milk
2 cups (480ml) whipping cream
1 pint shucked oysters with their liquor
2 tablespoons fresh lemon juice
1¼ teaspoons salt
¼ teaspoon Worcestershire sauce
Freshly ground pepper
Watercress leaves

SMOKED OYSTER SOUP WITH SPINACH AND WATERCRESS

This is richer than most of my soups and worth every calorie! Smoked oysters provide a counterpoint to the briny fresh oysters. I've served this both at an informal Sunday night supper and as a first course at Thanksgiving dinner.

Soak spinach and watercress in several changes of water until clean. Cook in 4-quart (4L) saucepan with only water clinging to leaves, until just wilted. Transfer to colander and hold under cold running water until completely cool. Wrap in towel and squeeze to remove as much water as possible. Spinach and watercress can be cooked 2 days in advance, wrapped airtight and refrigerated.

Metal Blade: Turn on machine, drop garlic through feed tube and process until minced. Add onion and leek and pulse until finely chopped.

Melt butter over medium heat in same saucepan used to cook greens. Add onions, leeks and garlic and cook gently until very soft — about 15 minutes. Do not let them brown.

Metal Blade: Process spinach, watercress, onion mixture and smoked oysters for 30 seconds, stopping once to scrape work bowl.

Transfer to pan and stir in milk, cream, shucked oysters with their liquor, lemon juice, salt, Worcestershire sauce and pepper. Cook until just heated through; do not boil. Serve immediately, garnished with watercress leaves.

Makes about 8 cups (2L).

To Clean Mussels

★ Mussels can be cleaned just before they're cooked, or they can be cleaned and drained, then refrigerated up to 6 hours. Sort through and discard any that are broken or unnaturally heavy (they're probably full of mud). If an open mussel doesn't close when tapped on the counter, it's dead. Throw it away. Scrub shells with a wire brush, under running water. Remove beards with a sharp tug, or cut them away with a small knife. Put mussels in a large pot and cover them with cold water. Add 1 teaspoon of salt. Let them soak for 30 minutes, then drain them well. Rinse all grit and sand from the pot.

FISH AND VEGETABLES IN BROTH WITH CILANTRO

While working at her Paris restaurant, l'Aquitaine, I had a memorable lunch with Christiane Massia, the chef and owner. She served this strikingly simple soup. A bottle of Bordeaux, an assortment of cheeses with French bread and a trio of fruit sorbets completed the menu. It rates as one of my favorites.

2 medium garlic cloves, peeled
4 large shallots (2 ounces total, 55g), peeled
2 medium onions (10 ounces total, 285g), peeled and cut to fit feed tube
3 cups (720ml) Fish Stock (see Index) or clam juice
6 cups (1.5L) water
2¼ teaspoons salt
Freshly ground white pepper
2 cups loosely packed cilantro leaves (see NOTE)
1½ sticks unsalted butter (6 ounces, 170g), softened
3 small zucchini (14 ounces total, 395g), cut into feed-tube lengths
2 medium tomatoes (12 ounces total, 340g), peeled, with seeds and pulp removed and outer shell cut into 1 by ¼-inch (2.5cm by 6mm) strips
1 pound (455g) grouper fillets, cut into 1½ by ¾-inch (4 by 2cm) strips
1 pound (455g) sole fillets, skinned and cut into 1½ by ¾-inch (4 by 2cm) strips

Metal Blade: Turn on machine, drop garlic and shallots through feed tube and process until minced.

Medium Slicing Disc (3mm): Use firm pressure to slice onions.

Transfer to 4-quart (4L) saucepan. Add Fish Stock or clam juice, water, salt and pepper and bring to boil. Reduce heat and simmer, uncovered, until onions are soft — about 20 minutes. Can be prepared to this point up to 2 days in advance, covered and refrigerated. Bring to boil before proceeding with recipe.

Put cilantro and butter into soup tureen and set aside.

Medium Slicing Disc (3mm): Stand zucchini in feed tube and use medium pressure to slice.

Add to saucepan with soup base and cook for 30 seconds. Add tomatoes and bring to full boil. Add fish and cook just until it turns opaque — about 40 seconds. Remove from heat, quickly ladle 2 cups (480ml) of hot broth into tureen and stir until butter melts. Gently ladle remaining soup into tureen, taking care not to break fillets. Stir only enough to blend, add pepper and adjust seasoning. Serve immediately.

Makes 8 servings.

NOTES: This is one recipe where cilantro is essential; there are no substitutes. Look for the herb in Oriental and Mexican groceries or large supermarkets; it is also called coriander or Chinese parsley.

You can substitute fillets of other types of white-fleshed ocean fish for either grouper or sole. Whatever you choose, use weight equal to that specified in recipe and be sure not to overcook it.

1 4-ounce (115g) piece salt pork,
  with rind removed
2 10¹/₄-ounce (290g) cans whole baby
  clams, drained, liquid reserved
3 medium onions (12 ounces total,
  340g), peeled and quartered
2 medium celery stalks (4 ounces
  total, 115g), strings removed
  with vegetable peeler, cut into
  1-inch (2.5cm) pieces
2 medium baking potatoes (14

ounces total, 395g), peeled and cut
  to fit feed tube
2 cups (480ml) water
1 whole bay leaf
¹/₂ teaspoon salt
¹/₂ teaspoon dried thyme
  Freshly ground white pepper
2 cups (480ml) milk
1 cup (240ml) whipping cream
3 tablespoons unsalted butter
3 tablespoons flour

*A New England
childhood firmly
established my
preference for
creamy clam
chowders — with
no tomatoes! This
version uses very
little flour as
thickener, and the
vegetables are
cooked briefly to
retain their fresh
crunch.*

Blanch salt pork in boiling water for 5 minutes. Drain, cool slightly and cut into 1-inch (2.5cm) cubes.

Metal Blade: Pulse to chop clams coarsely; remove and reserve. Pulse to chop salt pork, onions and celery coarsely. Transfer them to 3-quart (3L) saucepan.

Cook gently, stirring occasionally, until vegetables are soft — about 15 minutes.

French Fry Disc: Use firm pressure to cut potatoes. (If you do not have French Fry Disc, see page 229.)

Transfer to cutting board and cut into square dice. Add to saucepan with clam liquid, water, bay leaf, salt, thyme and pepper. Simmer until potatoes are cooked tender but still crisp — about 15 minutes. Add clams and milk and bring to simmer. Meanwhile, melt butter in small saucepan, stir in flour and cook gently for 1 minute; do not let mixture brown. Slowly whisk in 1 cup (240ml) of hot soup liquid. Increase heat and bring mixture to simmer, whisking constantly. Add to soup along with cream, whisk to combine, and adjust seasoning. Do not let it boil. Serve hot.

Makes 8 cups (2L).

NOTE: If you can get fresh clams, use them. Steam 1¹/₂ to 2 dozen in ¹/₄-inch (6mm) of water until their shells open. Shuck and strain liquid through coffee filter or triple thickness of paper towels. Add bottled clam juice or water to make 2 cups (480 ml). Chop clams coarsely by pulsing with metal blade.

CHICKEN STOCK

As you bone chicken breasts and clip tips from wings, freeze the bones. Supplement the frozen bones with backs and necks. Chicken stock cooks faster than other meat stocks. Unlike canned broth or bouillon cubes, your homemade stock will be without salt.

5 pounds (2.3kg) chicken bones
2 medium onions (8 ounces total, 225g), peeled and quartered
1 large leek (8 ounces, 225g), trimmed, and cut into thirds
1 large carrot (4 ounces, 115g), scrubbed and cut into 1-inch (2.5cm) pieces

2 medium celery stalks (4 ounces total, 115g), cut into 1-inch (2.5cm) pieces
8 parsley sprigs
1 bay leaf
2 whole cloves
1 teaspoon dried thyme

Combine all ingredients in 6-quart (6L) pot and add water to cover. Bring to boil, reduce heat and let simmer, uncovered, for 1 1/2 hours, skimming as necessary.

Discard bones and vegetables. Pour stock through strainer lined with double thickness of cheesecloth and refrigerate. When fat has solidified, remove and discard or reserve for another use.

Refrigerate up to 3 days or freeze up to 3 months.

Makes about 5 cups (1.2L).

BEEF OR VEAL STOCK

This recipe describes how to make stock in the oven, where you can let it cook overnight. If you prefer stove-top cooking, follow the procedure in the recipe for Lamb Stock. If this quantity is too large for your needs, it can be cut in half.

10 pounds (4.5kg) beef or veal bones, cut into 3 to 4-inch (7 to 10cm) pieces
4 large onions (1 pound total, 455g), peeled and quartered
4 medium carrots (1/2 pound total,

225g), peeled and cut into 1-inch (2.5cm) pieces
3 large celery stalks (1/2 pound total, 225g), cut into 1-inch (2.5cm) pieces
10 parsley sprigs

Fifteen minutes before baking, place rack in center of oven and preheat to 425°F (120°C).

Place bones in single layer in 1 or 2 large roasting pans. Bake for 1 hour, turning once after 30 minutes. Add onions and carrots to pan(s) and bake for 30 minutes longer. *Reduce oven temperature to 250°F (120°C).*

If you have used 2 pans, combine bones in one pan. Add boiling water to cover bottom of emptied pan and scrape up any browned bits and juices. Add to pan with bones. Add celery and enough water to cover bones. Bake uncovered for 12 hours. Skim surface and discard bones and vegetables. Pour stock through strainer lined with double thickness of cheesecloth and refrigerate. When fat has solidified, remove and discard it. Pour into containers of a practical size for your cooking needs and freeze up to 6 months.

Makes about 2 1/2 quarts (2.5L).

1½ pounds (680g) lamb bones, cut into 2-inch (5cm) pieces
1½ pounds (680g) chicken bones, cut into 2-inch (5cm) pieces
1½ pounds (680g) veal bones, cut into 2-inch (5cm) pieces
2 medium carrots (8 ounces total, 225g), scrubbed and cut into 1-inch (2.5cm) pieces
2 medium onions (12 ounces total, 340g), peeled and cut into 1-inch (2.5cm) pieces

2 medium tomatoes (12 ounces total, 340g), seeded and quartered
1 medium leek (6 ounces, 170g), trimmed and halved
2 medium celery stalks (4 ounces total, 115g), cut into 1-inch (2.5cm) pieces
½ head garlic, left whole
4 whole peppercorns
1 bay leaf
¼ teaspoon dried thyme

LAMB STOCK

This recipe describes the basic procedure for a stock cooked on top of the stove. If you prefer to cook it in the oven, follow the procedure described for Beef or Veal Stock.

Fifteen minutes before baking, place rack in center of oven and preheat to 425°F (220°C).

Place bones in single layer in one or two large roasting pans. Bake for 1 hour, turning once after 30 minutes. Add carrots and onions to pan(s) and cook for 30 minutes longer.

With slotted spoon, transfer bones and vegetables to 8-quart (8L) stockpot. Discard fat from roasting pan(s). Add water to cover bottom of roasting pan(s) and scrape bottom to release browned bits and juices. Add liquid to stockpot, then add water to cover.

Bring to boil over high heat, then reduce heat and simmer gently for 1 hour, skimming as necessary. Add remaining ingredients and simmer gently for 10 hours. As water evaporates during cooking, add more to maintain original level.

Discard bones and vegetables. Pour liquid through strainer lined with double thickness of cheesecloth. Return to pot and cook until reduced to 6 cups (1.5L) and refrigerate. When fat has solidified, remove and discard. Pour stock into containers of practical size for your cooking needs and freeze up to 6 months.

Makes about 6 cups (1.5L).

Green Peppercorns

★ Peppercorns harvested early are green; they turn black when they ripen and are allowed to dry. Green peppercorns are milder than the black and they have a unique pungency. They are available in jars or cans, packed in water or brine. Try to get the water-packed variety, which has no salt. Whichever you use, drain them and rinse them well under cold water before using them. Leftover peppercorns can be refrigerated indefinitely in water in a tightly covered jar. Drain them, rinse them and change the water every few weeks.

MEAT GLAZE (GLACE DE VIANDE)

3 quarts (3L) Lamb, Beef, Veal or Chicken Stock

Boil down any of these stocks to 1 1/2 cups (360ml) or less. This makes a glaze that becomes a hard jelly when cold. Less than 1 teaspoonful enhances sauce or soup; dissolved in hot water it becomes a stock. Divide into portions practical for your cooking needs, wrap airtight and freeze up to 6 months.

Makes 1 1/2 cups (360ml).

QUICK FISH STOCK

This is a well-flavored, time-saving substitute for stock made with fish heads and frames. Clam juice is usually salted, so taste carefully before adding additional salt to soups or sauces in which you use this quick fish stock.

1 large leek (8 ounces total, 225g), with coarse greens trimmed, cut into feed-tube lengths
2 small onions (8 ounces total, 225g), peeled

3 cups (720ml) clam juice
2 (480ml) cups water
1/4 (60ml) cup dry white wine
1 bay leaf
1/2 teaspoon dried thyme

All-Purpose Slicing Disc (4mm): Stand leek in feed tube and use medium pressure to slice. Use firm pressure to slice onions.

Transfer to 3-quart (3L) pan and add remaining ingredients. Bring to boil, reduce heat and let simmer uncovered for 20 minutes. Pour through strainer lined with double thickness of cheesecloth. Can be refrigerated up to 3 days or frozen up to 4 months.

Makes about 5 cups (3.5L).

FISH STOCK

Most fish markets will sell heads and bones from fish that has been cut up into fillets or steaks.

2 large shallots (1 ounce total, 30g), peeled
4 large garlic cloves, peeled
2 tablespoons extra virgin olive oil
1 large leek (10 ounces, 285g), trimmed and cut into 2-inch (5cm) pieces
1 medium onion (5 ounces, 140g), peeled and quartered
2 large tomatoes (1 pound total,

455g), seeded and quartered
2 pounds (1kg) heads and bones from non-oily fish, wrapped in cheesecloth
4 (1L) cups water
1 cup (240ml) dry white wine
20 sprigs parsley or parsley stems
2 bay leaves
1 teaspoon dried thyme

Metal Blade: Turn on machine, drop shallots and 2 garlic cloves through feed tube and process until minced.

Heat oil in 4-quart (4L) pot and add garlic and shallots.

Metal Blade: Pulse to mince leek and onion and add to pot. Pulse to chop tomatoes coarsely and add to pot along with fish bones.

Cover and cook gently over medium heat for 15 minutes. Add water and wine and bring to rapid boil over high heat, skimming as necessary. Wrap remaining 2 garlic cloves, parsley, bay leaves and thyme in double thickness of cheesecloth and tie to make bouquet garni. Add to pot, reduce heat and cook gently, uncovered, for 30 minutes. Discard bones and bouquet garni. Pour through strainer lined with double thickness of cheesecloth. Refrigerate up to 2 days or freeze up to 2 months.

Makes about 5 cups (3.5L).

2 quarts (2L) water
1 cup (240ml) dry white wine
1/4 cup (60ml) white wine vinegar
1 teaspoon confectioners' sugar
1 small celery stalk (2 ounces, 55g), including leafy top, cut in thirds
1 medium onion (5 ounces, 140g), peeled and stuck with 2 whole cloves
1 medium garlic clove, peeled
1 medium leek (8 ounces, 225g), trimmed and cut into thirds

1 teaspoon fresh thyme or 1/2 teaspoon dried
1 small sprig fresh rosemary or 1/2 teaspoon dried
1 teaspoon salt
1/4 teaspoon cayenne pepper
Freshly ground pepper
1 leafy green top of fennel bulb or 1/2 teaspoon dried fennel seed
2 mint leaves or 1/2 teaspoon dried
2 basil leaves or 1/2 teaspoon dried

Combine water, wine, vinegar, sugar, celery, onion, garlic, leek, thyme, rosemary, salt, cayenne and pepper in 6-quart (6L) pot. Cover and bring to boil over high heat. Reduce heat and simmer for 1 1/2 hours. Remove from heat, add fennel, mint and basil and steep for 1 hour. Pour through strainer lined with double thickness of cheesecloth. Refrigerate up to 1 week or freeze up to 6 months. This stock can be used over and over again. Strain it after each use and refreeze it.

Makes about 7 1/2 cups (1.8L).

4 medium leeks (1 1/4 pounds total, 570g), trimmed and cut into thirds
4 medium carrots (12 ounces total, 340g), scrubbed and cut into thirds
4 medium celery stalks (12 ounces total, 340g), cut into thirds
2 medium tomatoes (12 ounces total,

340g), halved and seeded
2 small bunches parsley
3 medium garlic cloves, peeled
6 whole peppercorns
2 bay leaves
4 quarts (4L) water
1 tablespoon cider vinegar

VEGETABLE STOCK

Frédy Girardet, of the restaurant of the same name in Crissier, Switzerland, created this light stock. He uses it in many sauces that accompany fish.

Combine all ingredients in 8-quart (8L) pot. Bring to boil, reduce heat and let simmer gently, uncovered, for 1 1/2 hours. Strain, pressing as much liquid from vegetables as possible. Refrigerate up to 5 days or freeze up to 6 months.

Makes about 5 quarts (3.5L).

PASTA, RICE & BEANS

Many foods soar to stardom and quickly run their course, but pasta is immortal. Americans have made this Italian staple their own. We serve it hot or cold; as the first course, the main course, a side dish or a salad. We even introduce Oriental touches, using Japanese noodles and Chinese stir-fry techniques. Now that we've learned to like pasta so much, there's good news — it's good for us. In fact, pasta, rice and beans are all great sources of complex carbohydrates, an important constituent of a balanced diet.

Try making your own pasta when time allows. It's a satisfying adventure, easy to master and actually fun! But when time is short, use one of the excellent packaged and fresh pastas that are now available. These pasta, rice and bean recipes have great versatility. There are hearty casseroles and cold salads. Most of the dishes will complement meat, fish, cheese, poultry or vegetables. Their style ranges from the elegance of Pasta Rolls with Scallops and Tomato Cream Sauce to the down-home informality of Red Beans and Rice with Creole Sauce.

PASTA, RICE AND BEANS

PASTA

Egg Pasta
Whole Grain Pasta
Basil and Cheese Pasta
Carrot Pasta
Tomato Basil Pasta
Bell Pepper Pasta
Semolina Pasta
Herbed Scallion Pasta
Tomato Pasta Sauce

ROLLING, CUTTING AND COOKING PASTA

PASTA DISHES

Pasta Carbonara
Pasta for All Seasons
Pasta with Cream and Spring Vegetables
Pasta with Four Cheeses
Pasta with Red Peppers and Anchovies
Pasta with Zucchini and Smoked Ham
Pasta Florentine
Pasta with Ratatouille and Sausage

Chinese Noodles Supreme
Pappardelle with Grilled Shrimp and Bell Peppers

Pasta Rolls with Scallops and Tomato Cream Sauce
Pasta Frittata with Cheese and Jalapeño Peppers

Pasta with Shrimp, Pea Pods and Dill
Italian Spinach Pasta Salad
Oriental Pasta Salad

RICE

Mushroom Pilaf
Rice Pilaf with Cashews and Currants
Fruit, Rice and Wheat Berry Pilaf
Fried Rice Salad
Colonial Rice Salad

BEANS

Red Beans with Rice and Creole Sauce
Vegetable Cassoulet

Oriental Pasta Salad
previous pages

MARDI GRAS GALA

Fresh Shucked Oysters
Red Beans and Rice with Creole Sauce
Orange, Red-Onion and Avocado Salad
Jalapeño Corn Griddle Bread
Maple Pecan Praliné Cheesecake

| 1³/₄ cups unbleached all-purpose or bread flour (8³/₄ ounces, 250g) | 3 large eggs
1 teaspoon salt | **EGG PASTA** |

Metal Blade: Process 1¹/₂ cups of flour (7¹/₂ ounces, 215g), eggs and salt until ball forms that moves easily around work bowl. If dough is too wet to form ball, add remaining flour by tablespoon through feed tube, letting each addition work in before adding more. Once desired consistency is reached, process dough until uniformly smooth — about 40 seconds.

Wrap in plastic and let rest for 30 minutes.

For rolling, cutting and cooking instructions, see page 94.

Makes 6 cups cooked pasta.

WHOLE WHEAT VARIATION: Substitute ³/₄ cup (3³/₄ ounces, 105g) each whole wheat flour and all-purpose flour for all-purpose flour. Proceed as directed above.

| ¹/₂ cup wheat berries (2¹/₂ ounces, 70g)
1¹/₂ cups unbleached all-purpose or bread flour (7¹/₂ ounces, 215g) | 2 large eggs
2 teaspoons safflower oil
1 teaspoon salt | **WHOLE-GRAIN PASTA**

Unlike commercial whole-grain pasta, this is a light, tawny brown, attractively flecked with tiny specks of grain. |

Put berries in dish and add water to cover by 3 inches (8cm). Soak for 12 hours or overnight. Drain well, then pat dry with paper towel. (see NOTE).

Metal Blade: Process wheat berries with 1 cup of flour (5 ounces, 140g) until berries are very finely ground — about 2 minutes. They will still be coarser than flour. Add eggs, oil and salt and process until ball forms that moves easily around work bowl. If dough is too wet to form ball, add remaining flour by tablespoon through feed tube, letting each addition work in before adding more. Once desired consistency is reached, process dough until uniformly smooth — about 40 seconds.

Wrap in plastic and let rest for 30 minutes.

For rolling, cutting and cooking instructions, see page 94.

Makes 6 cups cooked pasta.

NOTE: Soaked and drained berries can be sealed airtight and refrigerated up to 3 days or frozen up to 4 months. Bring to room temperature before using.

BASIL AND CHEESE PASTA

This pasta is vibrant in both color and flavor and can be served with the simplest sauces. It's a great addition to pasta salads, too!

¹/₂ cup firmly packed fresh spinach leaves (1 ounce, 30g)
¹/₂ cup firmly packed basil leaves (1 ounce, 30g)
3 ounces (85g) imported Parmesan cheese, at room temperature, cut into 3 pieces
3 large eggs
¹/₂ teaspoon salt
2¹/₄ cups unbleached all-purpose or bread flour (11¹/₄ ounces, 320g)

Metal Blade: Process spinach, basil and cheese until very finely minced. Add eggs and salt and process for 3 seconds. Add 2 cups of flour (10 ounces, 285g) and process until ball forms that moves easily around work bowl. If dough is too wet to form ball, add remaining flour by tablespoon through feed tube, letting each addition work in before adding more. Once desired consistency is reached, process dough until uniformly smooth — about 40 seconds.

Wrap in plastic and let rest for 30 minutes.

For rolling, cutting and cooking instructions, see page 94.

Makes 8 cups cooked pasta.

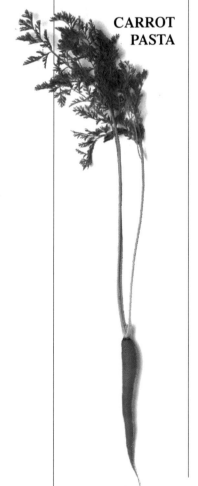

CARROT PASTA

2 medium carrots (4 ounces total, 115g), cut into 2-inch (5cm) pieces, cooked until very tender
1 large egg
¹/₂ teaspoon salt
1¹/₂ cups unbleached all-purpose or bread flour (7¹/₂ ounces, 215g)

Pat carrots dry.

Metal Blade: Process carrots until smooth. Add egg and salt and process for 2 seconds. Add 1¹/₄ cups of flour (6¹/₄ ounces, 180g) and process until ball forms that moves easily around work bowl. If dough is too wet to form ball, add remaining flour by tablespoon through feed tube, letting each addition work in before adding more. Once desired consistency is reached, process dough until uniformly smooth — about 40 seconds.

Wrap in plastic and let rest for 30 minutes.

For rolling, cutting and cooking instructions, see page 94.

Makes 5 cups cooked pasta.

1 6-ounce (170g) can tomato paste
2 large eggs
1 tablespoon dried basil

$^1/_2$ teaspoon salt
2$^1/_2$ cups unbleached all-purpose or bread flour (12$^1/_2$ ounces, 355g)

Metal Blade: Process tomato paste, eggs, basil and salt for 3 seconds. Add 2$^1/_4$ cups of flour (11$^1/_4$ ounces, 320g) and process until ball forms that moves easily around work bowl. If dough is too wet to form ball, add remaining flour by tablespoon through feed tube, letting each addition work in before adding more. Once desired consistency is reached, process dough until uniformly smooth — about 40 seconds.

Wrap in plastic and let rest for 30 minutes. For rolling, cutting and cooking instructions, see page 94.

Makes 8 cups cooked pasta.

TOMATO BASIL PASTA

This pasta has its own distinct flavor and needs only the simplest sauce of butter or olive oil, freshly grated Parmesan cheese and fresh herbs.

---

1 medium red or green bell pepper (6 ounces, 170g), peeled with vegetable peeler, cored and cut into 2-inch (5cm) pieces

1 large egg
1 teaspoon salt
2 cups unbleached all-purpose or bread flour (10 ounces, 285g)

Metal Blade: Process pepper until smooth, stopping several times to scrape work bowl. Add egg and salt and process for 3 seconds. Add 1$^3/_4$ cups of flour (8$^3/_4$ ounces, 250g) and process until ball forms that moves easily around work bowl. If dough is too wet to form a ball, add remaining flour by tablespoon through feed tube, letting each addition work in before adding more. Once desired consistency is reached, process dough until uniformly smooth — about 40 seconds.

Wrap in plastic and let rest for 30 minutes. For rolling, cutting and cooking instructions, see page 94.

Makes 6 cups cooked pasta.

BELL-PEPPER PASTA

Puréed bell pepper adds a dashing color and a subtle flavor to this pasta.

---

2 cups semolina pasta flour (12 ounces, 340g)
3 large eggs

4 teaspoons safflower oil
1 teaspoon salt

Metal Blade: Process 1$^3/_4$ cups of semolina (10$^1/_2$ ounces, 300g), eggs, oil and salt until ball forms that moves easily around work bowl. If dough is too wet to form ball, add remaining flour by tablespoon through feed tube, letting each addition work in before adding more. Once desired consistency is reached, process dough until uniformly smooth — about 40 seconds.

Wrap in plastic and let rest for 30 minutes. For rolling, cutting and cooking instructions, see page 94.

Makes 6 cups cooked pasta.

SEMOLINA PASTA

Semolina flour is now widely available and it is ideal for pasta making. It gives a chewy, yet tender bite.

HERBED SCALLION PASTA

Scallions and a fresh herb add tiny flecks of color to this pasta. Almost any herb can be substituted for parsley or cilantro. Dill, tarragon or chervil are possibilities.

6 large scallions (4 ounces total, 115g), including green tops, cut into 1-inch (2.5cm) pieces
$^{1}/_{4}$ cup loosely packed parsley or cilantro (fresh coriander) leaves

$2^{1}/_{4}$ cups unbleached all-purpose or bread flour (11$^{1}/_{4}$ ounces, 320g)
2 large eggs
1 teaspoon salt

Metal Blade: Process scallions and parsley or cilantro until minced. Add 2 cups of flour (10 ounces, 285g), eggs and salt and process until ball forms that moves easily around work bowl. If dough is too wet to form a ball, add remaining flour by tablespoon through feed tube, letting each addition work in before adding more. Once desired consistency is reached, process dough until uniformly smooth — about 40 seconds.

Wrap in plastic and let rest for 30 minutes.

For rolling, cutting and cooking instructions, see page 94.

Makes 7 cups cooked pasta.

Bell-Pepper Pasta

Carrot Pasta

2 large garlic cloves, peeled
2 tablespoons olive oil
2 tablespoons safflower oil
5 large tomatoes (2½ pounds total, 1.2kg), seeded and quartered
1 teaspoon sugar

1 teaspoon salt
Freshly ground pepper
2 tablespoons tomato paste, if necessary
1 tablespoon finely snipped fresh basil

Metal Blade: Turn on machine, drop garlic through feed tube and process until minced.

Gently heat both oils in 2-quart (2L) non-aluminum saucepan. Add garlic and cook until soft but not brown — about 10 minutes.

Metal Blade: Pulse to chop tomatoes coarsely, in 2 batches. Add to pan with sugar, salt and pepper. Cook gently until heated through — about 10 minutes. Add tomato paste if richer flavor is desired. Stir in basil and adjust seasoning.

Makes 3 cups (720ml).

TOMATO PASTA SAUCE

This summertime staple is quick and easy to prepare. It's delicious on pasta, fish, vegetables and chicken breasts. Make it only in the summer when tomatoes are really good. Extra batches freeze very well and will be welcomed at a winter table.

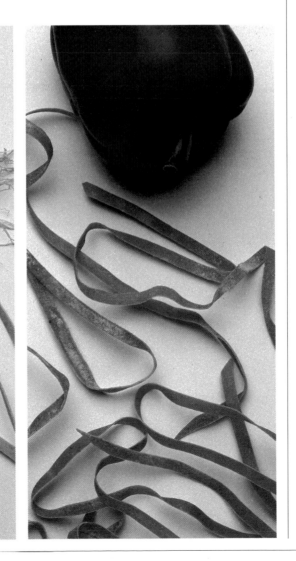

Herbed Scallion Pasta

Bell-Pepper Pasta

ROLLING IN ELECTRIC OR MANUAL PASTA MACHINE

Divide dough into 8 equal portions. Set rollers of electric or manual pasta machine at widest setting. Lightly dust one portion of dough with flour and put it through rollers once, pulling it gently as it comes through. Fold horizontally into thirds and put through rollers again. Repeat folding and rolling 6 more times, dusting dough with flour as necessary. Reset rollers at next setting. Without folding it, put dough through rollers, pulling gently as it comes out. Continue putting dough through at progressively smaller settings until it is very thin. If dough becomes too long to handle easily, cut it in half. I like pasta rolled very thin, about $1/32$-inch (less than 1mm) . It can be thicker if you prefer, but never more than $1/16$-inch (1.5mm). Make sure each portion of dough is rolled to uniform thickness so it will cook evenly.

CUTTING

Fettucine or Linguine: Cut each portion with fettucine or linguine cutter. Hang on pasta rack or lay on cloth towels. Separate strands.

Pasta Circles: Lay each rolled portion on floured board. Cut into rounds with fluted 3-inch (8cm) cutter or 3-inch (8cm) glass. Arrange in single layer on towels.

Pappardelle: Cut each piece of dough into thirds to make 12 by 4-inch (30 by 10cm) rectangles. Trim long sides with pastry wheel for ruffled effect. Then, use pastry wheel to cut into noodles $1/2$-inch (12mm) wide. Lay flat on towel.

Lasagna Noodles: Trim edges of each portion, then cut horizontally into thirds. Lay flat on towel.

Pasta can be cooked immediately or dried. If you are drying it, let sit at room temperature until dry. When dry, wrap airtight and store up to 2 weeks or freeze up to 3 months. Undried pasta can be stored in the refrigerator up to 3 days. Toss with light sprinkling of semolina or cornmeal, wrap airtight and refrigerate.

COOKING

Bring 8 quarts (8L) of water to rolling boil with 1 tablespoon of salt. Add pasta and stir gently. Fresh pasta will cook quickly and needs to be closely watched. Cook pasta until it is "al dente" — tender, but still firm — and drain immediately. Freshly made pasta will be cooked almost as soon as water returns to boil. Pasta can be cooked up to 2 days in advance. Remove any excess water and toss gently with 2 tablespoons of vegetable oil. Wrap airtight and refrigerate up to 3 days or freeze up to 6 months.

★ With cooked pasta from the refrigerator or freezer (see Cooking Pasta, page 94) and a handful of fresh vegetables, these simple combinations can be on the table in less than 10 minutes. It's also a good use of leftover vegetables.

Mince 1 or 2 large garlic cloves and sauté them in a 10-inch (25cm) skillet in 1 tablespoon of extra-virgin olive oil. Add one of the vegetable combinations suggested below, cover and cook until just tender but still crisp. Toss with 2 cups of cooked pasta and heat thoroughly. Add salt, pepper and nutmeg to taste. Serve immediately with shredded Parmesan cheese. Makes 2 to 4 servings.

★ 1 pound (455g) broccoli, with stems peeled and shredded; 1 cup (240ml) Chicken Stock (see Index) or broth; and 1 tablespoon fresh lemon juice

★ 1 28-ounce (795g) can whole tomatoes, drained; and 1 medium red onion (5 ounces, 140g), peeled and quartered, coarsely chopped together with metal blade

★ 6 scallions, including green tops (4 ounces, 115g), sliced; 2 carrots (8 ounces, 225g), shredded; and 1 cup (240ml) Chicken Stock (see Index) or broth

PASTA CARBONARA

I tested this recipe at least 20 different times until I was finally satisfied that the consistency was not that of scrambled eggs. Once the eggs and cream are added, careful cooking is essential to ensure a smooth sauce. Use gentle heat, and you won't have any trouble at all. Unlike many of the pasta recipes, this is a last-minute preparation and must be served immediately.

6 ounces (170g) slab bacon, cut into ¹/₂ by ¹/₂ by ¹/₁₆-inch (12 by 12 by 1.5mm) strips
4 ounces (115g) imported Parmesan cheese, at room temperature
²/₃ cup (160ml) whipping cream
2 large eggs
2 large egg yolks

¹/₂ to 1 teaspoon crushed red pepper flakes
¹/₂ teaspoon rubbed sage
¹/₂ teaspoon salt
    Freshly ground pepper
2 tablespoons unsalted butter
4 cups cooked Egg Pasta (see Index)

Slowly cook bacon in 12-inch (30cm) skillet until it is lightly browned and fat is rendered. Remove from skillet. Discard all but 1 tablespoon of fat from skillet.

Fine Shredding Disc or 2mm Julienne Disc: Use light pressure to shred cheese.

Remove and reserve ¹/₂ of cheese; leave remainder in work bowl.

Metal Blade: Add ¹/₃ cup (80ml) of cream, eggs, egg yolks, pepper flakes, sage, salt and pepper and pulse 3 times.

Add butter and remaining ¹/₃ cup (80ml) of cream to skillet and cook over high heat until butter is melted, stirring often. Add pasta and toss gently. Remove from heat and pour contents of work bowl directly onto hot pasta. Add bacon and toss gently. Briefly heat over very low heat, just until egg mixture thickens slightly and is heated through. Do not overcook. Adjust seasoning. Serve immediately, sprinkled with reserved cheese.

Makes 4 main-course servings.

PASTA FOR ALL SEASONS

Le Cirque Restaurant in New York City popularized Pasta Primavera in the United States; it was a great success. This recipe recreates the wonderful freshness and delicacy of spring, regardless of the season. Vegetables that are abundant all year are cooked until slightly tender but still crisp, then tossed with ribbons of pasta and lightly coated with cream. The food processor makes the presentation professionally perfect!

2 large garlic cloves, peeled
6 tablespoons unsalted butter
1 medium carrot (5 ounces, 140g), peeled and cut into feed-tube widths
1 large stalk broccoli (12 ounces, 340g), with flowerets trimmed and stems peeled, cut into feed-tube widths
1 medium leek (5 ounces, 140g), with coarse greens trimmed, cut into feed-tube lengths
$^1/_2$ teaspoon salt

32 large Chinese pea pods (6 ounces, 170g), with strings removed
1$^3/_4$ cups (420ml) chicken broth
$^1/_2$ cup (120ml) whipping cream
$^1/_4$ teaspoon freshly grated nutmeg
Freshly ground pepper
4 cups cooked Carrot, Herbed Scallion, Bell-Pepper or Egg Pasta (see Index)
1 tablespoon snipped fresh chives
2 tablespoons snipped fresh dill or
$^1/_2$ teaspoon dried dillweed

Metal Blade: Turn on machine, drop garlic through feed tube and process until minced.

In 12-inch (30cm) skillet, gently cook garlic in butter until soft but not brown — about 5 minutes.

3mm Julienne Disc: Lay carrot and broccoli stems in feed tube and use firm pressure to julienne. (If you do not have 3mm Julienne Disc, see page 229.)

Medium Slicing Disc (3mm): Stand leek in feed tube and use medium pressure to slice.

Add salt and all vegetables, including broccoli flowerets and pea pods, to skillet and cook over high heat, stirring constantly, until tender but still crisp — 3 to 4 minutes. Do not overcook. Remove from skillet and set aside. Add chicken broth, cream, nutmeg and pepper to skillet and cook over high heat until reduced to 1 $^1/_2$ cups (360ml) — about 10 minutes.

Can be prepared to this point in advance. Wrap vegetables airtight; cover sauce and refrigerate both. Reheat cream mixture before proceeding.

Toss pasta in sauce, heat thoroughly but do not overcook. Add vegetables and toss gently. When they are hot, add chives and dill. Adjust seasoning and serve immediately.

Makes 4 main-course servings.

2 large garlic cloves, peeled
2 large carrots (10 ounces total, 285g), peeled and cut into feed-tube widths
2 medium leeks (12 ounces total, 340g), trimmed and cut into feed-tube widths
12 ounces (340g) asparagus, with tips removed and stems peeled with

vegetable peeler (see NOTE)
2 tablespoons unsalted butter
1 cup (240ml) whipping cream
1 teaspoon salt
Freshly grated nutmeg
Freshly ground white pepper
6 cups cooked Whole-Grain fettucine (see Index)

Metal Blade: Turn on machine, drop garlic through feed tube and process until minced; remove and reserve.

3mm Julienne Disc: Lay carrots in feed tube and use firm pressure to julienne. (If you do not have Julienne Disc, see page 229.)

Thin Slicing Disc (2mm): Lay leeks in feed tube and use medium pressure to sliver.

Thick Slicing Disc (6mm): Stand asparagus stems in feed tube and use light pressure to slice.

Melt butter in 12-inch (30cm) skillet over medium heat. Cook garlic until soft but not brown — about 5 minutes. Add contents of work bowl and asparagus tips and cook over medium-high heat, stirring often, just until asparagus begins to soften — about 4 minutes. Add remaining ingredients and toss gently. Cook just until pasta is heated through — about 1 1/2 minutes. Adjust seasoning and serve immediately.

Makes 6 servings.

NOTE: To peel asparagus, lay each stalk down on counter and run swivel-bladed vegetable peeler down its length, starting just below tip. Rotate stalk until it is completely peeled.

PASTA WITH CREAM AND SPRING VEGETABLES

I developed this recipe for a popular series of classes featuring whole grains. Using whole-grain fettucine and fresh asparagus makes the dish extra-special. You can, of course, substitute seasonal vegetables and a basic egg fettucine, but I urge you to try it this way at least once.

Pasta for All Seasons

PASTA WITH FOUR CHEESES

Use this recipe as written, or improvise with pieces of cheese that gather in the refrigerator or freezer. Use a total of 1 pound (455g) of cheese, combining as many varieties as you like.

¹/₄ cup loosely packed parsley leaves, preferably Italian flat-leaf
4 ounces (115g) imported Parmesan cheese, quartered
4 ounces (115g) Asiago cheese, at room temperature
4 ounces (115g) Fontina cheese, chilled
3 tablespoons unsalted butter
1 cup (240ml) whipping cream
4 ounces (115g) Gorgonzola cheese, cut into 1-inch (2.5cm) cubes
6 cups cooked Bell-Pepper or Semolina Pasta (see Index)
¹/₄ teaspoon freshly grated nutmeg
Freshly ground white pepper

Metal Blade: Put parsley, Parmesan, Asiago and Fontina cheese in work bowl and pulse 6 times, then process continuously until chopped very fine. Melt butter in 12-inch (30cm) sauté pan. Add cream and Gorgonzola and cook gently, stirring occasionally, until cheese melts. Add pasta and toss to coat with sauce. Cover and cook gently until heated through — about 3 minutes. Remove from heat and add contents of work bowl, nutmeg and pepper. Toss gently until all cheese has melted. Adjust seasoning, and serve immediately or cheese will become too thick.

Makes 6 to 8 servings.

PASTA WITH RED PEPPERS AND ANCHOVIES

This recipe is always a hit when I teach it in class, especially surprising to those who think they don't like anchovies. The anchovies almost completely dissolve, giving a piquant edge to the sweet-sour sauce. It's beautiful as a first course, served at room temperature on a bed of sliced lettuce, or as part of an informal Italian buffet.

2 ounces (55g) imported Parmesan cheese, at room temperature
1 cup loosely packed parsley leaves
4 large shallots (2 ounces total, 55g), peeled
6 tablespoons unsalted butter
3 tablespoons sugar
¹/₄ cup (60ml) plus 2 tablespoons red-wine vinegar
3 large red peppers (18 ounces total,
510g)
2 teaspoons cornstarch
1¹/₂ cups (360ml) beef broth
6 cups cooked Egg Pasta (see Index)
8 anchovy fillets (1¹/₂ ounces total, 45g), cut into ¹/₂-inch (12mm) pieces
Freshly ground pepper
1 large head Boston lettuce (8 ounces, 225g), cored (optional)

2mm Julienne Disc or Fine Shredding Disc: Use light pressure to shred cheese; remove and reserve.

Metal Blade: Process parsley until minced; remove and reserve. Turn on machine, drop shallots through feed tube and process until minced.

Gently melt 4 tablespoons of butter in 12-inch (30cm) skillet. Add shallots and cook until soft but not brown — about 5 minutes. Add sugar and vinegar and continue cooking until mixture is thick and syrupy — about 5 minutes.

Stand peppers on cutting board. Use sharp knife to cut off sides in 3 or 4 vertical slices, leaving only core and stem. Remove any membrane from slices.

Medium Slicing Disc (3mm): Stack pepper slices and stand them lengthwise in feed tube, wedging them in tightly to hold. Use light pressure to slice.

Add to skillet and cook until soft but not limp — about 5 minutes. Transfer to mixing bowl. Can be prepared to this point in advance. Cover airtight and refrigerate.

Mix cornstarch into ¼ cup (60ml) of broth and stir into skillet with remaining broth. Bring to boil over high heat. Cut remaining 2 tablespoons of butter in half and whisk in, 1 piece at a time. Add pasta and heat through. Remove from heat and toss in peppers, anchovies and reserved parsley. Season with pepper and sprinkle with reserved cheese. Serve immediately.

Served as first course, hot or room temperature pasta can be placed on bed of sliced Boston lettuce.

Extra Thick Slicing Disc (8mm): Use light pressure to slice lettuce. Divide lettuce among 6 salad plates and place pasta in center, leaving small border of lettuce exposed.

Makes 6 servings.

PASTA WITH RED PEPPERS AND ANCHOVIES

2 ounces (55g) imported Parmesan cheese, at room temperature	saltiness of ham)
½ cup loosely packed parsley leaves	1 cup (240ml) whipping cream
2 large garlic cloves, peeled	1½ teaspoons fresh marjoram or ¾ teaspoon dried
2 tablespoons unsalted butter	Freshly ground pepper
4 medium zucchini (1¼ pounds total, 565g), cut into feed-tube lengths	4 cups cooked Basil and Cheese, Semolina, or Egg Pasta (see Index)
½ to ¾ teaspoon salt (depending on	1½ ounces (45g) imported smoked ham, cut into thin strips

2mm Julienne Disc or Fine Shredding Disc: Use light pressure to shred cheese; remove and reserve.

Metal Blade: Process parsley until minced; remove and reserve. Turn on machine, drop garlic through feed tube and process until minced.

Melt butter in 12-inch (30cm) skillet. Add garlic and cook gently until soft but not brown — about 5 minutes.

French Fry Disc: Stand zucchini in feed tube and use medium pressure to cut. (If you do not have French Fry Disc, see page 229.)

Add to skillet with salt and cook over medium heat, stirring often, until zucchini is tender but still crisp — about 4 minutes. Remove from skillet. Add cream, marjoram and pepper to skillet and bring to boil. Toss pasta in cream and heat gently. Stir in zucchini and ham, ½ of cheese and all of reserved parsley. Toss gently and adjust seasoning. Serve immediately, sprinkled with remaining cheese.

Makes 4 to 6 servings.

PASTA WITH ZUCCHINI AND SMOKED HAM

The subdued flavors in this attractive pasta dish work very well with simply broiled or grilled poultry, game or lamb. The ham must be a well flavored variety, such as Westphalian. If a similar type is not available, it's best to omit the ham; a domestic boiled ham will not add any interest to the dish.

PASTA FLORENTINE

Tender, young leaves of spinach are delicious when mixed with pasta, cream and a bit of garlic. Buy the freshest young spinach you can find, because nothing can mask the unpleasant flavor of tough, older spinach leaves, which tend to be bitter.

1 large garlic clove, peeled
10 ounces (285g) fresh, young spinach leaves, washed, with stems trimmed and reserved
3 tablespoons unsalted butter
1 teaspoon salt
1 cup (240ml) whipping cream
5 cups cooked Semolina Pasta (see Index)
Freshly ground pepper

Metal Blade: Turn on machine, drop garlic through feed tube and process until minced. Add spinach stems and process until minced.

Melt butter in 10-inch (25cm) sauté pan. Add garlic, spinach stems and salt and cook gently until very soft but not brown — about 8 minutes.

Metal Blade: Pulse spinach leaves in 4 batches to chop them coarsely.

Add to pan along with cream and bring to simmer over high heat. Add pasta and generous sprinkling of pepper. Cook just until heated through. Serve immediately.

Makes 6 side-dish servings.

PASTA WITH RATATOUILLE AND SAUSAGE

There are really two good recipes here. Freshly cooked pasta is tossed with finely minced garlic, olive oil and fresh parsley as a base for the robust topping of ratatouille, tomato and Italian sausage. Even by itself, the garlic, oil and parsley mixture is one of the most delicious — and certainly the easiest — ways to dress homemade pasta.

6 ounces (170g) hot or mild Italian sausage in casing
3 ounces (85g) imported Parmesan cheese, at room temperature
1/2 cup loosely packed parsley leaves
1 large garlic clove, peeled
1/4 cup (60ml) extra-virgin olive oil
3 medium tomatoes (18 ounces total, 510g), cored and halved
10 medium mushrooms (6 ounces total, 170g), with 2 opposite sides cut flat
2 teaspoons dried basil
1 teaspoon sugar
1 teaspoon salt
1 cup (240ml) plus 2 tablespoons tomato sauce
1 1/2 cups Ratatouille (see Index)
2 tablespoons red-wine vinegar
1 teaspoon dried oregano
12 Calamata olives
Freshly ground pepper
6 cups cooked Egg or Semolina Pasta (see Index)

Put sausage in 8-inch (20cm) skillet with 1/2 inch (12mm) of water. Let simmer, uncovered, until water has evaporated, turning once after 8 minutes. Then, brown on all sides. Cut sausage into 1/4-inch (6mm) slices.

Fine or Medium Shredding Disc: Use light pressure to shred cheese; remove and reserve.

Metal Blade: Put parsley in work bowl and turn on machine. Drop garlic through feed tube and process until minced.

Transfer to small dish and add 2 tablespoons of oil.

French Fry Disc: Use light pressure to cut tomatoes. (If you do not have French Fry Disc, see page 229.)

Heat remaining 2 tablespoons of oil in 12-inch (30cm) skillet. Use spoon to lift tomatoes from work bowl, leaving behind juice and seeds. Add tomato pieces to skillet. Discard seeds and juice.

All Purpose Slicing Disc (4mm): Stand mushrooms in feed tube flat side down and use light pressure to slice.

Add to skillet along with basil, sugar and $^{1}/_{2}$ teaspoon of salt and cook gently until vegetables are heated through but not limp — about 4 minutes. Add tomato sauce, Ratatouille, vinegar, oregano, olives and a generous sprinkling of pepper. Cook just until heated through. Add sausage and adjust seasoning.

In large serving bowl, toss hot pasta with reserved garlic-oil mixture and remaining $^{1}/_{2}$ teaspoon of salt. Add topping, garnish with reserved cheese and serve immediately.

Makes 4 to 6 servings.

*Pasta Florentine
and Pasta with
Ratatouille and
Sausage*

CHINESE NOODLES SUPREME

I first taught this recipe 8 years ago and time hasn't changed my taste for it. I've added cilantro, which is more readily available now than it was then, but otherwise the recipe has stayed intact. It's great to serve as part of an Oriental meal, but don't let its decidedly ethnic flavor stop you from offering it as part of a buffet or picnic. The pork can be replaced with an equal amount of diced chicken or turkey.

6 large dried Chinese mushrooms
1 12-ounce (340g) package Udon noodles, cooked al dente (see NOTE)
1 tablespoon Oriental sesame oil
2 medium garlic cloves, peeled
3/4 pound (340g) boneless pork, cut into 1-inch (2.5cm) cubes
1/2 cup cilantro, or fresh coriander, leaves
1 pound (455g) bok choy, cut into feed-tube lengths
12 large scallions (6 ounces total, 170g), cut into 2-inch (5cm) lengths
2 tablespoons safflower oil
2 cups fresh bean sprouts (7 ounces total, 200g)
1/4 cup (60ml) dry sherry
3/4 cup chicken broth
3 tablespoons soy sauce
1 tablespoon sugar

Cover mushrooms with warm water and let soak for 30 minutes; drain well. (If desired, strain liquid through strainer lined with paper towels or coffee filter. Freeze for use in soups or sauces.) Gently squeeze out excess moisture and cut stems from mushrooms. Reserve stems to flavor soups and sauces, if desired.

Toss noodles with sesame oil.

Can be prepared to this point 2 days in advance. Wrap mushrooms and noodles separately and refrigerate.

Metal Blade: Turn on machine, drop garlic through feed tube and process until minced; remove and reserve. Process pork, cilantro and mushrooms until finely chopped; remove and reserve.

All Purpose Slicing Disc (4mm): Stand bok choy in feed tube and use medium pressure to slice; remove and reserve. Lay scallions in feed tube and use light pressure to sliver.

In wok or 12-inch (30cm) skillet, heat safflower oil and gently cook garlic until soft — about 5 minutes. Add pork, cilantro and mushrooms and stir-fry over high heat until cooked — about 6 minutes. Add bok choy, bean sprouts, sherry and 1/2 of scallions and stir fry until heated through — about 2 minutes. Add chicken broth, soy sauce, sugar and noodles and cook over medium heat, stirring constantly, until heated through — about 2 minutes. Transfer to serving dish and garnish with remaining scallions. Serve hot, cold or at room temperature. Adjust seasoning before serving.

Makes 8 servings.

NOTE: Udon are long, flat Japanese noodles, which add an authentic touch. Many large supermarkets carry them, as do Oriental markets. Substitute an equal weight of linguine or spaghetti if you can't locate them.

16 extra large shrimp (1 1/2 pounds total, 680g), peeled, with black sand vein removed
4 tablespoons olive oil
4 ounces (115g) imported Parmesan cheese, at room temperature
4 large garlic cloves, peeled
1/4 cup pine nuts (1 ounce, 30g)
1 1/2 cups (360ml) dry vermouth or dry white wine
6 tablespoons whipping cream
1 teaspoon salt
1/2 teaspoon crushed red pepper flakes

Freshly grated nutmeg
Freshly ground pepper
2 large red peppers (14 ounces total, 395g), peeled with vegetable peeler
2 large green peppers (14 ounces total, 395g), peeled with vegetable peeler
2 large yellow peppers (14 ounces total, 395g), peeled with vegetable peeler
6 cups cooked Egg pappardelle (see Index)

PAPPARDELLE WITH GRILLED SHRIMP AND BELL PEPPERS

This elegant pasta dish is quite easy to make. The ruffled pappardelle noodles, grilled shrimp and colorful bell peppers are all bathed in a delicately flavored wine-and-cream sauce. It's a great first course because much of the work can be done in advance.

Brush shrimp with 1 tablespoon of oil. Grill over very hot fire (I use charcoal mixed with oak), turning them once, until opaque — about 3 minutes. Cut in half lengthwise.

Fine Shredding Disc: Use light pressure to shred cheese; remove and reserve.

Metal Blade: Turn on machine, drop garlic through feed tube and process until minced.

Heat remaining 3 tablespoons of oil in 12-inch (30cm) skillet over medium heat. Add pine nuts and cook until golden — about 4 minutes. Remove with slotted spoon and reserve. Add garlic and cook until soft but not brown — about 5 minutes. Add vermouth and bring to simmer. Add cream, salt, pepper flakes, nutmeg and pepper and cook until sauce has thickened slightly — about 7 minutes.

Can be prepared to this point 1 day in advance. Bring to simmer before proceeding.

Stand peppers on cutting board. Use sharp knife to cut off sides in 3 or 4 vertical slices, leaving only core and stem. Remove any membrane from slices.

Extra Thick (8mm) or Thick Slicing Disc (6mm): Stack pepper slices and stand lengthwise in feed tube, wedging them in tightly to hold. Use light pressure to slice.

Add peppers to skillet and let simmer for 3 minutes. Add shrimp and pasta and cook just until heated through — about 3 minutes. Sprinkle with pine nuts and pass cheese separately. Serve hot or at room temperature.

Makes 8 servings.

PASTA ROLLS WITH SCALLOPS AND TOMATO CREAM SAUCE

This is a light pasta dish. A cilantro-flecked scallop mousse is spread on tender homemade lasagna noodles which are rolled into cylinders, wrapped in plastic and gently baked at a very low temperature. The presentation is stunning — slices of the roll are placed on a rich, smooth Tomato-Cream Sauce and garnished with tiny bay scallops and cilantro leaves.

2 large shallots (1 ounce total, 30g), peeled
1 large garlic clove, peeled
3 tablespoons unsalted butter
2 pounds (910g) bay scallops, rinsed and patted dry
1 cup cilantro, or fresh coriander, leaves
1 slice white bread (1 ounce, 30g), with crust removed
2 teaspoons salt
Freshly ground white pepper
Freshly grated nutmeg
Pinch of cayenne pepper
1/2 cup (120ml) whipping cream, chilled
1 large egg
6 cooked and cooled Semolina lasagna noodles (see Index)
Tomato-Cream Sauce (recipe follows)
48 cilantro, or fresh coriander, leaves, for garnish

Metal Blade: Turn on machine, drop shallots and garlic through feed tube and process until minced.

Melt 1 tablespoon of butter in 6-inch (15cm) skillet. Gently cook shallots and garlic until soft but not brown — about 6 minutes. Transfer to work bowl.

Metal Blade: Add 1 pound (455g) of scallops, cilantro, bread, salt, pepper, nutmeg and cayenne and process until smooth, stopping once to scrape work bowl. Turn on machine and slowly pour cream through feed tube. Add egg and process until fluffy and smooth — about 30 seconds.

Transfer to mixing bowl and refrigerate for at least 30 minutes.

Melt remaining butter in 8-inch (20cm) skillet over high heat. Add remaining scallops and cook quickly, stirring often, until they begin to turn opaque — about 30 seconds. Immediately transfer to strainer placed over bowl. Reserve liquid for Sauce.

Lay lasagna noodles on towel and pat them dry. Spread each with 9 tablespoons of scallop mousse in smooth layer, going all the way to edges. Starting 1/2 inch (12mm) in from short side of noodle, place 10 sautéed scallops down short side. Roll up lasagna from short side, making roll as tight as possible without squeezing out filling. Smooth mousse on open ends with knife. Repeat with remaining noodles and filling. Reserve remaining scallops for sauce. Loosely wrap each roll in Saran wrap (see NOTE) and seal 1/2 inch (12mm) from end with twist-tie. Recipe can be prepared to this point 1 day in advance and refrigerated.

Fifteen minutes before baking, set rack in center of oven and preheat to 225°F (110°C). Place rolls on baking sheet and bake for 25 minutes, turning once after 13 minutes.

Fold remaining scallops into Tomato Cream Sauce and heat gently. Unwrap each roll and cut it into 8 slices. Divide Tomato Cream Sauce among 6 dinner plates, spreading it evenly over entire surface of plate. Arrange slices in circle over sauce. Garnish each plate with cilantro leaves and serve immediately.

Makes 6 main-course servings.

NOTE: I have spoken at length with the consumer products division of Dow Chemicals, makers of Saran plastic food wrap, about its cooking properties. They assure me that it is perfectly safe at temperatures lower than 250°F (120°C), with no transfer of particles between food and plastic. At 250°F (120°C), it will begin to melt, so watch your oven temperature carefully. They do not recommend use of Saran for cooking foods that have a high proportion of sugar or fat.

PASTA ROLLS WITH SCALLOPS AND TOMATO CREAM SAUCE

TOMATO CREAM SAUCE

4 large shallots (2 ounces total, 55g), peeled	Liquid from scallops (see preceding recipe)
1 tablespoon unsalted butter	1/2 cup (120ml) whipping cream
1 16-ounce (455g) can tomato wedges, undrained (see NOTE)	1/2 teaspoon Cognac
	Salt to taste
1/4 cup (60ml) tomato paste	Freshly ground pepper

In addition to its use with the Pasta Rolls, this is a good topping for pasta, broiled fish, sautéed chicken breasts or vegetables. Simply omit the juices from the scallops.

Metal Blade: Turn on machine, drop shallots through feed tube and process until minced.

Gently cook shallots and butter in 7-inch (18cm) skillet until soft but not brown — about 5 minutes.

Metal Blade: Process tomatoes and tomato paste for 10 seconds.

Add to shallots with reserved juice from scallops and let simmer, uncovered, for 10 minutes. Press through fine sieve and return to skillet with cream. Simmer gently, uncovered, until reduced to 1 cup (240ml). Add Cognac and adjust seasoning.

Sauce can be prepared up to 3 days in advance and refrigerated. Add liquid from scallops when it is reheated.

Makes 1 cup (240ml).

NOTE: When flavorful tomatoes are available, 2 medium tomatoes (12 ounces total, 340g), peeled, seeded and coarsely chopped, can be substituted for canned tomatoes.

FOR CELEBRATIONS

Pasta Rolls with Scallops and Tomato Cream Sauce
Boneless Leg of Lamb with Peppercorn Mustard Crust
Sautéed Spinach
Goat Cheese Salad with Julienned Beets
Whole-Wheat Nut Bread
French Apple Tart

PASTA FRITTATA WITH CHEESE AND JALAPENO PEPPERS

Leftover cooked pasta can spur culinary imagination, whether it's tossed with julienned vegetables for a hot or cold dish or transformed into a delicious frittata like this one. There is only enough egg to bind the pasta, so actually it's more like a pasta pancake. If you prefer a more typical frittata, use 4 eggs. Garnished with Salsa (see Index) and a dab of sour cream, it's an excellent dish for a brunch or light supper.

2 jalapeño peppers, halved, seeds removed if desired
6 large scallions (3 ounces total, 85g), including green tops, cut into 1-inch (2.5cm) pieces
1 cup cilantro, or fresh coriander, leaves
6 ounces (170g) Longhorn Colby cheese, cut into 1-inch (2.5cm) pieces
6 ounces (170g) Monterey Jack cheese, cut into 1-inch (2.5cm) pieces
1 large egg
³/₄ teaspoon salt (or to taste, depending on saltiness of cheeses)
1 medium red pepper (5 ounces, 140g)
3 cups cooked Egg or Semolina linguine (see Index)
2 tablespoons peanut oil
Salsa (see Index)

Fifteen minutes before broiling, place rack 6 inches (15cm) from heat and preheat broiler.

Metal Blade: Turn on machine, drop peppers through feed tube and process until minced. Add scallions, cilantro and both cheeses and process until minced. Add egg and salt and process for 3 seconds. Transfer to large mixing bowl.

Stand red pepper on cutting board. Use sharp knife to cut off sides in 3 or 4 vertical slices, leaving only core and stem. Remove any membrane from slices.

Thin Slicing Disc (2mm): Stack pepper slices and stand lengthwise in feed tube, wedging them in tightly to hold. Use light pressure to slice.

Add to bowl along with linguine and toss gently but thoroughly.

Heat 12-inch (30cm) griddle or ovenproof skillet over medium heat. Add oil and brush over bottom and up sides of pan. When pan is sizzling hot, add pasta mixture and use spatula to spread quickly in even layer. Cook for 6 minutes, then lift edges to see if bottom is lightly browned.

When bottom is browned, transfer to preheated broiler and broil until surface is set — about 2 to 3 minutes. Do not allow to brown.

Pasta with Shrimp, Pea Pods and Dill Bell-Pepper Pasta

Let rest for 5 minutes. Run thin spatula under frittata to loosen bottom and sides and slide onto serving plate. Use pizza cutter to cut into squares or wedges and serve immediately with Salsa.

Makes 6 to 8 servings.

PASTA WITH SHRIMP, PEA PODS AND DILL

I love this salad as much for its array of colors and textures as for its delicious flavor. It's dressed with a lemony vinaigrette, light enough so it doesn't mask the fresh ingredients. Fresh dill is especially nice in this salad, but dried dillweed can be used when it's not available.

2 pounds (910g) jumbo shrimp with shells on (if frozen, do not thaw)
2 to 4 tablespoons safflower oil
40 large snow peas (8 ounces total, 225g), trimmed, with strings removed
1 8-ounce (225g) can whole water chestnuts, drained

Lemon Dill Vinaigrette
1 cup loosely packed parsley leaves
6 tablespoons fresh dill or 1 tablespoon dried dillweed
2 large garlic cloves, peeled
6 large shallots (3 ounces total, 85g), peeled
²/₃ cup (160ml) safflower oil
¹/₃ cup (80ml) fresh lemon juice
1 teaspoon salt
Freshly ground pepper
6 cups cooked Egg or Bell-Pepper Pasta (see Index)

Rinse shrimp and pat dry. Heat 2 tablespoons of oil in 10-inch (25cm) sauté pan over high heat. Stir-fry shrimp in 4 batches, turning only once, just until opaque — about 3 to 4 minutes. Remove each shrimp as it is cooked; do not overcook. Add more oil as necessary. When shrimp are cool enough to handle, peel, remove black vein and cut in half lengthwise.

Bring 2 quarts (2L) of water to rolling boil with 1 teaspoon of salt. Add snow peas and cook for 60 seconds. Drain immediately and hold under cold running water until cool. Drain and pat dry.

All-Purpose Slicing Disc (4mm): Use medium pressure to slice water chestnuts; remove and reserve.

Metal Blade: Put parsley and dill in work bowl and turn on machine. Drop garlic and shallots through feed tube and process until minced. Add oil, lemon juice, salt and pepper and process for 3 seconds.

Toss hot pasta in large bowl with half of vinaigrette. Add water chestnuts and snow peas and toss gently. If salad is not being served immediately, add snow peas just before serving to keep them from discoloring. Heat remaining vinaigrette in 10-inch (25cm) sauté pan over high heat. Add shrimp and cook just until heated through — about 2 minutes. Toss with pasta and vegetables. Adjust seasoning and arrange snow peas over top. Serve warm or at room temperature.

Makes 6 servings.

ITALIAN SPINACH PASTA SALAD

This colorful and highly seasoned salad can be the first course of an Italian dinner or the focus of a light, refreshing supper or lunch. You can also make it without the pasta — it's delicious either way. I prefer to use pepperoni that's about 1 inch (2.5cm) in diameter. If only the 3-inch (8cm) variety is available, cut it in half lengthwise.

1¼ cups firmly packed tender, young spinach leaves (2½ ounces, 70g), with stems removed, cleaned
2 cups cooked Bell-Pepper or Herbed Scallion fettucine, with parsley (see Index)
½ cup loosely packed parsley leaves
1 tablespoon fresh oregano or ½ teaspoon dried
1 tablespoon fresh basil or ½ teaspoon dried
1 medium garlic clove, peeled
¼ cup (60ml) Balsamic vinegar
¼ cup (60ml) safflower oil
2 tablespoons olive oil
¾ teaspoon salt
Freshly ground pepper
5 ounces (140g) pepperoni, peeled, chilled and cut into thirds
1 medium red pepper (5 ounces, 140g)
2 small red onions (4 ounces total, 115g), peeled
1 6-ounce (170g) package sliced Provolone cheese, semi-frozen, quartered (see NOTE)
1 medium zucchini (7 ounces, 200g), cut into feed-tube lengths
12 Calamata olives

Tear spinach into bite-size pieces and combine with pasta in large salad bowl.

Metal Blade: Put parsley, oregano and basil in work bowl and turn on machine. Drop garlic through feed tube and process until minced. Add vinegar, oils, salt and pepper and process for 3 seconds. Leave in work bowl.

Thin Slicing Disc (2mm): Stand pepperoni in feed tube and use firm pressure to slice.

Stand red pepper on cutting board. Use sharp knife to cut off sides in 3 or 4 vertical slices, leaving only core and stem. Remove any membrane from slices.

Medium Slicing Disc (3mm): Stack pepper slices and stand them lengthwise in feed tube, wedging them in tightly to hold. Use light pressure to slice. Use firm pressure to slice onions. Stand cheese slices in feed tube, fitting in tightly to hold, and use light pressure to slice into matchsticks.

French Fry Disc: Stand zucchini in feed tube and use medium pressure to cut. (If you do not have French Fry Disc, see page 229.)

Transfer contents of work bowl to salad bowl, add olives and toss gently. Adjust seasoning and serve immediately.

Makes 6 servings.

NOTE: I rarely use sliced cheese but it works beautifully here for julienne strips. If you prefer, use bulk Provolone and shred it.

Marinade and Noodles

- ¹/₂ cup (120ml) white-rice vinegar
- ¹/₂ cup (120ml) safflower oil
- ¹/₄ cup (60ml) soy sauce
- 4 teaspoons sugar
- 2 teaspoons dry mustard
- 1 teaspoon peanut butter
- 1 teaspoon Oriental sesame oil
- 1 teaspoon ground ginger
- ¹/₄ teaspoon salt
- Freshly ground pepper
- 1 12-ounce package Udon noodles (see NOTE on page 102) or 6 cups Egg or Herbed Scallion Pasta (see Index), freshly cooked and still warm

Vegetables

- ¹/₄ cup sesame seeds
- 10 dried black Chinese mushrooms
- 16 large snow peas (4 ounces total, 115g), with strings removed, halved lengthwise
- 1 large red pepper (8 ounces, 225g)
- 4 large scallions (3 ounces total, 85g), including green tops, cut into 2-inch (5cm) lengths
- 1 large jicama (20 ounces, 565g), peeled and cut to fit feed tube
- 4 medium carrots (12 ounces total, 340g), peeled and cut into feed-tube widths

Metal Blade: Process vinegar, oil, soy sauce, sugar, mustard, peanut butter, sesame oil, ginger, salt and pepper for 2 seconds.

Toss with warm noodles or pasta and refrigerate for 2 hours or overnight.

Spread sesame seeds on jelly-roll pan and bake in preheated 350°F (175°C) oven until lightly browned — about 15 minutes.

Cover mushrooms with warm water and let soak until soft and spongy — about 20 minutes. Drain, remove stems and cut large mushrooms in half. (Reserve stems and liquid to use in soup.) Add mushrooms to noodles along with pea pods.

Stand red pepper on cutting board. Use sharp knife to cut off sides in 3 or 4 vertical slices, leaving only core and stem. Remove any membrane from slices.

Thin Slicing Disc (2mm): Stack pepper slices and stand them lengthwise in feed tube, wedging them in tightly to hold. Use light pressure to slice. Lay scallions in feed tube and use light pressure to sliver.

3mm Julienne Disc: Use firm pressure to julienne jicama and carrots. (If you do not have 3mm Julienne Disc, see page 229.) Toss vegetables with noodles.

At serving time, adjust seasoning and sprinkle with toasted sesame seeds. Serve at room temperature.

Makes 8 servings.

ORIENTAL PASTA SALAD

Jicama is a tuberous root native to Latin America; it has sweet, juicy flesh. It lends a marvelous crunchy sweetness to this salad and its flavor is far more interesting than that of water chestnuts. If jicama is not available, you can substitute water chestnuts.

MUSHROOM PILAF

The Ultra Thin Slicing Disc gives an entirely new look to this mushroom pilaf. Instead of cooking the mushrooms in the rice until they are dark and limp, you slice them so thin that they don't need to be cooked. They're gently folded into hot rice, which softens them, keeping their color, lovely shape and flavor.

2¹/₂ cups (600ml) water
1 teaspoon salt
1 cup long-grain white rice (7 ounces, 200g)
2 tablespoons unsalted butter

¹/₄ teaspoon ground cloves
10 large, firm white mushrooms (8 ounces total, 225g), with 2 opposite sides cut flat

Bring water and salt to boil in 2-quart (2L) saucepan. Add rice, butter and cloves, cover and cook over medium heat until water is absorbed — about 18 minutes.

Can be cooked up to 2 days in advance and refrigerated. Reheat in double boiler over gently simmering water before proceeding.

Ultra Thin Slicing Disc (1mm): Put mushrooms in feed tube flat side down and use light pressure to slice.

Toss gently into hot rice. Adjust seasoning and serve immediately.

Makes 6 servings.

RICE PILAF WITH CASHEWS AND CURRANTS

Rice is wonderfully versatile, but it is often passed over in favor of pasta. I serve this pilaf with Middle Eastern dishes, curries and simple meats. Though almonds are more commonly used with rice, I prefer cashews in this dish.

³/₄ cup cashews (3 ounces, 85g)
6 large shallots (3 ounces total, 85g), peeled
2 tablespoons unsalted butter
1 cup long-grain white rice (7 ounces, 200g)

2 cups (480ml) chicken broth
¹/₂ teaspoon cinnamon
¹/₂ teaspoon salt
¹/₃ cup dried currants (1²/₃ ounces, 50g)

Metal Blade: Pulse to chop cashews coarsely; remove and reserve. Turn on machine, drop shallots through feed tube and process until minced.

Melt butter in 2¹/₂-quart (2.5L) saucepan and add shallots. Cook gently until soft — about 8 minutes. Add rice, chicken broth, cinnamon, and salt and bring to boil. Cover and reduce to simmer. Cook until liquid is absorbed — about 20 minutes. Remove from heat and fold in cashews and currants.

Can be made 2 days in advance and refrigerated. Reheat in double boiler over gently simmering water.

Makes 6 to 8 servings.

Parmesan Cheese

★ The superior flavor of imported Parmesan cheese makes it worth the high price. As soon as you buy it, shred or finely chop all of it. Freeze in airtight plastic bags. Before processing, let it come to room temperature and remove any rind. Use the Fine Shredding Disc or the 2x2mm Julienne Disc for delicate strands to garnish fresh pasta, green salads or soups. Use the metal blade to chop it. First, cut it into 1-inch (2.5cm) cubes. Turn on the machine, drop cubes through feed tube and chop to the desired texture.

¹/₂ cup wheat berries (2¹/₂ ounces, 70g)

6 large shallots (3 ounces total, 85g), peeled

3 tablespoons unsalted butter

³/₄ cup long-grain white rice (5 ounces, 140g)

2 cups (480ml) chicken broth

1 large Granny Smith apple (8 ounces, 225g), unpeeled, cored and quartered

2 medium celery stalks (6 ounces total, 170g), strings removed with vegetable peeler, cut into 1-inch (2.5cm) pieces

¹/₃ cup dried currants (1²/₃ ounces, 50g)

1¹/₄ teaspoons salt

³/₄ teaspoon dried thyme

¹/₂ teaspoon ground allspice

FRUIT, RICE AND WHEAT BERRY PILAF

Tender, chewy kernels of wheat berries mixed into this pilaf set it apart from other fruit and rice stuffings. The wholesome and delicious berries are a perfect complement to fluffy, long-grain white rice.

Put berries in dish and add water to cover berries by 3 inches (8cm). Let soak for 12 hours or overnight. Drain well, then pat dry with paper towel. (See NOTE). Butter 1¹/₂-quart (1.5L) casserole.

Metal Blade: Turn on machine, drop shallots through feed tube and process until minced.

Melt butter in 2¹/₂-quart (2.5L) saucepan, add shallots and cook gently until soft but not brown — about 10 minutes. Add wheat berries, rice and chicken broth and bring to boil. Cover and reduce heat to low. Let simmer until rice is tender and liquid is absorbed — about 18 minutes. Remove from heat.

Fifteen minutes before baking, place rack in center of oven and preheat to 350°F (175°C).

Metal Blade: Pulse to chop apple and celery coarsely.

Stir into rice along with currants, salt, thyme and allspice. Transfer to prepared casserole.

Can be assembled up to 3 days in advance and refrigerated. Bring to room temperature before baking. Cover and bake until heated through — about 30 minutes.

Makes 4 to 6 servings.

NOTE: Soaked and drained berries can be sealed airtight and refrigerated up to 3 days or frozen up to 4 months. Bring to room temperature before using.

FRIED RICE SALAD

The inspiration for this salad comes from Oriental fried rice, but unlike that dish, it can be made in advance. Use it as a vehicle for leftovers, adding any bits of chicken, shrimp or vegetables that are on hand. It's delicious served hot or cold.

1 cup loosely packed parsley leaves
1 large carrot (5 ounces, 140g), peeled and cut into 1-inch (2.5cm) pieces
4 medium scallions (3 ounces total, 85g), including green tops, cut into thirds
4 large eggs
³/₄ teaspoon salt
5 tablespoons peanut oil
3 cups cooked long-grain white rice
1 cup tiny frozen peas, thawed

Vinaigrette
¹/₃ cup (80ml) rice-wine vinegar
1 tablespoon soy sauce
1 tablespoon safflower or peanut oil
1 teaspoon Oriental sesame oil
1 teaspoon sugar

Metal Blade: Process parsley until minced; remove and reserve. Process carrot until minced.

All Purpose Slicing Disc (4mm): Stand scallions in feed tube and use light pressure to slice. Remove and reserve carrot and scallions.

Metal Blade: Put eggs and ¹/₄ teaspoon of salt in work bowl and pulse 4 times.

Heat 3 tablespoons of oil in wok or 12-inch (30cm) skillet until hot. Add eggs and tilt pan as you push cooked part of eggs to side of wok; do not overcook. Remove from wok and scramble with fork to make coarse chunks. Add remaining 2 tablespoons of oil to wok. When hot, add carrot, scallions, parsley and remaining ¹/₂ teaspoon of salt and stir-fry just until heated through — about 30 seconds. Do not overcook. Remove from heat. Toss in rice, peas, cooked eggs and vinaigrette ingredients. Serve immediately or refrigerate for up to 3 days and serve chilled. Adjust seasoning before serving.

Makes 6 servings.

COLONIAL RICE SALAD

I spent a week working with Gaston Lenôtre at his laboratoire in the Paris suburb of Plaisir. Salads and baked goods are made there for his carry-out shops. The Colonial Rice Salad is one of Lenôtre's recipes. Sweet corn and red and green peppers give it an American look.

4¹/₂ cups cooked long-grain white rice
3 tablespoons safflower oil
3 tablespoons olive oil
3 tablespoons red-wine vinegar
1 small red pepper (3 ounces, 85g)
1 small green pepper (3 ounces, 85g)
3 large scallions (2 ounces total, 55g), including green tops, cut into thirds
1 cup fresh or frozen sweet corn kernels (6 ounces, 170g)
Salt
Freshly ground pepper

Put rice in large mixing bowl and add both oils and vinegar. Stand peppers on cutting board. Use sharp knife to cut off sides in 3 or 4 vertical slices, leaving only core and stem. Remove any membrane from slices.

Medium Slicing Disc (3mm): Stack pepper slices and stand them lengthwise in feed tube, wedging them in tightly to hold. Use light pressure to slice. Stand scallions in feed tube and use light pressure to slice.

Add processed vegetables and corn to rice and toss gently. Can be refrigerated up to 4 days. Adjust seasoning and serve at room temperature.

Makes 8 to 10 servings.

<table>
<tr><td>

¹/₂ pound (225g) dried red kidney beans
¹/₂ cup loosely packed parsley leaves
1 large garlic clove, peeled
1 medium onion (4 ounces, 115g), peeled and quartered
1 small smoked ham hock (³/₄ pound, 340g)
1 bay leaf
1¹/₄ teaspoons salt
¹/₄ teaspoon freshly ground pepper
¹/₄ teaspoon dried thyme
¹/₄ teaspoon dried basil
2¹/₄ cups (540ml) water

</td><td>

5 ounces (140g) Longhorn Colby cheese, chilled
3 medium scallions (1¹/₂ ounces total, 45g), including green tops, cut into 1-inch (2.5cm) pieces
¹/₂ small green pepper (2 ounces, 55g), cut into 1-inch (2.5cm) pieces
2 cups cooked long-grain white rice
1 medium carrot (3 ounces, 85g), cut into 1-inch (2.5cm) pieces
¹/₂ teaspoon Worcestershire sauce
¹/₂ teaspoon crushed red pepper flakes
¹/₄ teaspoon Tabasco sauce
Creole Sauce (recipe follows)

</td></tr>
</table>

RED BEANS AND RICE WITH CREOLE SAUCE

This earthy and substantial dish is an adaptation of a simple, though highly esteemed, dish of the American South. I've modified it considerably by cutting back on the ham and pork and adding crisp vegetables so it's more healthy and appealing. And authentic or not, I love to serve it with Creole Sauce and shredded Colby cheese.

Soak beans overnight in cold water to cover. Drain and transfer to 3-quart (3L) pan.

Metal Blade: Process parsley until minced; remove and reserve. Turn on machine, drop garlic through feed tube and process until minced. Add onion and process until minced.

Add to beans with ham hock, bay leaf, salt, pepper, thyme, basil and water. Bring to boil, then reduce heat and cook gently, uncovered, until beans are tender — about 1¹/₂ hours. Do not overcook; the beans should not be mushy. If necessary, add ¹/₂ to ³/₄ (120 to 180ml) cup more water to keep mixture very moist. Remove ham hock and cut meat from it. Add meat to beans and discard bone and bay leaf.

Can be prepared to this point 3 days in advance and refrigerated. Reheat gently before proceeding.

Fine Shredding Disc: Use light pressure to shred cheese; remove and reserve.

Metal Blade: Process scallions and green pepper until minced. Add to rice. Process carrots until minced and add to rice with reserved parsley.

Stir rice into hot beans and add Worcestershire sauce, crushed red pepper and Tabasco sauce. Cook just until heated through. Adjust seasoning.

Serve with Creole Sauce and cheese.

Makes 6 servings.

CREOLE SAUCE

2 large garlic cloves, peeled
1 small onion (2 ounces, 55g), peeled
1 small celery rib (1 ounce, 30g), strings removed with vegetable peeler, cut into feed-tube lengths
1 small green pepper (3 ounces, 85g)
1 tablespoon unsalted butter
1 16-ounce (455g) can whole tomatoes, undrained
1 bay leaf
1/4 teaspoon dried thyme
1 teaspoon chili powder
1 teaspoon Tabasco sauce
1 teaspoon Worcestershire sauce
1/4 teaspoon sugar
1/8 teaspoon salt

Metal Blade: Turn on machine, drop garlic through feed tube and process until minced.

Thin Slicing Disc (2mm): Stand onion and celery in feed tube and use medium pressure to slice.

Stand pepper on cutting board. Use sharp knife to cut off sides in 3 or 4 vertical slices, leaving only core and stem. Remove any membrane from slices.

Medium Slicing Disc (3mm): Stack slices and stand lengthwise in feed tube, wedging them in tightly to hold. Use light pressure to slice.

Melt butter in 8-inch (20cm) skillet. Add vegetables and cook gently until soft — about 5 minutes.

Metal Blade: Pulse to chop tomatoes coarsely.

Add to skillet with remaining ingredients. Bring to boil, then let simmer, uncovered, for 15 minutes. Discard bay leaf.

Can be made in advance and refrigerated or frozen. Reheat gently at serving time.

Makes 1 1/2 cups (360ml).

VEGETABLE CASSOULET

If this reminds you of lasagna, it's no accident; I've replaced noodles with protein-packed navy beans in my favorite lasagna recipe. You can cut the recipe in half and bake it in a smaller casserole.

1 pound (455g) dried navy beans
1 medium onion (4 ounces, 115g), peeled and halved
2 large garlic cloves, peeled and halved
1 tablespoon salt
Freshly ground pepper
2 pounds (910g) fresh spinach, with stems trimmed
1 medium garlic clove, peeled
1 medium onion (5 ounces, 140g), peeled and quartered
1 tablespoon safflower oil
16 large mushrooms (1 pound total, 455g), with 2 opposite sides cut flat
4 large carrots (1 pound total, 455g), peeled and cut into feed-tube widths
1 15-ounce (425g) can tomato sauce
1 6-ounce (170g) can tomato paste
1 1/2 teaspoons dried oregano
1/2 teaspoon salt
Freshly ground pepper
1 3/4 pounds (795g) Monterey Jack cheese, chilled
1 ounce (30g) imported Parmesan cheese, at room temperature
2 cups (480ml) small-curd cottage cheese, well drained

Soak beans overnight in cold water to cover. Drain and put in saucepan with onion, garlic, salt, pepper and fresh water to cover. Bring to boil, cover and let simmer until beans are tender but not mushy — about 55 minutes. Do not overcook. Drain and discard onion and garlic.

Fifteen minutes before baking, place rack in center of oven and preheat to 375°F (190°C). Have 4-quart (4L) casserole ready.

In 8-quart (8L) non-aluminum pot, cook spinach in 2 batches with only water clinging to its leaves, just until wilted. Immediately hold under cold running water until completely cool. Drain, wrap in towel and squeeze firmly to remove as much water as possible. Spinach can be cooked 1 day in advance, wrapped airtight and refrigerated.

Metal Blade: Turn on machine, drop garlic through feed tube and process until minced. Add onion and pulse until finely chopped.

In 10-inch (25cm) skillet, gently cook onion and garlic in oil until they begin to soften — about 4 minutes.

Medium Slicing Disc (3mm): Put mushrooms in feed tube flat side down and use light pressure to slice.

Add to skillet and cook gently until mushrooms are soft, and most of moisture has cooked away — about 15 minutes.

Medium Shredding Disc: Use firm pressure to shred carrots.

Add to skillet and cook gently until wilted — about 4 minutes. Stir in tomato sauce, tomato paste, oregano, salt and pepper and remove from heat.

Medium Shredding Disc: Use light pressure to shred Monterey Jack cheese; remove and reserve. Use light pressure to shred Parmesan cheese.

Line bottom of baking dish with 1/2 of beans. Spread 1 cup (240ml) of cottage cheese evenly over beans, then divide 1/2 of spinach over cottage cheese. Season with freshly ground pepper. Top spinach with 1/3 of Monterey Jack cheese, then 1/2 of vegetable mixture. Repeat layering and top with last 1/3 of Monterey Jack cheese. Sprinkle with Parmesan cheese. Can be assembled 1 day in advance, covered and refrigerated. Bring to room temperature before baking. Bake, uncovered, for 1 hour. Let stand for 5 minutes before serving.

Makes 10 to 12 servings.

PIZZA

Long before I initiated my first food processor by putting it to the pizza-making test, I loved pizza with a passion that bordered on addiction. Living in Chicago, the undisputed pizza capital of American cities, gave me a running start. Whenever a new pizza parlor opened, I was on my way, in an endless search for the best.

But the best always comes from home. And after the food processor arrived, making pizza at home became less frenzied. What would have taken most of an afternoon and lots of helping hands, I could now do quickly, by myself. The machine that mixed and kneaded the dough in three minutes also made short work of the ingredients for toppings.

These recipes show that I don't slavishly follow tradition. I think the definition of pizza should encompass anything you can bake on a crisp, chewy crust. Sometimes this means a jump into new territory, where pizza is a combination of paper-thin slices of vegetables on a cracker-like crust. Or Tex-Mex ingredients on a cornmeal crust. But just as often, I stick to conventional Italian ways. For evidence, look at Pepperoni, Green-Pepper and Onion Pizza or Deep-Dish Sausage, Mushroom and Green-Pepper Pizza.

PIZZA

CRUSTS
Thin Crust
Thick Crust
Deep-Dish Crust
Double Crust for Stuffed Pizza
Paper-Thin Crust
Cornmeal Crust

SAUCES
Fresh Tomato Pizza Sauce
Pizza Sauce with Canned Tomatoes

PIZZA
Pepperoni, Green Pepper and Onion
  Pizza
Escarole, Garlic and Three-Cheese Pizza
Ratatouille Pizza
Mexican Pizza
Fresh Vegetable Pizza

Deep-Dish Sausage, Mushroom and
  Green Pepper Pizza
Deep-Dish Eggplant and Pepperoni Pizza
Deep-Dish Broccoli and Red Pepper Pizza

Stuffed Spinach Pizza

Smoked Salmon Pizza with Scallions and
  Mozzarella
Shrimp, Fennel and Leek Pizza
Leek, Zucchini and Red Pepper Pizza
Four Seasons Pizza
Pizza Nicoise
Clam and Mussel Pizza

SOUTH OF THE BORDER
SUPPER
Tex-Mex Gazpacho
Mexican Pizza
Fresh Coconut Rum Cake
Sliced Papaya

Mexican Pizza
previous pages

2 teaspoons olive or safflower oil
2 teaspoons cornmeal
1 package active dry yeast
1 teaspoon sugar
$^1/_2$ cup (120ml) plus 2 tablespoons

warm water (105 to 115°F, 40 to 46°C)
1 $^1/_2$ cups plus 2 tablespoons unbleached all-purpose or bread flour (8 ounces, 225g)
$^3/_4$ teaspoon salt

Rub 1 teaspoon of oil over one 14-inch (36cm) or two 9-inch (23cm) pizza pans, preferably black metal, and sprinkle pan(s) with cornmeal. Stir yeast and sugar into warm water and let stand until foamy.

Metal Blade: Put flour, salt and remaining oil into work bowl and turn on machine. Pour yeast mixture through feed tube and process until dough cleans inside of work bowl. If it sticks, add more flour by tablespoon through feed tube, letting each addition work in before adding more. If dough is crumbly, add water by teaspoon through feed tube, letting each addition work in before adding more. Once desired consistency is reached, process dough until uniformly supple and elastic — about 40 seconds.

This dough does not need to rise. It can be rolled immediately and used as is, in the recipes for Pepperoni, Green Pepper and Onion Pizza, and Ratatouille Pizza. If dough is allowed to rise until doubled in size, crust will be slightly chewier.

On heavily floured board, roll dough to 14-inch (36cm) circle or divide dough in half and roll each half to 9-inch (23cm) circle. Reflour board as necessary and rotate dough as you roll it. If dough resists, let it rest for 5 minutes to relax gluten, then try again.

If you prefer to let dough rise, transfer to oiled bowl and rotate to coat entire surface with oil. Cover with oiled plastic wrap and let rise in warm spot (75 to 80°F, 40 to 46°C) until doubled — about 1 hour. Then, roll as above.

Use soft brush to remove excess flour. Fold dough in half, then in quarters and place in prepared pan with point of dough in center. Unfold dough and lightly press into place, working from center to edge. Pinch edge together or fold over edge to form $^1/_3$-inch (8mm) rim. Proceed with pizza recipe of your choice.

Makes one 14-inch (36cm) or two 9-inch (23cm) thin crusts.

WHOLE WHEAT VARIATION: Use $^3/_4$ cup plus 1 tablespoon (4 ounces, 115g) each of unbleached all-purpose or bread flour, *and* whole wheat flour. Proceed as directed.

WHOLE-GRAIN WHEAT VARIATION: Put $^1/_2$ cup of wheat berries (2 $^1/_2$ ounces, 70g) in dish and add water to cover by 3 inches (8cm). Soak for 12 hours or overnight. Drain well, then pat dry with paper towel.

Stir 1 package of active dry yeast and 1 teaspoon of sugar into $^1/_3$ cup (80ml) of warm water (105 to 115°F, 40 to 46°C) and let stand until foamy.

Metal Blade: Process soaked wheat berries with 1 cup plus 2 tablespoons of bread flour (5 $^1/_2$ ounces, 155g) until very finely ground — about 2 minutes. Add 1 teaspoon of oil and $^3/_4$ teaspoon salt and proceed as directed above.

THICK CRUST

1 1/2 tablespoons olive or safflower oil
2 teaspoons cornmeal
1 package active dry yeast
1 teaspoon sugar
1 cup (240ml) warm water (105 to

115°F, 40 to 46°C)
2 1/3 cups unbleached all-purpose or
   bread flour (12 ounces, 340g)
1 teaspoon salt

Rub 1 teaspoon of oil over 14-inch (36cm) or two 9-inch (23cm) pizza pans, preferably black metal, and sprinkle pan(s) with cornmeal. Stir yeast and sugar into warm water and let stand until foamy.

Metal Blade: Put flour, salt and remaining oil into work bowl and turn on machine. Pour yeast mixture through feed tube and process until dough cleans inside of work bowl. If it sticks, add more flour by tablespoon through feed tube, letting each addition work in before adding more. If dough is crumbly, add water by teaspoon through feed tube, letting each addition work in before adding more. Once desired consistency is reached, process dough until uniformly supple and elastic — about 40 seconds.

Transfer to oiled bowl and rotate to coat entire surface with oil. Cover with oiled plastic wrap and let rise in warm spot (75 to 80°F, 24 to 26°C) until doubled — about 1 hour.

Punch dough down on heavily floured board and roll into 14-inch (36cm) circle or divide dough in half and roll each half to 9-inch (23cm) circle. Reflour board as necessary and rotate dough as you roll it out. If dough resists, let it rest for 5 minutes to relax gluten, then try again.

Use soft brush to remove excess flour. Fold dough in half, then in quarters and place in prepared pan with point of dough in center. Unfold dough and lightly press into place, working from center to edge. Add topping of your choice, then roll edge over to form 1/3-inch (8mm) rim. Let rest at room temperature until edge of dough is puffy — from 1 to 2 hours — before baking. Proceed with pizza recipe of your choice.

Makes one 14-inch (36cm) or two 9-inch (23cm) thick crusts.

WHOLE WHEAT VARIATION: Use 1 cup plus 2 tablespoons (6 ounces, 170g) each of unbleached all-purpose or bread flour, *and* whole wheat flour. Proceed as directed.

DEEP-DISH CRUST

1 1/2 tablespoons olive or safflower oil
2 teaspoons cornmeal
1 package active dry yeast
1 teaspoon sugar
1 cup (240ml) warm water (105 to

115°F, 40 to 46°C)
2 1/3 cups unbleached all-purpose or
   bread flour (12 ounces, 340g)
1 teaspoon salt

Rub 2 teaspoons of oil on sides and bottom of 14-inch (36cm) deep-dish pizza pan, two 9-inch (23cm) layer-cake pans, or 11 1/2 by 17 1/2-inch (29 by 44cm) jelly-roll pan (preferably black metal pans). Sprinkle pan(s) with cornmeal. Stir yeast and sugar into warm water and let stand until foamy.

Metal Blade: Put flour, salt and remaining oil into work bowl and turn on machine. Pour yeast mixture through feed tube and process until dough cleans inside of work bowl. If it sticks, add more flour by tablespoon through feed tube, letting each addition work in before adding more. If dough is crumbly, add water by teaspoon through feed tube, letting each addition work in before adding more. Once desired consistency is reached, process dough until uniformly supple and elastic — about 40 seconds.

Transfer to oiled bowl and rotate to coat entire surface with oil. Cover with oiled plastic wrap and let rise in warm spot (75 to 80°F, 24 to 26°C) until doubled — about 1 hour.

Punch dough down on heavily floured board and roll into 20-inch (50cm) circle or divide dough in half and roll each half to 12-inch (30cm) circle. For jelly-roll pan, roll to rectangle 18 by 22 inches (45 by 55cm). Reflour board as necessary and rotate dough as you roll it. If dough resists, let it rest for 5 minutes to relax gluten, then try again.

Use soft brush to remove excess flour and fold dough in half, then in quarters and place in prepared pan with point of dough in center. Unfold dough and lightly press into bottom and sides of pan, working from center to edge. Gently ease dough so it extends $1/2$-inch (12mm) beyond rim of pan, then cut away any excess.

Distribute filling of your choice over crust. Fold dough over to filling and pinch to form finished edge. Proceed as directed in pizza recipe of your choice.

Makes one 14-inch (36cm), two 9-inch (23cm) or one $11^{1}/_{2}$ by $17^{1}/_{2}$ (29 by 44cm) deep-dish crust.

WHOLE WHEAT VARIATION: Use 1 cup plus 2 tablespoons (6 ounces, 170g) each of unbleached all-purpose or bread flour, *and* whole wheat flour. Proceed as directed.

Pizza Pointers

★ Black metal pans produce the best crust. They transmit more heat than a shiny pan, making the outside of the crust dark and crisp, while the inside stays chewy.

★ To prepare the pizza pan, brush it with olive oil. Use only enough oil to coat it, not so much that it collects in pools.

★ Except when making paper-thin crusts, sprinkle the oiled pan with cornmeal; it improves the texture of the crust.

★ For a hot baking surface that closely approximates the stone-lined ovens of pizza parlors, line the oven with unglazed quarry tiles or a pizza stone. If you don't have either, use a heavy, preferably dark-colored, baking sheet.

★ Pizza with thin crust or thick crust can be baked directly on quarry tiles or a pizza stone. Pizza with paper-thin crust, deep-dish pizza or stuffed pizza cannot.

★ At least fifteen minutes before baking pizza, preheat the oven to the specified temperature. The tiles, stones or baking sheet must be preheated also.

DOUBLE CRUST FOR STUFFED PIZZA

2 tablespoons olive or safflower oil
2 teaspoons cornmeal
1 package active dry yeast
1 teaspoon sugar
1¹/₄ cups (300ml) warm water (105 to

115°F, 40 to 46°C)
3 cups plus 2 tablespoons unbleached all-purpose or bread flour (16 ounces, 455g)
1¹/₂ teaspoons salt

Rub 2 teaspoons of oil on sides and bottom of 14-inch (36cm) deep-dish pizza pan or two 9-inch (23cm) layer-cake pans, preferably of black metal, and sprinkle pan(s) with cornmeal.

Stir yeast and sugar into warm water and let stand until foamy.

Metal Blade: Put flour, salt and remaining oil into work bowl and turn on machine. Pour yeast mixture through feed tube and process until dough cleans inside of work bowl. If it sticks, add more flour by tablespoon through feed tube, letting each addition work in before adding more. If dough is crumbly, add water by teaspoon through feed tube, letting each addition work in before adding more. Once desired consistency is reached, process dough until uniformly supple and elastic — about 40 seconds.

Transfer to oiled bowl and rotate to coat entire surface with oil. Cover with oiled plastic wrap and let rise in warm spot (75 to 80°F, 24 to 26°C) until doubled — about 1 hour.

Punch dough down on heavily floured board. For one 14-inch (36cm) pizza, divide dough into 2 portions, one of 20 ounces (565g), the other of 8 ounces (225g). (For two 9-inch (23cm) pizzas, divide dough in half, then divide each half into two portions of 10 ounces (285g) and 4 ounces (115g).) Roll larger portion to 20-inch (50cm) circle or 14-inch (36cm) circle. Reflour board as necessary and rotate dough as you roll it out. If dough resists, let it rest for 5 minutes to relax gluten, then try again.

Use soft brush to remove excess flour and fold dough in half, then in quarters and place in prepared pan(s) with point of dough in center. Unfold dough and lightly press into bottom and sides of pan, working from center to top edge. Gently ease dough so it extends 1 inch (2.5cm) beyond rim of pan, then cut away any excess. Roll smaller portion of dough to 14-inch (36cm) circle or 9-inch (23cm) circle.

Proceed with pizza recipe of your choice.

Makes one 14-inch (36cm) or two 9-inch (23cm) double crusts for stuffed pizza.

WHOLE WHEAT VARIATION: Use 1¹/₂ cups plus 1 tablespoon (8 ounces, 225g) each of unbleached all-purpose or bread flour, *and* whole wheat flour. Proceed as directed above.

1 teaspoon active dry yeast
½ teaspoon sugar
½ cup (120ml) plus 1 teaspoon warm
    water (105 to 115°F, 40 to 46°C)
2¼ cups bread flour (11¼ ounces,

320g)
1 large egg
1 teaspoon salt
1 teaspoon olive oil for each pizza

This recipe makes enough dough for five 12-inch (30cm) crusts that are much thinner and crisper than most. The dough freezes well, so all crusts needn't be used at once. Heavy pizza toppings are not appropriate with this crust; use it for recipes that specify paper-thin crust.

Stir yeast and sugar into warm water and let stand until foamy. For each pizza, rub 1 teaspoon of olive oil on 15-inch (38cm) round black metal pizza pan.

Metal Blade: Put flour, egg and salt into work bowl and turn on machine. Pour yeast mixture through feed tube and process until dough cleans inside of work bowl. If it sticks, add more flour by tablespoon through feed tube, letting each addition work in before adding more. If dough is crumbly, add water by teaspoon through feed tube, letting each addition work in before adding more. Once desired consistency is reached, process dough until uniformly supple and elastic — about 40 seconds.

Transfer to oiled bowl and rotate to coat surface with oil. Cover with oiled plastic wrap and let rise in warm spot (75 to 80°F, 24 to 26°C) until doubled — about 1 hour.

Punch dough down on floured board and divide into 5 equal pieces, each weighing about 3½ ounces (100g) (see NOTE). Cover loosely with plastic wrap and let rest for 30 minutes before rolling.

On very heavily floured board, shape one piece of dough with your hands to 4-inch (10cm) circle, then roll to 9- to 10-inch (23 to 25cm) circle. Brush off excess flour. Place on prepared pan. Easing dough from center, gently stretch to 12-inch (30cm) circle. Press edges onto pan so dough holds its shape. If dough resists rolling, process with metal blade for 3 seconds, then roll. Proceed with paper-thin pizza recipe of your choice (see Index).

Makes five 12-inch (30cm) paper-thin crusts.

NOTE: Dough can be refrigerated up to 3 days or frozen up to 3 months; wrap each piece airtight. Refrigerated dough can be rolled immediately after removal from refrigerator. If dough is frozen, let it thaw at room temperature just until pliable, 1 to 1½ hours.

WHOLE-WHEAT VARIATION: Use 1 cup plus 2 tablespoons (5½ ounces, 14g) each of whole-wheat and bread flour. Proceed as directed above.

WHOLE GRAIN VARIATION: Put 1 cup of wheat berries (5 ounces, 140g) in dish and add water to cover by 3 inches (8cm). Let soak for 12 hours or overnight. Drain well, then pat dry with paper towel.

Stir 1 teaspoon of active dry yeast and ½ teaspoon of sugar into ⅓ cup (80ml) of warm water (105 to 115°F, 40 to 46°C) and let stand until foamy.

Metal Blade: Process soaked wheat berries with 1¼ cups of bread flour (6¼ ounces, 180g) until very finely ground — about 2 minutes. Add egg and salt and proceed as directed above.

CORNMEAL CRUST

1 tablespoon safflower oil
1/2 cup plus 2 teaspoons yellow cornmeal (3 1/2 ounces, 100g)
1 package active dry yeast
1 teaspoon sugar
3/4 cup (180ml) plus 1 tablespoon warm water (105 to 115°F, 40 to 46°C)
1 1/2 cups plus 2 tablespoons unbleached all-purpose or bread flour (8 ounces, 225g)
2 tablespoons cilantro, or fresh coriander, leaves (optional)
3/4 teaspoon salt

Rub 1 teaspoon of oil over 14-inch (36cm) pizza pan or two 9-inch (23cm) pizza pans, preferably of black metal, and sprinkle pan(s) with 2 teaspoons of cornmeal.

Stir yeast and sugar into warm water and let stand until foamy.

Metal Blade: Put flour, cilantro and salt into work bowl with remaining oil and cornmeal and turn on machine. Pour yeast mixture through feed tube and process until dough cleans inside of work bowl. If it sticks, add more flour by tablespoon through feed tube, letting each addition work in before adding more. If dough is crumbly, add water by teaspoon through feed tube, letting each addition work in before adding more. Once desired consistency is reached, process dough until uniformly supple and elastic — about 40 seconds.

Transfer to oiled bowl and rotate to coat entire surface with oil. Cover with oiled plastic wrap and let rise in warm spot (75 to 80°F, 24 to 26°C) until doubled — about 1 hour.

Punch dough down on heavily floured board and roll into 14-inch (36cm) circle or divide dough in half and roll each half to 9-inch (23cm) circle. Reflour board as necessary and rotate dough as you roll it out. If dough resists, let it rest for 5 minutes to relax gluten, then try again.

Use soft brush to remove excess flour. Fold dough in half, then in quarters and place on prepared pan(s) with point of dough in center. Unfold dough and lightly press into place, working from center to edge. Pinch edge together or fold over edge to form 1/3-inch (8mm) rim.

Proceed with pizza recipe of your choice.

Makes one 14-inch (36cm) or two 9-inch (23cm) crusts.

2½ pounds (1kg) plum tomatoes,
    halved and seeded
1½ tablespoons extra-virgin olive oil
¼ cup (60ml) tomato paste
¾ teaspoon salt

½ teaspoon crushed red pepper
    flakes
¼ teaspoon sugar
2 tablespoons finely snipped fresh
    basil, or 1½ teaspoons dried

*This pizza sauce
and the one that
follows are
interchangeable in
all the pizza
recipes. Make this
one when tomatoes
are vine-ripened
and abundant, and
the second one at
other times. Either
sauce freezes well.*

Metal Blade: Pulse to chop tomatoes fine, in 3 batches.

Heat oil in 2½-quart (2.5L) saucepan. Add tomatoes, tomato paste, salt, pepper flakes and sugar and cook over medium heat, uncovered, until reduced to 2⅔ cups (640ml) — about 45 minutes.

Can be refrigerated 4 days or frozen 3 months. Just before using, add basil and mix thoroughly.

Makes 2⅔ cups (640ml).

1 16-ounce (455g) can plum
    tomatoes, drained
2 tablespoons tomato paste
2 teaspoons snipped fresh basil or ½
    teaspoon dried

2 teaspoons snipped fresh oregano
    or ½ teaspoon dried
½ teaspoon sugar
½ teaspoon crushed red pepper flakes
½ teaspoon salt

**PIZZA SAUCE
WITH CANNED
TOMATOES**

Metal Blade: Process all ingredients for 10 seconds.

Can be stored up to 5 days in refrigerator or up to 4 months in freezer. Stir well before using.

Makes 1⅛ cups (270ml).

CHICAGO-STYLE PIZZA
PARTY
Spinach-Stuffed Pizza
Deep-Dish Sausage, Mushroom
and Green Pepper Pizza
Julienned Zucchini and Red
Peppers with Anchovy Vinaigrette
Spiaggi's Mascarpone Cream

PEPPERONI, GREEN PEPPER AND ONION PIZZA

When I first taught this recipe, my students ecstatically dubbed it "The 28-Minute Pizza." It takes less than a half hour from food processor to table, so it's quicker than having one delivered. The dough doesn't rise at all — it's rolled and baked as soon as it's mixed.

Rolled dough for one 14-inch (36cm) or two 9-inch (23cm) Thin Crusts (see Index)
12 ounces (340g) mozzarella cheese, well chilled
2 ounces (55g) pepperoni, peeled and cut into thirds
4 ounces (115g) imported Parmesan cheese, quartered
1 small onion (3 ounces, 85g), peeled
1 small tomato (4 ounces, 115g), cored
1 medium green pepper (4 ounces, 115g), cored
6 tablespoons Pizza Sauce (see Index)
Salt
Freshly ground pepper
Pinch of sugar
1/2 teaspoon dried oregano
1/2 teaspoon dried basil

Fifteen minutes before baking, place rack in center of oven and preheat to 425°F (220°C). If you are using quarry tiles or pizza stone, place on center rack to preheat.

Prick prepared and rolled crust(s) in several places with fork. Bake in preheated oven until very lightly browned — about 5 minutes. Let cool for 5 minutes before adding topping. Leave oven at 425°F (220°C).

As each ingredient is processed, remove from work bowl and reserve separately.

Medium Shredding Disc: Use light pressure to shred mozzarella; remove and reserve.

Metal Blade: Pulse to chop pepperoni and Parmesan coarsely; remove and reserve.

Thin Slicing Disc (2mm): Use medium pressure to slice onion; remove and reserve.

All Purpose Slicing Disc (4mm): Use light pressure to slice tomato; remove and reserve. Stand green pepper in feed tube, cut end down, and use light pressure to slice.

Spread sauce evenly over partially baked crust(s). Separate onion into rings and distribute over sauce. Sprinkle with mozzarella, then arrange tomatoes over. Season with salt, pepper and sugar. Distribute pepperoni/Parmesan mixture, then green pepper rings over top. Sprinkle oregano and basil over top. Bake until bottom of crust is well browned, about 15 minutes. Let stand for 5 minutes before serving.

Makes one 14-inch (36cm) or two 9-inch (23cm) pizzas.

ESCAROLE, GARLIC AND THREE-CHEESE PIZZA

The slightly bitter flavor of escarole becomes almost sweet when blanched.

Rolled dough for one 11 1/2 by 17 1/2-inch (29 by 44cm) Deep-Dish Crust pizza (see Index)
4 large garlic cloves
2 pounds (1kg) escarole, with thick white center ribs removed
5 tablespoons extra-virgin olive oil
3/4 teaspoon salt
Freshly ground pepper
5 ounces (140g) mozzarella cheese, cut into thirds
5 ounces (140g) Asiago cheese, cut into thirds (see NOTE)
1/2 cup (120ml) ricotta cheese, well drained

Fifteen minutes before baking, place rack in center of oven and preheat to 475°F (245°C). If you are using quarry tiles or pizza stone, place on center rack to reheat.

Bring 8 quarts (8L) of salted water to rolling boil. Add escarole and cook for 3 minutes. Drain immediately and hold under cold running water until completely cool. Wrap in cloth towel and squeeze to remove as much moisture as possible. (You should have about 1²/₃ cups of firmly packed escarole.)

Metal Blade: Turn on machine, drop garlic through feed tube and process until minced.

Heat 4 tablespoons of oil in 10-inch (30cm) skillet. Add garlic and cook gently until soft but not brown — about 5 minutes.

Metal Blade: In 2 batches, chop escarole coarsely by pulsing 6 to 8 times.

Add to skillet and continue to cook until heated through — about 3 minutes. Add salt and pepper and remove from heat.

Metal Blade: Process mozzarella and Asiago cheeses until minced.

Brush bottom and sides of prepared crust with remaining oil. Put 16 scant tablespoons of escarole over crust, spacing them evenly. Separate and flatten clumps slightly. Place about 1¹/₂ teaspoons of ricotta cheese on each one and smooth out slightly but do not flatten. Fill in spaces with remaining escarole. Sprinkle mozzarella and Asiago cheeses evenly over entire surface.

Bake until bottom of crust is well browned and golden — about 18 minutes. Serve immediately.

Makes one 11¹/₂ by 17¹/₂-inch (29 by 44cm) pizza.

NOTE: If Asiago cheese is not available, substitute imported Parmesan cheese.

Escarole, Garlic and Three-Cheese Pizza

RATATOUILLE PIZZA

Rich melted cheese and a freshly sliced tomato transform the hearty vegetable stew into a top-notch pizza topping. With ratatouille on hand, it's a cinch to make this pizza in under 30 minutes.

Rolled dough for one 14-inch (36cm) or two 9-inch (23cm) Thin Crusts (see Index)

9 ounces (255g) mozzarella cheese, well chilled

5 ounces (140g) imported Parmesan cheese, at room temperature

1 medium tomato (6 ounces, 170g), cored

6 tablespoons Pizza Sauce (see Index)

1¹/₂ cups (360ml) well drained Ratatouille (see Index)

1 teaspoon dried oregano

¹/₂ teaspoon dried basil

¹/₂ teaspoon salt

Pinch of sugar

Freshly ground pepper

Fifteen minutes before baking, place rack in center of oven and preheat to 425°F (220°C). If you are using quarry tiles or pizza stone, place on center rack to preheat.

Prick crust(s) in several places with fork. Bake in preheated oven until very lightly browned, about 5 minutes. Let cool for 5 minutes before adding topping. Leave oven at 425°F (220°C).

Medium Shredding Disc: Use light pressure to shred both cheeses.

Transfer to mixing bowl and toss together.

All Purpose Slicing Disc (4mm): Use light pressure to slice tomato.

Spread sauce evenly over partially baked crust(s). Sprinkle ¹/₂ of cheese over, then all of ratatouille. Arrange tomato slices over top and season with pinch of salt and pepper. Add remaining cheese and sprinkle with oregano, basil, salt, sugar and pepper. Bake until bottom of crust is well browned, about 15 minutes. Let stand for 5 minutes before serving.

Makes one 14-inch (36cm) or two 9-inch (23cm) pizzas.

MEXICAN PIZZA

Tex-Mex ingredients make marvelous pizza. Here, a cornmeal crust, similar to a tortilla, is smothered with cheese, fresh vegetables and hot peppers, then garnished with avocado and sour cream.

Rolled dough for one 14-inch (36cm) or two 9-inch (23cm) Cornmeal Crusts (see Index)

2 jalapeño or serrano chiles, with stems and seeds removed

3 large onions (1 pound total, 455g), peeled and quartered

3 tablespoons water

2 tablespoons safflower oil

2 cups (480ml) Pizza Sauce (see Index)

1 medium green pepper (5 ounces, 140g), cored

4 large scallions (2 ounces total, 55g), including green tops, cut into 1-inch (2.5cm) pieces

¹/₄ cup loosely packed cilantro or parsley leaves

1 pound (455g) Monterey Jack cheese, chilled and cut into 10 pieces

1 large avocado (8 ounces, 225g), peeled and cut lengthwise into 12 slices

1 cup (240ml) sour cream

Fifteen minutes before baking, place rack in center of oven and preheat to 425°F (220°C). If you are using quarry tiles or pizza stone, place on center rack to preheat.

Metal Blade: Turn on machine, drop chiles through feed tube and process until minced; remove and reserve. Pulse to chop onions coarsely.

Put water, oil and onions in 10-inch (25cm) skillet. Cover and cook over medium-high heat until soft — about 5 minutes. Uncover and cook until all moisture has evaporated. Remove from stove and stir in reserved chiles and pizza sauce.

Medium Slicing Disc (3mm): Stand green pepper in feed tube, cut end down, and use light pressure to slice; remove and reserve.

Metal Blade: Process scallions, cilantro or parsley, and cheese until minced.

Spread onion/tomato mixture over crust(s), leaving 1/2-inch (12mm) edge of dough exposed. Top with green pepper slices, then cheese. Bake until bottom of crust is well browned — about 20 minutes. Let rest for 10 minutes. Arrange avocado slices on top in radial design and serve with sour cream.

Makes one 14-inch (36cm) pizza.

NOTE: If making two 9-inch (23cm) pizzas, place them in preheated 475°F (245°C) oven and *immediately decrease temperature to 450°F (230°C)*. Bake for 22 minutes.

Ratatouille Pizza

FRESH VEGETABLE PIZZA

If you have preconceived notions that pizza means cheese and sausage, here's an alternate to change your thinking. A thick, chewy crust is topped with fresh vegetables and rich melted cheese.

Rolled dough for one 14-inch (36cm) Thick Crust (see Index)
1 large garlic clove, peeled
1 small onion (3 ounces, 85g), peeled and quartered
1 tablespoon safflower oil
12 large mushrooms (12 ounces total, 340g), with 2 opposite sides cut flat
3 medium carrots (8 ounces total, 225g), peeled and cut into 2-inch (5cm) lengths

1 medium zucchini (7 ounces, 200g), cut into 2-inch (5cm) lengths
2 cups (480ml) Pizza Sauce (see Index)
1½ teaspoons dried oregano
½ teaspoon salt
12 ounces (340g) Monterey Jack cheese, well chilled
4 ounces (115g) imported Parmesan cheese, at room temperature

Metal Blade: Turn on machine, drop garlic through feed tube and process until minced. Add onion and pulse until chopped finely.

Heat oil in 10-inch (25cm) skillet. Cook garlic and onion over high heat, stirring often, until they begin to soften — about 2 minutes.

All Purpose Slicing Disc (4mm): Put mushrooms in feed tube flat side down and use light pressure to slice.

Add to skillet and cook gently until most of moisture has evaporated — about 15 minutes.

Medium Shredding Disc: Lay carrots in feed tube and use firm pressure to shred.

French Fry Disc: Lay zucchini in feed tube and use light pressure to cut. (If you do not have French Fry Disc, see page 229.)

Add carrots and zucchini to skillet and continue to cook, stirring occasionally, until they begin to soften — about 4 minutes. Remove from heat and stir in pizza sauce, oregano and salt.

Medium Shredding Disc: Use light pressure to shred Monterey Jack; remove and reserve. Use light pressure to shred Parmesan.

Spread vegetable mixture over prepared crust, leaving ½ inch (12mm) of edge exposed. Sprinkle Monterey Jack then Parmesan cheese over surface. Let pizza rest at room temperature for 1 to 2 hours before baking.

Fifteen minutes before baking, place rack in center of oven and preheat to 425°F (220°C). If you are using quarry tiles or pizza stone, place on center rack to preheat. Bake until bottom of crust is deep golden-brown, about 20 to 22 minutes. Let rest for 10 minutes before serving. For neat slices, cut through cheese and vegetables with serrated knife, then finish slicing with pizza cutter.

Makes one 14-inch (36cm) pizza.

Rolled dough for one 14-inch (36cm) or two 9-inch (23cm) Deep-Dish Crusts (see Index)
1 pound (455g) mild or hot Italian sausage, with casing removed
1 large green pepper (6 ounces, 170g)
10 ounces (285g) Herkimer or white cheddar cheese, chilled
1 pound (455g) mozzarella cheese, well chilled
2 tablespoons flour
1/2 teaspoon fennel seed
1/2 teaspoon dried oregano
1/2 teaspoon crushed red pepper flakes
1/4 teaspoon salt
4 large mushrooms (3 ounces total, 85g), with 2 opposite sides cut flat
2 cups (480ml) Pizza Sauce (see Index)
2 tablespoons safflower oil

DEEP-DISH SAUSAGE, MUSHROOM AND GREEN PEPPER PIZZA

Pizzas are a natural for the food processor and almost unthinkable without one. Imagine making this Chicago-style pizza without a food processor to knead the dough, slice the vegetables, shred the cheese and make the sauce.

Fifteen minutes before baking, place rack in center of oven and preheat to 425°F (220°C). If you are using quarry tiles or pizza stone, place on center rack to preheat.

Crumble sausage and cook in 8-inch (20cm) skillet until browned. Drain off fat and transfer to large mixing bowl.

Stand green pepper on cutting board. Use sharp knife to cut off sides in 3 or 4 vertical slices, leaving only core and stem. Remove any membrane from slices.

Medium Slicing Disc (3mm): Stand pepper slices lengthwise in feed tube, wedging them tightly to hold. Use light pressure to slice.

Medium Shredding Disc: Use light pressure to shred cheeses.

Add cheeses and green pepper to mixing bowl along with flour, fennel, oregano, pepper flakes and salt and combine thoroughly.

Thin Slicing Disc (2mm): Put mushrooms in feed tube flat side down and use light pressure to slice.

Gently fold mushrooms into pizza sauce.

Brush bottom and sides of rolled crust(s) with oil. Add filling in even layer. Spread tomato topping over, leaving rim exposed. Fold upper edge of dough over and pinch to form decorative edge.

Bake until bottom is well browned, about 20 to 22 minutes. Let rest for 10 minutes before serving.

Makes one 14-inch (36cm) or two 9-inch (23cm) deep-dish pizzas.

DEEP-DISH EGGPLANT AND PEPPERONI PIZZA

Traditional dictates about pizza are no longer meaningful. Now anything goes, including eggplant. Its neutral character picks up the flavor of the other ingredients, while its meaty texture adds substance.

Rolled dough for one 14-inch (36cm) or two 9-inch (23cm) Deep-Dish Crusts (see Index)
1 small eggplant (12 ounces, 340g), unpeeled and cut to fit feed tube
1 teaspoon salt
2 large garlic cloves, peeled
1 medium onion (5 ounces, 140g), peeled and quartered
3 tablespoons safflower oil
3 tablespoons flour
1 teaspoon dried oregano
2 1/2 ounces (70g) pepperoni, peeled, cut into thirds and chilled
12 ounces (340g) mozzarella cheese, well chilled
2 small tomatoes (8 ounces total, 225g), cored
2 cups (480ml) Pizza Sauce (see Index)
1/4 teaspoon sugar
Freshly ground pepper

Fifteen minutes before baking, place rack in center of oven and preheat to 425°F (220°C). If you are using quarry tiles or pizza stone, place on center rack to preheat.

Thick Slicing Disc (6mm): Stand eggplant in feed tube and use light pressure to slice.

Transfer to colander, toss with salt and let drain for 30 minutes. Rinse with cold water, then wrap in towel and squeeze firmly to remove as much liquid as possible.

Metal Blade: Turn on machine, drop garlic and onion through feed tube and process until minced.

Heat 1 tablespoon of oil in 10-inch (25cm) skillet. Add garlic, onion and eggplant, cover and cook over medium-high heat, shaking pan often, until eggplant is cooked through — about 8 minutes. Transfer to large mixing bowl and toss with flour and oregano.

Metal Blade: Pulse to chop pepperoni coarsely.

Medium Shredding Disc: Use light pressure to shred cheese.

Add to mixing bowl and combine.

All Purpose Slicing Disc (4mm): Stand tomatoes in feed tube and use light pressure to slice.

Brush bottom and sides of crust(s) with remaining oil. Add filling in even layer and top with sauce. Distribute tomato slices over top and sprinkle with sugar and pepper. Fold upper edge of dough over and pinch to form decorative border.

Bake until bottom is well browned, about 25 minutes.

The pizza may look juicy, but juices will be absorbed as it rests. Let it rest for 10 minutes before serving.

Makes one 14-inch (36cm) or two 9-inch (23cm) deep-dish pizzas.

Rolled dough for one 14-inch
(36cm) or two 9-inch (23cm)
Deep-Dish Crusts (see Index)
3 large garlic cloves, peeled
1 medium onion (4 ounces, 115g),
  peeled and quartered
3 tablespoons safflower oil
2 medium broccoli stalks (1 pound
  total, 455g), with flowerets
  removed and stems peeled, cut into
  1-inch (2.5cm) pieces

½ teaspoon salt
2 tablespoons flour
  Freshly ground pepper
1 large red pepper (6 ounces, 170g)
1 pound (455g) mozzarella cheese,
  well chilled
6 ounces (170g) Provolone cheese,
  well chilled
4 ounces (115g) imported Parmesan
  cheese, at room temperature

**DEEP-DISH
BROCCOLI
AND RED
PEPPER PIZZA**

*This recipe takes
liberty with the
definition of pizza
and does it so well
that you may
permanently
rethink what
constitutes a great
pizza. There's no
tomato sauce, but
enough crunchy
fresh vegetables
and cheese so you
won't miss it a bit.*

Fifteen minutes before baking, place rack in center of oven and preheat to 425°F
(220°C). If you are using quarry tiles or pizza stone, place on center rack to preheat.

Metal Blade: Turn on machine, drop garlic and onion through feed tube and process
until minced.

Heat 1 tablespoon of oil in 8-inch (20cm) skillet. Add garlic and onion and cook over
medium heat, stirring often, until soft but not brown — about 5 minutes.

Metal Blade: Pulse to chop broccoli stems coarsely.

Add to skillet with salt. Break flowerets into small pieces and add to skillet. Cook over
high heat, stirring often, until broccoli turns bright green, but is still crisp — about 6
minutes. Transfer to large mixing bowl and toss with flour and ground pepper.

Stand red pepper on cutting board. Use sharp knife to cut off sides in 3 or 4 vertical
slices, leaving only core and stem. Remove any membrane from slices.

Medium Slicing Disc (3mm): Stand pepper slices lengthwise in feed tube, wedging
them tightly to hold. Use light pressure to slice. Add to mixing bowl.

Medium Shredding Disc: Use light pressure to shred cheeses.

Add to mixing bowl and mix thoroughly.

Brush bottom and sides of prepared crust(s) with remaining oil. Add filling in even
layer. Roll upper edge of crust down and pinch to form decorative border. Bake until
bottom of crust is well browned — about 20 to 22 minutes. Let rest for 10 minutes
before serving.

Makes one 14-inch (36cm) or two 9-inch (23cm) deep-dish pizzas.

CANADIAN BACON VARIATION: Omit red peppers. Remove rind from 7 ounces
(200g) of Canadian Bacon and cut bacon into 6 pieces. Use Metal Blade to pulse until
bacon is chopped to size of peas; add it to remaining ingredients.

SPINACH-STUFFED PIZZA

A gooey cheese filling, flecked with fresh spinach leaves, is set off by a chewy crust. Basil-scented tomato sauce tops it off, making this a Chicago-style pizza at its best.

Rolled dough for one 14-inch (36cm) or two 9-inch (23cm) Double Crusts (see Index)
3 large garlic cloves, peeled
1 small onion (3 ounces, 85g), peeled and quartered
2 cups firmly packed fresh spinach (4 ounces total, 115g), washed and well dried
2 tablespoons flour

20 ounces (570g) mozzarella cheese, well chilled
8 ounces (225g) Herkimer or white cheddar cheese, chilled
12 ounces (340g) Monterey Jack cheese, chilled
2 tablespoons safflower oil
2 cups (480ml) Pizza Sauce (see Index)

Fifteen minutes before baking, place rack in center of oven and preheat to 450°F (220°C). If you are using quarry tiles or pizza stone, place on center rack to preheat.

Metal Blade: Turn on machine, drop garlic and onion through feed tube and process until minced. Add spinach and pulse to chop it coarsely. Add flour and pulse twice. Carefully remove metal blade.

Medium Shredding Disc: Use light pressure to shred half of mozzarella. Remove shredding disc and insert metal blade.

Metal Blade: Pulse 3 times to combine spinach mixture and mozzarella.

Transfer to large bowl.

Medium Shredding Disc: Use light pressure to shred all remaining cheeses.

Add to bowl and mix thoroughly.

Brush bottom and sides of prepared crust(s) with oil. Spread filling evenly inside crust. Lightly brush upper edge of crust with water. Place smaller circle of dough on top, gently easing it, if necessary, to join edge of bottom crust. Trim dough from bottom crust 1/4 inch (6mm) beyond edge of pan, then pinch top and bottom crusts together tightly to seal them. Roll dough over onto top, outside edge of pizza. Pinch decoratively and press into place. Cut about 20 random 1-inch (2.5cm) slits in top crust.

Bake until top crust begins to brown, about 12 minutes. Spread sauce evenly over top, leaving rolled edge exposed. Continue baking until side and bottom of crusts are well browned — about 23 more minutes. Let rest for 15 minutes before serving.

Makes one 14-inch (36cm) or two 9-inch (23cm) stuffed pizzas.

Rolled dough for one 12-inch (30cm) Paper-Thin Crust (see Index)

7 ounces (200g) mozzarella cheese, cut into 1-inch (2.5cm) cubes

3 medium scallions (1³/₄ ounces total, 50g), including green tops, **cut into 1-inch (2.5cm) pieces**

Freshly ground pepper

2 ounces (55g) Nova Scotia salmon, cut into ¹/₄-inch (6mm) diagonal strips

2 teaspoons snipped fresh dill or ¹/₄ teaspoon dried dillweed

Fifteen minutes before baking, place rack in center of oven and preheat to 475°F (245°C). If you are using quarry tiles or pizza stone, place on center rack to preheat.

Metal Blade: Process cheese and scallions until very fine.

Distribute cheese mixture evenly over crust, leaving ¹/₄-inch (6mm) border. Sprinkle top with pepper. Bake for 5 minutes. Arrange salmon over pizza and bake until bottom of crust is deep brown and cheese is melted but not brown — about 3 more minutes. Remove from oven and sprinkle with dill. Serve immediately.

Makes one 12-inch (30cm) pizza.

This simple pizza is only as good as its components. Use the best mozzarella you can find, good quality salmon and fresh dill, and the pizza will be superb. Serve as an hors d' oeuvre or light lunch.

SHRIMP, FENNEL AND LEEK PIZZA

This pizza is more sophisticated than some of the heartier ones. The green vegetables and pink shrimp on red sauce are as attractive as they are tasty. Paired with a crisp salad of Mixed Greens with Cheese and Walnuts (see Index), it's a perfect dinner for two.

Rolled dough for one 12-inch (30cm) Paper-Thin Crust (see Index)

12 medium peeled shrimp (4 ounces total, 115g), if frozen do not thaw

2 tablespoons plus 1 teaspoon extra-virgin olive oil

1 small fennel bulb (7ounces, 200g), stalks and greens trimmed (reserve 2 tablespoons greens)

1 small leek (4 ounces, 115g), with coarse greens trimmed, cut into feed-tube lengths

1/4 teaspoon salt
Freshly ground pepper

2 ounces (55g) imported Parmesan cheese, in 2 pieces

2 tablespoons fennel greens

1/4 cup (60ml) Fresh Tomato Pizza Sauce (see Index)

Fifteen minutes before baking, place rack in center of oven and preheat to 475°F (245°C). If you are using quarry tiles or pizza stone, place on center rack to preheat.

Rinse shrimp and pat dry. Heat 1 tablespoon of oil in 8-inch (20cm) skillet. When hot, add shrimp and cook over high heat just until they begin to turn opaque. Do not fully cook at this time. Remove shrimp from skillet. When cool enough to handle, cut in half lengthwise and reserve. Leave juice in pan and remove from heat. Quarter fennel bulb lengthwise.

All Purpose Slicing Disc (4mm): Stand fennel and leek in feed tube and use medium pressure to slice.

Heat 1 tablespoon of oil in skillet used for shrimp. Add fennel, leek, salt and pepper and cook over medium heat, stirring occasionally, until soft — about 10 minutes. Remove from heat.

Metal Blade: Process cheese and fennel greens until minced.

Spread thin layer of pizza sauce over prepared crust, leaving 1/4-inch (8mm) border. Add fennel and leeks, then arrange shrimp over. Sprinkle with cheese.

Bake in preheated oven until bottom of crust is golden — about 10 minutes. Serve immediately.

Makes one 12-inch (30cm) pizza.

LEEK, ZUCCHINI AND RED-PEPPER PIZZA

A colorful combination of fresh vegetables with creamy Monterey Jack cheese and tomato sauce tops this paper-thin crust. It's great for a weekend lunch or a light supper.

Rolled dough for one 12-inch (30cm) Paper-Thin Crust (see Index)

1 medium red pepper (5 ounces, 140g)

1/2 medium leek (4 ounces, 115g), split, cleaned and cut in half

1/2 small zucchini (2 ounces, 55g)

1 1/2 teaspoons extra-virgin olive oil

1/2 teaspoon dried basil

1/2 teaspoon dried marjoram

1/4 teaspoon salt

8 ounces (225g) Monterey Jack cheese, cut into 1-inch (2.5cm) cubes

1/4 cup (60ml) Pizza Sauce (see Index)

1/4 teaspoon crushed red pepper flakes

Fifteen minutes before baking, place rack in center of oven and preheat to 475°F (245°C). If you are using quarry tiles or pizza stone, place on center rack to preheat.

Stand red pepper on cutting board. Use sharp knife to cut off sides in 3 or 4 vertical slices, leaving only core and stem. Remove any membrane from slices.

All Purpose Slicing Disc (4mm): Stack pepper slices and stand lengthwise in feed tube, wedging them tightly to hold. Use light pressure to slice. Stand leek and zucchini in fccd tube and use medium pressure to slice.

Heat oil in 8-inch (20cm) skillet. Add contents of work bowl and basil, marjoram and salt and cook over medium heat, stirring occasionally, until vegetables are heated through — about 4 minutes.

Metal Blade: Process cheese until minced.

Use back of spoon to spread sauce over prepared crust, leaving ¼-inch (6mm) border. Distribute cheese, then vegetables, evenly over top. Sprinkle with pepper flakes. Bake until bottom is deep brown, about 8 to 9 minutes. Serve immediately.

Makes one 12-inch (30cm) pizza.

LEEK, ZUCCHINI AND RED-PEPPER PIZZA

Rolled dough for one 12-inch (30cm) Paper-Thin Crust (see Index)
1 medium onion (4 ounces, 115g), peeled
1 tablespoon extra-virgin olive oil
6 ounces (170g) mozzarella cheese, cut into 6 pieces
1 ounce (30g) imported Parmesan cheese
6 tablespoons Pizza Sauce (see Index)
5 anchovies, washed, patted dry and halved
12 Niçoise olives, pitted
½ teaspoon dried basil
½ teaspoon dried oregano
Freshly ground pepper

Fifteen minutes before baking, place rack in center of oven and preheat to 475°F (245°C). If you are using quarry tiles or pizza stone, place on center rack to preheat.

Thin Slicing Disc (2mm): Use firm pressure to slice onion.

Heat oil in 6-inch (15cm) skillet. Add onion and cook gently until very soft but not brown — about 8 minutes.

Metal Blade: Process both cheeses until minced.

Use back of spoon to spread sauce over prepared crust, leaving ¼-inch (6mm) border. Distribute cheese, then onions, evenly over top. Arrange anchovies in radial design around pizza and dot top with olives. Sprinkle with basil, oregano and pepper. Bake until bottom is deeply browned — about 8 to 9 minutes. Serve immediately.

Makes one 12-inch (30cm) pizza.

PIZZA NICOISE

Paper-thin crusts are perfectly suited to light pizza toppings that would be lost on a more typical thick pizza crust. I first had such typically French pizza at La Potinière, a small café in Cannes, France. I was so enthusiastic that I persuaded the chef to give me his recipe. This and other paper-thin pizzas must be served with a knife and fork. The crust is too delicate for finger food.

FOUR SEASONS PIZZA

This delicate creation is the first paper-thin pizza I sampled, the one that made me question my devotion to Chicago-style pizza with thick crusts. But there's room in this world for both, as any ardent pizza fan knows.

Rolled dough for one 12-inch (30cm) Paper-Thin Crust (see Index)
3½ tablespoons Pizza Sauce (see Index)
6 ounces (170g) mozzarella cheese, cut into 6 pieces
1 ounce (30g) imported Parmesan cheese
3 medium mushrooms (1¾ ounces total, 50g), with 2 opposite sides cut flat

1 tablespoon extra-virgin olive oil
¼ teaspoon salt
5 frozen artichoke quarters, thawed, squeezed dry and halved lengthwise
10 large capers, drained
½ teaspoon dried basil
½ teaspoon dried oregano
2 thin slices good-quality smoked ham (1¼ ounces total, 35g), halved lengthwise
Freshly ground pepper

Fifteen minutes before baking, place rack in center of oven and preheat to 475°F (245°C). If you are using quarry tiles or pizza stone, place on center rack to preheat.

Use back of spoon to spread sauce evenly over prepared crust, leaving ¼-inch (6mm) border.

Metal Blade: Process both cheeses until minced. Distribute over sauce.

Thick (6mm) or All Purpose Slicing Disc (4mm): Put mushrooms in feed tube flat side down and use light pressure to slice.

Toss mushrooms with 2 teaspoons of oil and ⅛ teaspoon of salt. Toss artichokes with remaining oil and salt. Arrange mushrooms, artichokes and capers over cheese. Sprinkle entire pizza with basil and oregano, then arrange pieces of ham at equal intervals over top. Sprinkle with pepper. Bake until bottom of crust is deep brown, about 8 to 9 minutes. Serve immediately.

Makes one 12-inch (30cm) pizza.

LATE AUTUMN DINNER
Four Seasons Pizza
Roast Cornish Hens with Caramelized Garlic
Braised Turnips with Bacon and Cream
Whole-Grain Country Bread
Prune Armagnac Mousse

Rolled dough for one 12-inch (30cm) Paper-Thin Crust (see Index)

4 dozen small mussels (2¼ pounds total, 1kg)

4 dozen Littleneck clams (2¼ pounds total, 1kg)

¼ cup loosely packed parsley leaves

1 large garlic clove, peeled

3 tablespoons extra-virgin olive oil

¼ teaspoon salt

6 tablespoons Pizza Sauce (see Index)

½ teaspoon dried basil

½ teaspoon dried oregano

Freshly ground pepper

Fifteen minutes before baking, place rack in center of oven and preheat to 475°F (245°C). If you are using quarry tiles or pizza stone, place on center rack to preheat.

Scrub mussels and remove their beards. Discard any that are open and do not close when tapped on counter. Transfer to 7-quart (7L) pot with 1 teaspoon of salt and cover with cold water. Let soak for 30 minutes. Wash several times until water is clean, then drain well.

Put clams in 7-quart (7L) pot with enough water to measure ½ inch (12mm). Cover and cook over high heat just until shells open. Remove from pot with slotted spoon. Add mussels to pot and cook, covered, just until shells open. Discard any that don't open. Remove with slotted spoon and cool slightly. Strain cooking liquid and freeze for soups or Quick Fish Stock (see Index).

Metal Blade: Put parsley in work bowl and turn on machine. Drop garlic through feed tube and process until minced. Add oil and salt and process for 3 seconds.

Remove mussels and clams from shells and place in mixing bowl. Toss with garlic-parsley mixture.

Use back of spoon to spread sauce over prepared crust, leaving ¼-inch (6mm) border. Arrange mussels and clams over top, making sure to use all garlic and parsley. Sprinkle with basil, oregano and pepper. Bake until bottom crust is deeply browned — about 9 minutes. Serve immediately.

Makes one 12-inch (30cm) pizza.

CLAM AND MUSSEL PIZZA

Another triumph of La Potinière in Cannes, France. Pristine shellfish —fresh and sweet — a bit of garlic-flavored oil and a chunky tomato sauce stand out superbly against the thin, crisp crust. You can use mussels alone, if you prefer; just make sure they're small ones.

TARTS, SAVORY SOUFFLES & EGGS

Tarts, flans, soufflés and frittatas — a list of seemingly diverse dishes with one common element: the egg. Eggs are essential in all styles of cooking. Devotees of haute cuisine applaud their magical ability of puff soufflés, bind sauces and enrich cakes and pastries. Home cooks use them for impromptu meals. I'm all for both approaches. As a home cook, I love eggs for their endless menu possibilities. As a professional, I rely on their almost miraculous chemical properties.

The many virtues of the egg have been overshadowed lately by fears about their cholesterol count. I'm mindful about limiting them in my diet, but I haven't lost sight of their nutritional value. They supply protein and  generous amounts of vitamins and minerals. Try Puffy Baked Eggs for breakfast or Tomato Marmalade Soufflé for lunch, a Red Pepper and Lettuce Frittatta at a picnic or the Tart Rio Grande for a late-night snack.

TARTS

Fresh Spinach and Mussel Tart
Cheese and Onion Tart with Sweet and
 Sour Red Peppers
Middle Eastern Lamb and Ratatouille
 Custard Tart
Tart Rio Grande with Salsa

SOUFFLES

Eggplant Soufflé
Fresh Broccoli Soufflé
Tomato Marmalade Soufflé

EGGS

Red Pepper and Lettuce Frittata
Smoked Salmon Flan
Puffy Baked Eggs in Casserole
Shirred Eggs in Canadian-Bacon-and-
 Spinach Cups with Hollandaise Sauce
Ragout of Spring Vegetables with Eggs
 and Watercress-Hollandaise Sauce

COUNTRY-STYLE BREAKFAST

Freshly Squeezed Orange Juice
Puffy Baked Eggs in Casserole
McIntosh Breakfast Sausage
Whole-Grain Gingerbread Muffins

Tomato
Marmalade Soufflé
previous pages

1 11-inch (28cm) prebaked Shallot
   Pastry shell (see Index)
32 small mussels (2 pounds total,
   910g)
2 pounds (910g) fresh young
   spinach, with stems trimmed,
   washed
4 large shallots (2 ounces total, 55g),

peeled
3 tablespoons unsalted butter
1 cup (240ml) Half and Half or light
   cream
3 large eggs
1/2 teaspoon salt
   Freshly grated nutmeg
   Freshly ground pepper

**FRESH
SPINACH AND
MUSSEL TART**

*This is a simple
pairing of fresh,
sweet-tasting
mussels and
tender young
spinach in a flaky
pastry crust. The
recipe is Roger
Vergé's, from his
restaurant in
Mougins, France.*

Scrub mussels and remove their beards. Discard any that are open and do not close
when tapped on counter. Transfer to 4-quart (4L) pot, add 1 teaspoon of salt and cover
with cold water. Soak for 30 minutes. Wash several times, then drain well. Return to
pot with only water clinging to them. Cover and cook over high heat just until shells
open — about 6 to 7 minutes. Discard any that do no open. When cool enough to
handle, remove mussels from shells.

Put spinach in large non-aluminum pot with only water clinging to leaves. Cook,
stirring several times, just until wilted. Immediately transfer to colander and hold
under cold running water until completely cool. Wrap in towel and squeeze firmly to
release as much moisture as possible. Can be cooked 1 day in advance. Wrap airtight
and refrigerate.

Fifteen minutes before baking, place rack in center of oven and preheat to 350°F
(175°C).

Metal Blade: Turn on machine, drop shallots through feed tube and process until
minced.

Melt butter in 10-inch (25cm) sauté pan. Add shallots and cook gently until soft —
about 6 minutes. Add spinach and continue to cook, stirring often, until all moisture
has cooked from spinach, about 8 minutes. Transfer to work bowl.

Metal Blade: Pulse spinach mixture 4 times to chop coarsely. Spread in even layer in
pastry shell and arrange mussels over spinach. Process cream, eggs, salt, nutmeg and
pepper for 5 seconds to mix, and pour over tart.

Place tart on baking sheet and bake until custard is just set — about 35 minutes. Cool
on wire rack for 10 minutes. Remove side of pan and serve hot or at room temperature.

Makes 8 servings.

To Clean Spinach

★ Nothing is more unpleasant than gritty spinach. It's important to clean every trace
of sand and grit from it before you cook it. This is the best method I've found for
accomplishing that. Fill a large pot with cold water and put in the spinach. Let it soak
for 10 minutes, then lift it out into a colander. Rinse the pot thoroughly, add fresh cold
water and the spinach. Repeat the procedure until there is no sand at the bottom of the
pot when you remove the spinach.

CHEESE AND ONION TART WITH SWEET AND SOUR RED PEPPERS

The sweet and sour red peppers offset the richness of the cheese. Although the recipe calls for a large quantity of onions, their flavor is not strong, but mildly sweet from the gentle sautéeing. If you prefer, bake the tart without pastry in a shallow, buttered 6-cup (1.5L) baking dish.

1 11-inch (28cm) prebaked Herb Pastry shell (see Index)
4 medium onions (1¼ pounds total, 570g), peeled and cut to fit feed tube, if necessary
4 tablespoons unsalted butter
2 large red peppers (12 ounces total, 340g)
1 tablespoon red-wine vinegar
1 tablespoon sugar

6 ounces (170g) Monterey Jack cheese, chilled
3 ounces (85g) imported Parmesan cheese, at room temperature
2 large eggs
½ cup (120ml) whipping cream
1 teaspoon dried basil
½ teaspoon salt
Freshly ground pepper

Medium Slicing Disc (3mm): Use firm pressure to slice onions.

Melt 2 tablespoons of butter in 10-inch (25cm) sauté pan and add onions. Place circle of waxed paper directly on onions and cook gently for 10 minutes. Remove paper and continue to cook gently until onions are completely soft, but not brown — about 25 minutes.

Fifteen minutes before baking, place rack in center of oven and preheat to 325°F (160°C). Have baking sheet ready.

Stand peppers on cutting board. Use sharp knife to cut off sides in 3 or 4 vertical slices, leaving only core and stem. Remove any membrane from slices.

Medium Slicing Disc (3mm): Stack slices and stand them lengthwise in feed tube, wedging them in tightly to hold. Use light pressure to slice.

Melt remaining 2 tablespoons of butter in 8-inch (20cm) skillet and add peppers. Cook over medium heat just until peppers begin to soften — about 4 minutes. Add vinegar and sugar and continue to cook until liquid becomes thick and syrupy — about 5 minutes. Remove from heat.

Medium Shredding Disc: Use light pressure to shred cheeses. Leave in work bowl.

Metal Blade: Add eggs, cream, basil, salt, ground pepper and any liquid from cooked peppers and pulse twice. Add onions and process for 3 seconds.

Pour egg mixture into pastry. Arrange red peppers over top and press them gently in so they are partially submerged. Place on baking sheet and bake until very lightly browned and set in center — about 42 minutes. Let cool on wire rack for 10 minutes before serving.

Makes 6 to 8 main-course or 12 first-course servings.

2 tablespoons unsalted butter,
softened
4 ounces (115g) imported Parmesan
cheese, at room temperature
4 ounces (115g) mozzarella cheese,
chilled
1/4 cup parsley leaves
6 large scallions (3 ounces total,
85g), including green tops, cut into
thirds
2 medium garlic cloves, peeled
1 small onion (3 ounces, 85g), peeled
and halved

1 tablespoon safflower oil
8 ounces (225g) cooked or raw lamb,
cut into 3/4-inch (2cm) cubes (see
NOTE)
1 1/2 teaspoons dried oregano
1 teaspoon cinnamon
1 cup (240ml) whipping cream
4 large eggs
1/2 teaspoon salt
1/3 cup (80ml) plain yogurt
3 cups Ratatouille (see Index), well
drained

MIDDLE EASTERN LAMB AND RATATOUILLE CUSTARD TART

The ingredients used in ratatouille — zucchini, eggplant, tomatoes and onions — are often used in Middle-Eastern cooking. Ground lamb, seasonings and a tangy custard base turn the French vegetable stew into a Turkish-style main course. The crust is not a pastry, but a delicious mix of shredded cheeses. You can omit it if you prefer.

Fifteen minutes before baking, place rack in center of oven and preheat to 375°F (190°C). Grease shallow, round 6-cup (1.5L) baking dish with 2 tablespoons of butter.

Medium Shredding Disc: Use light pressure to shred cheeses.

Toss cheeses together and press onto sides and bottom of prepared dish to form crust.

Metal Blade: Process parsley until minced; remove and reserve.

Medium (3mm) or All Purpose Slicing Disc (4mm): Stand scallions in feed tube and use light pressure to slice; remove and reserve.

Metal Blade: Turn on machine, drop garlic and onion through feed tube and process until minced.

Heat oil in 8-inch (20cm) skillet. Gently cook garlic and onion until soft — about 5 minutes.

Metal Blade: Add lamb, oregano and cinnamon and pulse until lamb is coarsely chopped.

Add to skillet and cook gently for 10 minutes.

Metal Blade: Process cream, eggs and salt for 3 seconds to mix. Add yogurt and pulse twice.

Spread Ratatouille evenly over crust, then add lamb. Pour custard over and sprinkle with reserved parsley and scallions. Bake until custard is just set — about 40 minutes. Transfer to wire rack and let rest for 10 minutes before serving. Serve hot or at room temperature.

Makes 6 main-course servings.

NOTE: 8 ounces (225g) of beef, pork, chicken or turkey can be substituted for lamb.

TART RIO GRANDE

All the elements of this tart are drawn from Tex-Mex cuisine: the cornmeal crust, the mix of savory vegetables in the filling, and the puffy topping of Monterey Jack cheese. The tart contains no egg yolks or cream, so it's lighter than most.

1 11-inch (28cm) prebaked Cornmeal Pastry shell (see Index)
3 medium onions (14 ounces total, 395g), peeled and halved lengthwise
2 large green peppers (12 ounces total, 340g), cored
1 tablespoon safflower oil
3/4 teaspoon salt
1 cup (240ml) plus 3 tablespoons Salsa (recipe follows), drained
2 tablespoons tomato paste
3 large egg whites
1 tablespoon red-wine vinegar

12 ounces (340g) Monterey Jack cheese, chilled and cut into 1-inch (2.5cm) cubes
4 large scallions (4 ounces total, 115g), including green tops, cut into 1-inch (2.5cm) pieces
Freshly ground pepper
2 tablespoons yellow cornmeal
2 ripe avocados (1 pound total, 455g), peeled and cut lengthwise into 1/4-inch (6mm) slices
1/2 to 1 cup (120 to 240ml) sour cream (optional)

Medium Slicing Disc (3mm): Stand onions in feed tube and use firm pressure to slice. Stand peppers cut side down in feed tube and use light pressure to slice.

Heat oil in 10-inch (25cm) skillet. Add onions, peppers and 1/2 teaspoon of salt. Put circle of waxed paper directly on vegetables and cook over medium-high heat until very soft, but not brown — about 15 minutes. Remove paper and cook gently, stirring often, until all moisture has evaporated — about 10 minutes. Stir in 3 tablespoons of Salsa and tomato paste and remove from heat.

Fifteen minutes before broiling, place rack 8 inches (20cm) from heat and preheat broiler. Have baking sheet ready.

Metal Blade: Process egg whites for 8 seconds. With machine running, pour vinegar through feed tube and process until egg whites are whipped and hold their shape — about 45 seconds.

Use spatula to transfer gently to mixing bowl. It is not necessary to wash work bowl.

Metal Blade: Process cheese, scallions, 1/4 teaspoon of salt and pepper for 10 seconds, stopping once to scrape work bowl. Add 1/4 of egg whites and pulse twice. Run spatula around inside of work bowl to loosen mixture and spoon remaining egg whites in ring onto cheese. Pulse 3 times. Run spatula around inside of work bowl and pulse just until combined, 1 or 2 more times. Do not overprocess.

Sprinkle cornmeal over bottom of pastry. Add vegetables in even layer, then spread cheese mixture evenly on top. Place on baking sheet. Broil until top is puffy and golden — about 5 minutes. Arrange avocado slices in spiral pattern over top. Cut into wedges and serve with remaining Salsa and sour cream.

Makes 8 servings.

¹/₂ cup cilantro, or fresh coriander,
   leaves and stems
1 large garlic clove, peeled
1 jalapeño pepper, halved
1 small onion (1¹/₂ ounces,
   45g),peeled and quartered

2 medium tomatoes (12 ounces total,
   340g), seeded and quartered
¹/₄ cup (60ml) tomato paste
¹/₂ teaspoon salt

Metal Blade: Put cilantro in work bowl and turn on machine. Drop garlic and pepper through feed tube and process until minced. Add onion, tomatoes, tomato paste and salt and process for 15 seconds, stopping once to scrape work bowl.

Can be refrigerated up to 5 days.

Makes 2 cups (480ml).

*Tart Rio Grande
with Salsa*

EGGPLANT SOUFFLE

Soufflés no longer have an aura of mystery, nor a reputation for unpredictability. With a food processor, they're always easy and successful. My revived enthusiasm for them led to this light and airy concoction, based on egg whites whipped in the food processor and eggplant puréed in it. The delicate flavor of eggplant is bolstered by hints of garlic and cheese.

1 small eggplant (12 ounces, 340g)
1 large garlic clove, peeled
2 tablespoons unsalted butter
3 tablespoons flour
³/₄ cup (180ml) milk
³/₄ teaspoon dried thyme
³/₄ teaspoon salt
2 dashes of Tabasco sauce
Freshly ground pepper
6 large egg whites
1 tablespoon white vinegar
1 tablespoon water
1 ounce (30g) imported Parmesan cheese, at room temperature
4 large egg yolks

Fifteen minutes before baking eggplant, place rack in center of oven and preheat to 350°F (175°C).

Place eggplant in baking pan and bake until very wrinkled and soft — about 1 hour. When cool enough to handle, peel and cut flesh into 3-inch (8cm) chunks. Can be cooked up to 2 days in advance and refrigerated.

Fifteen minutes before baking soufflé, place rack in center of oven and preheat to 375°F (190°C). Butter a 5- or 6-cup (1.5L) soufflé dish.

Metal Blade: Turn on machine, drop garlic through feed tube and process until minced.

In 1¹/₂-quart (1.5L) saucepan, gently cook garlic in butter until soft, but not brown — about 5 minutes. Stir in flour and cook for 1 minute, stirring often. Do not let brown. Add milk, thyme, salt, Tabasco sauce and pepper. Whisk rapidly, taking care to reach edges of pan, until mixture thickens to medium paste. Keep warm until needed. If it becomes too thick, add several drops of milk.

Metal Blade: Process cooked eggplant until smooth. Measure ³/₄ cup to use in this recipe and set aside; reserve remainder for another use (see NOTE.) It is not necessary to wash work bowl. Process egg whites for 8 seconds. With machine running, pour vinegar and water through feed tube and process until egg whites are whipped and hold their shape — about 2 minutes and 20 seconds.

Use spatula to transfer gently to mixing bowl.

Metal Blade: Process cheese until very fine. Add egg yolks and process for 5 seconds. Add ³/₄ cup of eggplant purée and warm flour mixture and process for 5 seconds. Spoon egg whites onto mixture in circle and pulse twice. Run spatula around inside of work bowl and pulse just until ingredients are combined, 1 or 2 more times. Do not overprocess; some streaks of white will be visible.

Gently transfer to prepared soufflé dish and bake until well browned — about 38 minutes. Serve immediately.

Makes 4 to 6 servings.

NOTE: Any remaining eggplant purée is a bonus. I season it with herbs, garlic, chopped olives and a bit of olive oil, and spread it on French bread for a snack.

1 large stalk broccoli (12 ounces, 340g)
1 tablespoon safflower oil
1½ tablespoons flour
½ cup (120ml) skim milk
1½ tablespoons instant nonfat dry-milk powder
½ teaspoon salt
¼ teaspoon freshly grated nutmeg
1 drop Tabasco sauce
5 large egg whites
1 tablespoon white vinegar
1 tablespoon water

This low-fat, low-calorie soufflé was inspired by the Framingham Institute's study on heart disease and the American Cancer Society's dietary guidelines. It's so good, you'll never guess its good for you.

Fifteen minutes before baking, place rack in center of oven and preheat to 400°F (205°C). Butter 5-cup (1.2L) soufflé dish.

Cut flowerets from broccoli. Peel stem with vegetable peeler and cut into feed-tube lengths.

All Purpose Slicing Disc (4mm): Stand broccoli stem in feed tube and use medium pressure to slice.

Put flowerets and stem in steamer insert and steam until tender, about 10 minutes. Set aside until cool enough to handle, then wrap in towel and squeeze gently to remove as much moisture as possible. You should have about 1¾ cups cooked broccoli. Broccoli can be cooked 1 day in advance. Pat dry before using.

Heat oil in 1-quart (1L) saucepan and stir in flour. Cook gently and stir for 1 minute. Add milk, milk powder, salt, nutmeg and Tabasco sauce and increase heat to medium. Cook, stirring constantly, until mixture comes to boil and thickens. Remove from heat and proceed with recipe. Sauce must be warm when combined with beaten egg whites.

Metal Blade: Process egg whites for 8 seconds. With machine running, pour vinegar and water through feed tube and process until they are whipped and hold their shape, about 1 minute and 30 seconds. Use spatula to transfer them gently to mixing bowl.

Metal Blade: Process broccoli and warm sauce until combined — 5 seconds. Add ¼ of egg whites and process to combine — 2 seconds. Scrape work bowl, spoon remaining egg whites onto mixture in circle and pulse just until combined, about 2 or 3 times. Do not overprocess; some streaks of white will be visible.

Use spatula to transfer to prepared dish. Bake until golden and set in center, about 32 minutes. Serve immediately.

Makes 4 servings.

1. Whipping Egg Whites

2. Combining egg whites with broccoli

3. Transferring mixture to soufflé dish

4. Fresh Broccoli Soufflé

TOMATO MARMALADE SOUFFLE

The intense flavor of tomato marmalade makes it a good base for a soufflé. This one is puffy and light — picture-perfect every time. Pair it with a crisp cooked vegetable and bread or rolls for a pleasingly light meal.

2 tablespoons unsalted butter
3 tablespoons flour
3/4 cup (180ml) milk
3/4 teaspoon salt
3/4 teaspoon dried basil
   Freshly ground pepper

6 large egg whites
1 tablespoon white vinegar
1 tablespoon water
3/4 cup (180ml) Tomato Marmalade
   (see Index)
4 large egg yolks

Fifteen minutes before baking, place rack in center of oven and preheat to 350°F (175°C). Butter 6-cup (1.5L) soufflé dish.

Melt butter in 1 1/2-quart (1.5L) saucepan. Stir in flour and cook gently for 1 minute, stirring often. Add milk, salt, basil and pepper. Whisk rapidly, taking care to reach edges of pan, until mixture thickens to medium paste. Keep it warm; if it becomes too thick, add several drops of milk before using.

Metal Blade: Process egg whites for 8 seconds. With machine running, pour vinegar and water through feed tube and process until egg whites are whipped and hold their shape — about 2 minutes.

Use spatula to transfer gently to bowl. It is not necessary to wash work bowl.

Metal Blade: Process marmalade, egg yolks and warm flour mixture for 5 seconds. Spoon egg whites onto mixture in circle and pulse twice. Run spatula around inside of work bowl and pulse just until combined, 1 or 2 more times. Do not overprocess; some streaks of white will be visible.

Gently transfer to prepared soufflé dish and bake until well browned — about 35 minutes. Serve immediately.

Makes 4 to 6 servings.

RED PEPPER VARIATION: Substitute 3/4 cup (180ml) Red Pepper Marmalade (see Index) for Tomato Marmalade.

Red Pepper and Lettuce Frittata

5 ounces (140g) mozzarella cheese,
preferably imported, cut into
1-inch (2.5cm) cubes

¹/₄ cup fresh basil leaves or 2
teaspoons dried

³/₄ cup parsley leaves

1 slice firm white bread (1 ounce,
30g), broken into pieces

1 medium red pepper (6 ounces,
170g)

1 medium onion (4 ounces, 115g),
peeled and halved vertically

2 tablespoons unsalted butter

¹/₂ medium head Romaine lettuce (6
ounces, 170g), cut into feed-tube
lengths

2 tablespoons red-wine vinegar

8 large eggs

1 teaspoon Worcestershire sauce
Dash of Tabasco sauce

¹/₂ teaspoon salt
Freshly ground pepper

2 tablespoons peanut oil

A frittata, the Italian version of an omelette, is less demanding of the cook than its French relative. Almost any combination of meat, cheese and vegetables can be mixed with eggs to make the hearty egg pancake. No matter what ingredients you choose, your food processor will be invaluable when it comes to slicing, chopping, shredding and mixing them together.

Fifteen minutes before broiling, place rack 6 inches (15cm) from heat and preheat broiler. Have 10-inch (25cm) ovenproof skillet ready.

Metal Blade: Process cheese until very finely chopped; remove and reserve. Process basil, parsley and bread until finely chopped; remove and reserve.

Stand pepper on cutting board. Use sharp knife to cut off sides in 3 or 4 vertical slices, leaving only core and stem. Remove any membrane from slices.

Medium Slicing Disc (3mm): Stack pepper slices and stand them lengthwise in feed tube, wedging them in tightly to hold. Use light pressure to slice. Stand onion in feed tube and use firm pressure to slice.

Melt butter in skillet and add red pepper and onion. Cook gently until soft but not limp — about 5 minutes.

All Purpose Slicing Disc (4mm): Stand lettuce in feed tube and use light pressure to slice.

Add to pan with vinegar and continue to cook until lettuce is wilted, but still green — about 2 minutes. Remove pan from heat.

Metal Blade: Pulse 3 times to combine eggs, Worcestershire and Tabasco sauces, salt and pepper. Add cooked vegetables, reserved herb mixture and ¹/₂ of cheese and pulse 3 more times. Can be prepared to this point several hours in advance and held at room temperature.

Brush oil over bottom and sides of same skillet and heat until very hot. Reduce heat to medium-low and add contents of work bowl. Use spatula to distribute vegetables evenly. Cook gently until bottom and sides are set, but center is still loose — about 12 minutes. As it cooks, run small knife around pan several times to loosen frittata from sides of pan. Remove from heat and sprinkle with remaining cheese. Immediately transfer to broiler and broil until eggs are set and top is just lightly colored — about 2 minutes. Let rest for 5 minutes, then cut into wedges. Serve hot or at room temperature.

Makes 6 servings.

SMOKED SALMON FLAN

The proportions of cream, milk and eggs in this custard are the same as used by Frédy Girardet for his famous onion tart. The smooth texture is just right for this adaptation, which combines the rich flavors of onion and smoked salmon. The flan is easy to make and perfect for brunch or Sunday supper.

2 medium onions (8 ounces total, 225g), peeled and halved lengthwise
2 tablespoons unsalted butter
9 large eggs
3 ounces (85g) smoked Nova Scotia salmon

1 1/2 cups (360ml) whipping cream
6 tablespoons milk
3/4 teaspoon salt
1/8 teaspoon freshly grated nutmeg
Freshly ground pepper
1 tablespoon snipped fresh chives

Fifteen minutes before baking, place rack in center of oven and preheat to 300°F (150°C). Butter shallow round 6-cup (1.5L) baking dish.

Thin (2mm) or Medium Slicing Disc (3mm): Use firm pressure to slice onions.

Melt butter in 8-inch (20cm) skillet. Add onions and cook gently until very soft, about 12 minutes. Do not brown.

Metal Blade: Pulse 4 times to combine eggs, salmon, 1/2 cup (120ml) of cream, milk, salt, nutmeg and pepper.

Transfer to large mixing bowl and stir in remaining cream. (If your work bowl diameter is 7 inches (18cm) or more, all the cream can be processed with eggs.)

Arrange onions in bottom of prepared baking dish and add egg mixture. Can be prepared to this point 1 day in advance and refrigerated. (If preparing in advance, do not add salmon until just before baking.) Bring to room temperature before baking.

Sprinkle with chives and bake in preheated oven until just set in center, about 60 minutes. Let set 10 minutes before serving. Serve warm or at room temperature.

Makes 6 servings.

HOLIDAY BRUNCH
Mimosa Cocktails
Smoked Salmon Flan
Pasta Florentine
Cranberry-Streusel Muffins
Dresden Stollen
Prunes in Port-Wine Syrup

6 large scallions, including green
    tops (6 ounces total, 170g), cut into
    1-inch (2.5cm) pieces
12 small mushrooms (4 ounces total,
    115g), with 2 opposite sides cut flat
1 tablespoon unsalted butter
10 ounces (285g) Muenster cheese, cut
    into 1-inch (2.5cm) cubes
1/4 cup cilantro, or fresh coriander,
    leaves
1/4 cup loosely packed parsley leaves

1 1/2 slices white bread (1 1/2 ounces
    total, 45g), with crust removed,
    broken into pieces
12 large eggs
1 cup (240ml) milk
1/2 to 3/4 teaspoon salt, amount
    depending on saltiness of cheese
    Freshly ground pepper
1/3 cup (80ml) water
    Salsa (see Index), optional

PUFFY BAKED EGGS IN CASSEROLE

This casserole of softly scrambled eggs with Muenster cheese, scallions and mushrooms brings to mind the flavors of a filled omelette and the lightness of a soufflé. Unlike either, it can be assembled in advance.

Fifteen minutes before baking, place rack in center of oven and preheat to 400°F (205°C). Butter shallow 6-cup (1.5L) baking dish.

Metal Blade: Process scallions until minced.

All Purpose Slicing Disc (4mm): Put mushrooms in feed tube on flat side and use light pressure to slice.

Melt butter in 10-inch (25cm) skillet. Add scallions and mushrooms and cook gently until mushrooms are soft, but still hold their shape — about 8 minutes. Remove pan from heat.

Metal Blade: Process cheese, cilantro and parsley until very finely chopped; remove and reserve. Process bread until finely crumbed. Add eggs, milk, salt and pepper and pulse to mix, about 4 times.

Transfer to large mixing bowl and stir in water. (If your work bowl has diameter of 7 inches (18cm) or more, water can be processed with eggs.)

Return vegetables to medium heat and add egg mixture. Cook, stirring often, until very soft and runny with large, semi-liquid curds.

Transfer 1/2 of mixture to prepared baking dish, and sprinkle with 1/2 of cheese. Repeat layers. Bake until lightly browned and puffy — about 28 minutes. Serve with Salsa, if desired. Can be prepared up to 3 hours in advance and held at room temperature. Do not refrigerate.

Makes 6 to 8 servings.

SHIRRED EGGS IN CANADIAN BACON-AND-SPINACH CUPS WITH HOLLANDAISE SAUCE

A savory mixture of finely chopped Canadian bacon and spinach is used to shape edible containers for shirred eggs. The cups can be assembled a day in advance so that last-minute preparations are minimal.

2 cups tightly packed fresh spinach leaves (4 ounces total, 115g), washed

2 large shallots (1 ounce total, 30g), peeled

2 tablespoons unsalted butter

2 slices white bread (2 ounces total, 55g), broken into pieces

6 ounces (170g) Canadian bacon, cut into 1-inch (2.5cm) pieces

1 teaspoon Dijon mustard

1 large egg white

8 large eggs, at room temperature

Hollandaise Sauce (recipe follows)

Fifteen minutes before baking, place rack in center of oven and preheat to 375°F (190°C). Butter eight ¹/₃-cup (80ml) muffin cups or individual baking dishes.

Put spinach, with only water clinging to its leaves, in non-aluminum pot over high heat and cook just until wilted. Immediately transfer to colander and hold under cold running water until completely cool. Wrap in towel and squeeze firmly to remove as much moisture as possible. Spinach can be cooked 1 day in advance, wrapped airtight and refrigerated.

Metal Blade: Turn on machine, drop shallots through feed tube and process until minced.

Melt butter in 6-inch (15cm) skillet. Add shallots and cook until soft but not brown — about 6 minutes.

Metal Blade: Pulse about 8 times to chop cooked shallots, spinach, bread, bacon and mustard.

Use electric mixer to beat egg white until firmly whipped, but still glossy. Gently fold contents of work bowl into egg white.

Divide mixture between prepared muffin cups and press against sides and bottom to form ¹/₈-inch (3mm) crust. Bake for 10 minutes. Cups can be baked 1 day in advance. Leave in pan and refrigerate. Bring to room temperature before proceeding.

Decrease oven temperature to 350°F (175°C).

Crack egg into each cup and bake until whites are softly set and yolks still soft — about 12 to 15 minutes. Let rest for 5 minutes. Carefully run small spatula or knife around each cup and lift onto serving plate. Spoon Hollandaise Sauce over each and pass any remaining sauce separately.

Makes 4 servings of 2 eggs each.

2 sticks unsalted butter (8 ounces total, 225g)
3 large egg yolks
1 tablespoon hot water

$^1/_2$ teaspoon dry mustard
$^1/_2$ teaspoon salt
Freshly ground white pepper
1 tablespoon fresh lemon juice

Melt butter and keep it bubbling hot.

Metal Blade: Process egg yolks, water, mustard, salt and pepper for 1 minute. With machine running, slowly pour butter through feed tube in thin, steady stream. Add it only as quickly as it is incorporated into egg yolks. Stop machine, add lemon juice and process for 3 seconds. Adjust seasoning.

Sauce can be kept warm up to 15 minutes by placing in pan of hot, not boiling, water.

Makes about 1 $^1/_4$ cups (300ml).

Makes 6 servings.

WATERCRESS VARIATION: Blanch 1 cup of watercress leaves in 3 cups (720ml) of boiling water for 30 seconds. Drain and hold under cold running water until cool. Drain, wrap in towel and squeeze to remove as much moisture as possible. You will have about 1 tablespoon of watercress. Proceed as above, adding watercress with lemon juice and processing for 15 seconds.

FATHERS' DAY
BRUNCH
Spicy Bloody Marys
Ragout of Spring
Vegetables with Eggs and
Watercress
Hollandaise Sauce
Popovers
Whole-Wheat Honey Buns

RAGOUT OF SPRING VEGETABLES WITH EGGS AND WATERCRESS-HOLLANDAISE SAUCE

A crisp, colorful assortment of spring vegetables forms the base for baked eggs. The dish has lots of color and style and is great for brunch or lunch-time entertaining. Much of the preparation can be done in advance, making it even more appealing.

12 medium asparagus spears (12 ounces total, 340g), stems peeled with vegetable peeler
3 small yellow summer squash (12 ounces total, 340g)
40 small snow peas (4 ounces total, 115g), with strings removed
1 large garlic clove, peeled
6 large scallions (4 ounces total, 115g), including green tops, cut into feed-tube lengths
2 tablespoons unsalted butter
2 tablespoons flour

2 large red peppers (12 ounces total, 340g)
1 large head Boston lettuce (5 ounces, 140g), cored and cut to fit feed tube
1¼ teaspoons dried basil
1 teaspoon dried thyme
¾ teaspoon salt
Freshly ground pepper
½ cup tiny frozen peas, not thawed
6 large eggs
Watercress Hollandaise Sauce (see Index)

Fifteen minutes before baking, place rack in center of oven and preheat to 375°F (190°C). Have ready 8-cup (2L) gratin pan or 6 individual casseroles of about 10 ounce (285g) capacity. Bring 4 quarts (4L) of salted water to boil.

Cut 2½-inches (6cm) from tips of asparagus, then cut stems into feed-tube lengths.

Thick Slicing Disc (6mm): Stand asparagus stems in feed tube and use medium pressure to slice; remove and reserve. Stand squash in feed tube and use medium pressure to slice.

Add squash to boiling water and cook for 1½ minutes. Remove with slotted spoon and hold under cold running water until completely cool. Let water return to boil. Cook asparagus stems and tips until tender but still crisp — about 5 minutes. Remove with slotted spoon and hold under cold running water until completely cool. Let water return to boil. Add snow peas and cook until tender but still crisp — about 3 minutes. Drain and hold under cold running water until completely cool. Wrap squash in towel and press gently to remove moisture. Pat asparagus and snow peas dry.

Metal Blade: Turn on machine, drop garlic through feed tube and process until minced.

Thick Slicing Disc (6mm): Stand scallions in feed tube and use light pressure to slice.

Melt butter in 12-inch (30cm) skillet. Add garlic and ½ of scallions and cook gently until soft — about 5 minutes. Add flour and mix together.

Stand peppers on cutting board. Use sharp knife to cut off sides in 3 or 4 vertical slices, leaving only core and stem. Remove any membrane from slices.

Thick Slicing Disc (6mm): Stack pepper slices and stand them lengthwise in feed tube, wedging them in tightly to hold. Use light pressure to slice. Stand lettuce in feed tube and use light pressure to slice.

Add to skillet with basil, thyme, salt and pepper. Cover and cook until lettuce is wilted — about 5 minutes. Remove from heat and add peas, asparagus stems (reserve tips), squash, remaining scallions and snow peas and mix thoroughly. There will be a slight film on bottom of pan; make sure to mix it into vegetables. Taste and adjust seasoning.

Spread vegetables in even layer in gratin pan and make 6 evenly spaced indentations for eggs. Or divide vegetables among 6 casserole dishes and make indentation in center of each that goes to bottom of dish. Recipe can be prepared to this point 1 day in advance. Cover airtight and refrigerate. Bring to room temperature before proceeding.

Carefully crack egg into each indentation and place reserved asparagus tip on each side of egg. Bake in preheated oven until eggs are just set — about 28 minutes. Serve immediately with Watercress Hollandaise Sauce.

Makes 6 servings.

NOTE: 6 ounces (170g) of Canadian bacon, cut into 3 by $^1\!/_4$ by $^1\!/_4$-inch (8cm by 6mm by 6mm) strips, can be added to vegetables.

RAGOUT OF SPRING VEGETABLES WITH EGGS AND WATERCRESS-HOLLANDAISE SAUCE

Ragout of Spring Vegetables with Eggs

MEATS & POULTRY

Americans are changing their classic pattern of meat and potatoes for dinner. Big steaks, chops and roasts are giving place to more nutritionally balanced alternatives — dishes that combine meat with fresh vegetables, pasta, beans or rice. Use of poultry, especially chicken, is increasing while consumption of red meat declines. Today's cooks appreciate the versatility and economy of chicken, which also is low in fat and calories.

Meanwhile, the popularity of hearty one-pot stews and ragouts is reviving. They're easy and adaptable to a busy life. Many, like Veal Ragout and Roast Pork with Fennel, are appropriate for informal entertaining. These recipes vary widely in style and complexity of preparation. Some, like Ginger-Beef Stir-Fry or Chicken Breasts with Oriental Vegetables are ideal for spur-of-the-moment dining. Others, like stews, require planning, but they freeze well. Grilling is a preparation I often use. I love the various aromatic woods that give subtlety of flavor. To complement the simplicity of grilled meats and poultry, I've included several savory and exotic condiments.

MEATS AND POULTRY

CHICKEN

Chicken Breasts with Oriental Vegetables
Supremes of Chicken with Chicken Mousse, Vegetables and Madeira Sauce
Chicken in Vinegar with Green Peppercorns
Orange Chicken Jambalaya
Baked Chicken Marsala
Stir-Fry of Chicken with Broccoli and Red Peppers
Chicken Breasts with White Port Sauce on Braised Leeks
Roast Chicken with Garden Vegetables
Curried Chicken
Chicken Hash with Wild Rice
Curried Chicken Medallions with Buttered Cucumbers

Glazed Cornish Hens Stuffed with Fruit Pilaf
Roast Cornish Hens with Caramelized Garlic
Roast Capon with Green Peppercorns and Lime

TURKEY

Roast Turkey with Sausage and Chestnut Stuffing
Turkey Breast with Fresh Orange and Port Sauce
Marinated Turkey Breast with Lemon and Caper Sauce

DUCK

Breast of Duck with Honey and Lemon
Duck Curry with Cabbage and Apples

BEEF

Ginger-Beef Stir-Fry
Beef Stew with Cranberries
Rio Grande Tostado Casserole
Flemish Beef Carbonnade
Sliced Beef Miroton
Fillet of Beef with Green Peppercorn Sauce
Sliced Corned Beef with Horseradish Cream

VEAL

Veal Ragout with Mushrooms, Tomatoes and Lamb

LAMB

Navarin of Lamb with Spring Vegetables
Roast Lamb with Port Wine and Garlic Sauce
Middle Eastern Skewered Lamb with Leeks, Beans and Tomatoes
Lamb Medallions with Sherry Vinegar
Marinated Lamb with Provençal Beans
Boneless Leg of Lamb with Peppercorn Mustard Crust

PORK

Roast Pork with Fennel, New Potatoes and Leeks
Savory Stuffed Cabbage
Saucisson
McIntosh Breakfast Sausage
Chili Pork Stew

CONDIMENTS

Fresh Cranberry Chutney
Onion Compote
Mushroom Marmalade Sauce
Apple Raisin Chutney
Tarragon Shallot Mayonnaise
Sweet Mustard Sauce
Texas Barbecue Sauce

FARMHOUSE SUPPER
Corn and Parsnip Chowder
Roast Chicken with Garden Vegetables
Sliced Tomatoes and Onion with Garlic Cheese Vinaigrette
Carrot Torte

4 large dried shiitake mushrooms
2 large whole chicken breasts, split, boned and skinned (about 1¼ pounds, 565g meat)
1 large garlic clove, peeled
6 medium scallions (3 ounces, 85g), including tops, cut into feed-tube lengths

1 large carrot (6 ounces total, 85g), peeled, cut into feed-tube widths
4 teaspoons Oriental sesame oil
1¼ teaspoons soy sauce
4 ounces (115g) large snow peas, trimmed, with strings removed
2 tablespoons water

Colorful and low in calories, this dish can be prepared in well under thirty minutes. I keep a supply of the flattened chicken breasts in the freezer so that only a bit of supplemental marketing is necessary to produce a delicious and healthy meal.

Cover mushrooms with hot water and soak for 20 minutes, then drain and squeeze dry. Discard stems and cut caps into thin strips.

Place each chicken breast between 2 sheets of plastic wrap. With meat pounder or side of chef's knife, flatten to uniform thickness of about ³/₁₆ inch (4mm).

Metal Blade: Turn on machine, drop garlic through feed tube and process until minced; remove and reserve.

Medium Slicing Disc (3mm): Stand scallions in feed tube and use light pressure to slice; remove and reserve. Use double-slicing technique to slice carrot as follows. Lay carrot horizontally in feed tube and use firm pressure to slice. Gather slices, stack them together and reinsert them in feed tube, with slices perpendicular to slicing disc. Slice again, using medium pressure, to produce julienne strips.

Heat oil and 1 teaspoon of soy sauce in 10-inch (25cm) skillet over medium-high heat. Add garlic and chicken, cover and cook, turning only once, just until opaque — about 2½ minutes total. Remove from skillet and keep warm while cooking vegetables.

Add water, ¼ teaspoon of soy sauce, carrots and snow peas to skillet and cook, stirring constantly, until vegetables are tender but still crisp — about 3 minutes. Toss in scallions and remove from heat. Adjust seasoning.

Divide most of vegetables among 4 dinner plates, arranging as bed for chicken. Top with chicken and arrange remaining vegetables over top. Serve immediately.

Makes 4 servings.

1. Flattening chicken breast

2. Slicing carrots

3. Double slicing carrots

4. Individual serving

SUPREMES OF CHICKEN WITH CHICKEN MOUSSE, VEGETABLES AND MADEIRA SAUCE

Pierre Wynants of Comme Chez Soi in Brussels uses whole boneless squab for this recipe. I've substituted boneless chicken breasts to make the recipe more practical for home cooking. Make sure each chicken breast weighs at least 5 ounces (140g), so it can easily envelop the stuffing. Wynants serves this with Sautéed Mushrooms and Sautéed Spinach (see Index).

Chicken
4 large chicken breasts, split and boned, with skins left intact (8 halves, each weighing 5 ounces, 140g, after boning)
Salt
Freshly ground white pepper

Mousse
2 small turnips (2 ounces total, 55g), peeled and cooked until tender but crisp
2 large fresh artichoke bottoms (2 ounces total, 55g), cooked until tender but crisp (see page 32)
2 large chicken thighs and 1 large chicken breast half with skin, bones and tendons removed, chilled
1 large egg white
1/4 cup (60ml) whipping cream, chilled
1/2 teaspoon salt
Freshly ground white pepper
Freshly grated nutmeg
2 tablespoons unsalted butter

Sauce
4 large shallots (2 ounces total, 55g), peeled
1/2 cup (120ml) Chicken Stock (see Index), or chicken broth
1/4 cup (60ml) Madeira wine
6 tablespoons unsalted butter, chilled and cut into sixths
Salt to taste

Fifteen minutes before baking, place rack in center of oven and preheat to 450°F (230°C). Have 12-inch (30cm) stove-to-oven gratin dish ready.

Place breast half between two sheets of waxed paper and press with meat pounder to uniform 1/4-inch (6mm) thickness. Repeat with remaining breasts. Place on baking sheet, skin side down, season lightly with salt and pepper and refrigerate.

French Fry Disc: Use medium pressure to cut turnips and artichoke bottoms. Put processed vegetables on cutting board and cut into square dice. Put in small bowl. (If you do not have French Fry Disc, use knife to cut vegetables into 1/4-inch, 6mm, dice.)

Metal Blade: Process meat from chicken thighs and breast half until smooth, stopping once to scrape work bowl. Turn on machine, pour egg white through feed tube and process for 30 seconds. Pour cream and salt, pepper and nutmeg through feed tube and process for 30 seconds, stopping once to scrape work bowl.

Combine chicken mixture with diced vegetables and refrigerate for at least 30 minutes or overnight. Put 2 rounded tablespoons of chicken mixture in strip down center of each chilled breast piece. Bring up sides, then ends, to make neat package and skewer with round toothpicks. Season with salt and pepper.

Melt 2 tablespoons of butter over high heat in gratin pan. When it is sizzling, add chicken breasts, seam side up, and cook until well browned — about 2 minutes. Turn breasts carefully with tongs and place pan in preheated oven. Bake until flesh is firm to touch, but not stiff — about 18 minutes. Do not overcook. Remove breasts from pan, cover with tent of aluminum foil and keep in warm place while preparing sauce. Discard all but 1 tablespoon of fat from pan.

Metal Blade: Turn on machine, drop shallots through feed tube and process until minced.

Add to pan and cook over medium-high heat for 2 minutes, loosening particles from bottom of pan. Add stock or broth and Madeira and simmer until reduced to ¹/₃ cup (80ml). Strain sauce and return it to pan. Whisk in butter, 1 tablespoon at a time, waiting until each piece is fully incorporated before adding another. Adjust seasoning. Spoon 1¹/₂ to 2 tablespoons of sauce over each breast and serve immediately.

Makes 8 servings.

2 large frying chickens (6 pounds total, 2.8kg), cut into serving pieces
1 teaspoon salt
Freshly ground pepper
2 tablespoons safflower oil
1 tablespoon unsalted butter
3 large garlic cloves, peeled
6 large shallots (3 ounces total, 85g), peeled
¹/₄ cup (60ml) red-wine vinegar
2 cups (480ml) dry red wine
1 bay leaf

¹/₂ teaspoon dried thyme
3 large tomatoes (18 ounces total, 510g), seeded and quartered
2 cups (480ml) Beef Stock (see Index), or beef broth
3 tablespoons tomato paste
1 teaspoon sugar
4 tablespoons unsalted butter, chilled and quartered (optional)
1 to 2 tablespoons green peppercorns, drained (see NOTE on page 83)

Chicken in vinegar is a classic French recipe, which is served in bistros and cafés as well as 3-star restaurants. This version from Roger Vergé is by far the best I've tasted. Despite its 3-star heritage, it's very easy to prepare. Butter, whisked in just before serving, enriches the sauce and makes it smooth and velvety. You can omit it if you're counting calories; even without it, the sauce is robust and well flavored.

Season chicken with salt and pepper. Heat oil and butter in 12-inch (30cm) sauté pan over high heat. When it is sizzling, add half the chicken, skin side down. Cook, turning once with tongs, until each side is well browned — about 5 minutes per side. Remove and reserve; cook remaining chicken. Discard grease and reserve pan.

Metal Blade: Turn on machine, drop garlic and shallots through feed tube and process until minced. Return pan to high heat. When it is hot, add vinegar and loosen particles from bottom of pan. Add garlic, shallots, wine, bay leaf and thyme and boil, uncovered, until reduced to ²/₃ cup (160ml) — about 15 minutes.

Metal Blade: Add tomatoes and pulse until coarsely chopped. Add to skillet with stock or broth, tomato paste, sugar and dark chicken meat. Cook, uncovered, for 20 minutes. Add white meat and cook until meat is firm but not stiff — about 13 minutes longer. Transfer chicken to serving platter and cover with tent of aluminum foil.

Strain sauce, return to skillet and cook over high heat until reduced to 1¹/₂ cups (360ml) — about 8 minutes. Whisk in butter, one piece at a time, waiting until each is incorporated. Add peppercorns, adjust seasoning and pour over chicken.

Can be prepared up to 3 days in advance. For best results, slightly undercook chicken in advance preparation. To reheat, cover and cook gently until heated through.

Makes 6 to 8 servings.

ORANGE CHICKEN JAMBALAYA

Foods that have style and great taste don't need to cost a lot of or take all day to prepare. Fifteen minutes of preparation and fifteen minutes of cooking are the total for this fresh and appealing dish. It's easy enough for family and special enough for guests. Serve with buttered rice or pasta.

3 large, whole chicken breasts, split, skinned and boned (about 22 ounces of meat total, 625g)
2 large garlic cloves, peeled
1 medium red pepper (6 ounces, 170g)
1 medium green pepper (6 ounces, 170g)
3 small onions (5 ounces total, 140g), peeled
3 tablespoons unsalted butter
2 ounces (55g) smoked

ham, cut into $^1/_8$-inch (3mm) dice
Zest of 1 large orange, removed with zester or grater
$^1/_8$ teaspoon cayenne pepper
4 medium scallions (3 ounces total, 85g), cut into feed-tube lengths
$^1/_2$ teaspoon salt
Juice of 2 large oranges (1$^1/_4$ cups, 300g)
$^1/_4$ cup (60ml) Cognac
$^1/_2$ cup tiny frozen peas, not thawed

Trim fat from chicken and tuck thin ends under to form compact shape of uniform thickness. Wrap each individually in plastic wrap and place on baking sheet. Freeze until firm but not solid. To be ready for processing, they should feel uniformly firm but you should be able to pierce them through with tip of sharp knife. (The meat can be frozen up to 2 months. When solid, wrap airtight and return to freezer. When ready to use, thaw to firmness described above.)

Extra Thick (8mm) or Thick Slicing Disc (6mm): Unwrap chicken. Stand pieces in feed tube, fitting them in tightly, and use firm pressure to slice. (If you do not have an Extra Thick or Thick Slicing Disc, slice chicken into slices $^1/_3$ inch (8mm) thick.)

Metal Blade: Turn on machine, drop garlic through feed tube and process until minced.

Stand peppers on cutting board. Use sharp knife to cut off sides in 3 or 4 vertical slices, leaving only core and stem. Remove any membrane from slices.

Medium Slicing Disc (3mm): Stack pepper slices and stand them lengthwise in feed tube, wedging them in tightly to hold. Use light pressure to slice. Stand onions in feed tube and use firm pressure to slice.

Melt 2 tablespoons of butter in 12-inch (30cm) skillet over medium heat. Add garlic, peppers, onions, ham, orange zest and cayenne and cook, uncovered, stirring often, until vegetables are very soft — about 12 minutes. Remove from skillet and reserve.

All Purpose Slicing Disc (4mm): Stand scallions in feed tube and use light pressure to slice; remove and reserve.

Heat remaining tablespoon of butter in same skillet over high heat. Season chicken slices with salt, add to skillet and cover. Cook, shaking pan often to prevent sticking, just until chicken turns opaque — about 2 minutes. Do not overcook. Remove with slotted spoon and set aside with vegetables. Add orange juice to juices in skillet and cook over high heat until reduced to $^2/_3$ cup (160ml) — about 8 minutes. Add Cognac and cook for 1 more minute. Return chicken and vegetables to skillet along with peas and scallions and cook just until heated through. Adjust seasoning and serve immediately.

Makes 6 servings.

*Orange Chicken
Jambalaya and
Baked Chicken
Marsala*

BAKED CHICKEN MARSALA

A delicious dish for entertaining Italian-style. The flavors of prosciutto, Marsala wine and sage will remind you of classic Italian cooking; the convenience and do-ahead ease are totally contemporary. Start the meal with your favorite antipasto, and add a simple tossed green salad and Glazed Pears with Gorgonzola and Walnuts (see Index).

3 large, whole chicken breasts (3 pounds total, 1.4kg), split, skinned and boned
5 ounces (140g) thinly sliced prosciutto
3 tablespoons unsalted butter
2 tablespoons olive oil
1 medium onion (4 ounces, 115g), peeled and quartered
18 small mushrooms (8 ounces total, 225g), with 2 opposite sides cut flat
1 cup (240ml) Marsala wine
1 1/4 teaspoons dried crumbled sage
1/2 teaspoon salt
1/2 cup (120ml) whipping cream
6 ounces (160g) mozzarella cheese, chilled and cut into 6 pieces
5 ounces (140g) imported Parmesan cheese, at room temperature, in 4 pieces

Have 12-inch (30cm) oval gratin dish ready. Tuck thin ends of chicken breasts under to form compact shape of uniform thickness. Wrap each one individually in plastic wrap and place on baking sheet. Freeze until firm but not solid. To be ready for processing, they should feel uniformly firm but you should be able to pierce them through with tip of sharp knife. (The meat can be frozen up to 2 months. When solid, wrap airtight and return to freezer. When ready to use, thaw to firmness described above.)

Fifteen minutes before baking, place rack in center of oven and preheat to 425°F (220°C).

Extra Thick (8mm) or Thick Slicing Disc (6mm): Place chicken horizontally in feed tube and use firm pressure to slice.

Cut 1/2 of prosciutto into strips 1/4 inch (6mm) wide. Melt 2 tablespoons each of butter and oil in 12-inch (30cm) skillet over medium-high heat. When hot, add chicken and prosciutto strips and cook, stirring constantly, for 1 minute. Cover and cook until chicken turns opaque — about 2 minutes. Remove meat with slotted spoon and reserve. Discard fat from skillet and set skillet aside.

Metal Blade: Turn on machine, drop onion through feed tube and process until minced.

All Purpose Slicing Disc (4mm): Stand mushrooms in feed tube, flat side down, and use light pressure to slice.

Melt remaining tablespoon of butter in skillet and add onion and mushrooms. Cover and cook over medium-high heat, stirring several times, until soft — about 4 minutes. Add Marsala and cook, uncovered, for 1 minute. Use slotted spoon to lift vegetables from skillet and set them aside with chicken. Add sage, salt and cream to juices in pan and simmer until consistency of very heavy cream. Remove pan from heat.

Metal Blade: Process both cheeses and remaining prosciutto until finely chopped.

Discard liquid from chicken and mushrooms and place in gratin pan. Recipe can be prepared 6 hours in advance, covered airtight and refrigerated. Bring to room temperature and carefully drain any liquid before baking. Add reduced cream mixture and sprinkle cheese and prosciutto over top. Bake in preheated oven until cheese is melted and lightly browned — about 10 minutes. Serve immediately.

Makes 6 servings.

2 large whole chicken breasts (1³/₄ pounds total, 795g), split, skinned and boned
1¹/₂ teaspoons cornstarch
¹/₂ cup (120ml) cold water
1 tablespoon dry sherry
4 teaspoons soy sauce
1 large garlic clove, peeled
1 ¹/₂-inch (12mm) cube fresh ginger, peeled
2 medium red peppers (8 ounces total, 225g)
12 ounces (340g) fresh broccoli, with flowerets cut off and stems peeled with vegetable peeler, cut into feed-tube lengths
12 medium scallions (3 ounces total, 85g), including green tops, cut into feed-tube widths
¹/₄ cup (60ml) safflower oil
¹/₄ cup cashews (1 ounce, 30g)
2 teaspoons Oriental sesame oil

This recipe is typical of my everyday cooking. It's an easily prepared combination of chicken and vegetables, cooked and seasoned in an Oriental style. Since I always have chicken breasts wrapped and ready to slice in the food processor, I can get dinner ready in no time. I vary the meat and vegetables according to what's on hand, and urge you to do the same. Turkey and pork are both delicious; for the vegetables, just about anything goes.

Trim fat from chicken and tuck thin ends under to form compact shapes of uniform thickness. Wrap individually in plastic wrap and place on baking sheet. Freeze until firm, but not solid. To be ready for processing, they should feel uniformly firm but you should be able to pierce them through with tip of sharp knife. (Can be frozen up to 4 months. When solid, wrap airtight and return to freezer. When ready to use, thaw to firmness described above.) Dissolve cornstarch in water, sherry and soy sauce.

Metal Blade: Turn on machine, drop garlic and ginger through feed tube and process until minced. Leave in work bowl.

If necessary, cut chicken in half horizontally to fit feed tube.

Extra Thick (8mm) or Thick Slicing Disc (6mm): Fit chicken lengthwise in feed tube, wedging it in tightly to hold. Use firm pressure to slice. Reserve in freezer.

Stand peppers on cutting board. Use sharp knife to cut off sides in 3 or 4 vertical slices, leaving only core and stem. Remove any membrane from slices.

Medium Slicing Disc (3mm): Stack pepper slices and stand them lengthwise in feed tube, wedging them in tightly to hold. Use light pressure to slice. Stand broccoli stems in feed tube and use firm pressure to slice. Lay scallions in feed tube and use light pressure to sliver.

Heat 2 tablespoons of safflower oil in 12¹/₂-inch (31cm) skillet over high heat. Lightly brown cashews; remove with slotted spoon and reserve.

Add chicken, garlic and ginger to skillet. Cover and cook just until opaque — about 2 minutes. Shake pan to prevent chicken from sticking; do not overcook. Remove and reserve.

Heat remaining 2 tablespoons of safflower oil and sesame oil in same skillet and add sliced vegetables and broccoli flowerets. Stir-fry over high heat until tender but crisp — about 3 minutes. Do not overcook.

Stir reserved sauce mixture and add to skillet along with chicken. Cook until sauce is clear and thickened — about 1 minute. Garnish with cashews and serve immediately.

Makes 4 servings.

CHICKEN BREASTS WITH WHITE PORT SAUCE ON BRAISED LEEKS

Vividly attractive, light and delicious, this dish inspired by Frédy Girardet is one of the most popular in my cooking classes. It meets my students' never-ending demands for stylish ways to serve chicken for entertaining. Prepare the leeks first and keep them warm while you cook the chicken; don't prepare them too far in advance or they will lose their bright color.

Leeks

4 medium leeks (2 pounds total, 910g), with coarse greens trimmed away
2 tablespoons unsalted butter

1 cup (240ml) whipping cream
1 teaspoon salt
Freshly ground pepper

Chicken

1¹/₂ ounces (45g) dried European mushrooms
6 large whole chicken breasts, split, skinned and boned
Salt
Freshly ground pepper

1 cup (240ml) white Port
1 cup (240ml) Beef Stock (see Index), or beef broth
1 stick unsalted butter (4 ounces, 115g), chilled and cut into 8 pieces

Split leeks lengthwise to within ¹/₂ inch (12mm) of their roots. Rinse under cold water, fanning leaves open to clean each layer. Drain and cut into feed-tube lengths.

Thick Slicing Disc (6mm): Stand leeks upright in feed tube and use medium pressure to slice.

Melt butter in 4-quart (4L) saucepan. Add leeks and cook gently, stirring occasionally, until soft — about 10 minutes. Add cream, salt and pepper and cook over medium-high heat until cream is thick enough to coat leeks. Keep warm while preparing chicken.

Soak mushrooms in hot water to cover for 1 minute and drain. Pat chicken dry and season with salt and pepper.

Put mushrooms, Port and stock or broth in 12-inch (30cm) sauté pan. Arrange as many chicken breasts as possible in single layer without letting them touch. Cut circle of aluminum foil to fit pan and place directly on chicken. Cook over high heat just until chicken is firm to touch — 6 to 8 minutes. Transfer to plate and cover loosely with aluminum foil. Cook remaining chicken breasts.

Boil liquid over high heat until reduced to ¹/₄ cup (60ml). Whisk in butter, one piece at a time, waiting until each piece is incorporated before adding another. Adjust seasoning.

Spoon leeks onto platter and arrange chicken breasts over them. Drizzle with sauce and garnish with mushrooms.

Makes 4 to 6 servings.

1¼ teaspoons salt
¼ teaspoon Hungarian paprika
　　Freshly ground pepper
2 frying chickens, 2½ to 3 pounds
　　(1.2 to 1.4kg) each
2 large sprigs parsley
2 whole bay leaves
　　Leafy celery tops
3 tablespoons safflower oil
½ cup loosely packed parsley leaves
2 large garlic cloves, peeled
1 medium onion (4 ounces, 115g),
　　peeled and quartered
4 medium carrots (12 ounces total,
340g), peeled and cut into
　　feed-tube lengths
3 large celery stalks (10 ounces total,
　　285g), strings removed with
　　vegetable peeler, cut into feed-tube
　　lengths
6 small red new potatoes (12 ounces
　　total, 340g), unpeeled
2 teaspoons fresh thyme or ½
　　teaspoon dried
½ teaspoon salt
2 small zucchini (6 ounces total,
　　170g), cut into feed-tube lengths

This is a contemporary version of the old-fashioned chicken roasted in a covered pot. Broiling the chicken briefly before baking it produces golden-brown skin and succulent, juicy meat. Choose vegetables that reflect the season — tiny peas or asparagus in the spring, diced turnips and rutabaga in the fall.

Fifteen minutes before broiling, place rack 9 inches (23cm) from heat and preheat broiler. Have casserole or roasting pan just large enough to hold chickens ready.

Combine salt, paprika and pepper in small dish. Sprinkle cavities of chickens with half of seasoning mixture. Divide parsley sprigs, bay leaves and celery tops between birds and place in cavities. Rub skin with 1 tablespoon of oil and sprinkle with remaining seasoning. Fold wings up over neck and tuck legs in close to body. Place in roasting pan and broil for 6 minutes, turning pan around after 3 minutes to color chickens evenly. (If broiler is shallow, broil chickens on broiler pan and transfer to casserole or roasting pan.)

Metal Blade: Put parsley in work bowl and turn on machine. Drop garlic and onion through feed tube and process until minced.

Thick (6mm) or All Purpose Slicing Disc (4mm): Stand carrots in feed tube and use firm pressure to slice. Stand celery in feed tube and use medium pressure to slice.

Place vegetables in mixing bowl with potatoes, remaining oil, thyme, salt and pepper and toss gently. Arrange around outer edge of roasting pan.

Place rack in center of oven and preheat to 400°F (205°C). Cover pan and bake for 60 minutes.

Thick (6mm) or All Purpose Slicing Disc (4mm): Stand zucchini in feed tube and use medium pressure to slice.

Add to other vegetables in pan. Cover and bake until chicken thighs feel firm and juices run clear — about 10 minutes longer. Serve immediately.

Makes 6 to 8 servings.

CURRIED CHICKEN

This delicious curry sauce is flavored to please American palates; it's complex and mildly spicy, but it won't bring tears to your eyes. Commercially blended curry powders vary widely from mild to searingly hot. Experience will tell you which one suits your taste; I use one imported from India. Condiments are a must with curry, adding wonderful taste and textural contrast to the meal. For entertaining, I offer all of them; for family dinners, just two or three.

Curry Sauce
- 2 large garlic cloves, peeled
- 3 medium onions (1 pound total, 455g), peeled and quartered
- 2 tablespoons unsalted butter
- 2 tablespoons flour
- 1 large Granny Smith apple (8 ounces, 225g), unpeeled, cored and quartered
- 2 medium carrots (12 ounces total, 340g), trimmed and cut into 1-inch (2.5cm) pieces
- 3 medium celery stalks (7 ounces total, 200g), strings removed with vegetable peeler and cut into 1-inch (2.5cm) pieces
- 3 cups (720ml) Chicken Stock (see Index), or chicken broth
- 3/4 cup (180ml) plain yogurt
- 1/2 cup dried currants (2 1/2 ounces, 70g)
- 1/4 cup (60ml) tomato paste
- 1 tablespoon curry powder, or to taste
- 1/2 teaspoon cinnamon
- 1/2 teaspoon salt
- Freshly ground pepper

Chicken
- 1 tablespoon unsalted butter
- 1 tablespoon safflower oil
- 4 whole chicken breasts (3 1/2 to 4 pounds total, 1.5 to 1.8kg), skinned, boned and cut into 1 1/2-inch (4cm) cubes

Garnish
- 2 tablespoons cilantro, or fresh coriander, leaves

Condiments (list follows)

Metal Blade: Turn on machine, drop garlic through feed tube and process until minced. Add onion and pulse to mince.

Melt butter in 12-inch (30cm) sauté pan and add contents of work bowl. Cook gently until soft but not brown — about 10 minutes. Stir in flour and remove from heat.

Metal Blade: Process apple, carrots, and celery in separate batches until minced; add them to pan.

Add stock or broth, yogurt, currants, tomato paste, curry powder, cinnamon, salt and pepper and stir to combine. Cover and cook gently, stirring often, for 40 minutes.

Sauce can be refrigerated up to 2 days. Reheat gently, adding more stock or broth if it is too thick.

Melt butter and oil in 12-inch (30cm) skillet and add chicken. Cover and cook, shaking pan several times, just until chicken turns opaque — about 1 1/2 minutes. Do not overcook. Chicken can be cooked 1 day in advance and refrigerated.

Fold chicken into sauce and cook only until heated through. Do not overcook. Serve with rice and garnish with cilantro. Serve with an assortment of condiments.

Makes 8 servings.

NOTE: Lamb and shrimp are also good in this sauce. Cook them separately, like chicken, and reheat briefly in sauce just before serving. This method keeps meat tender and juicy.

Condiments

1 cup dry roasted peanuts (5 ounces, 140g)
Whites of 3 hard-cooked eggs
Yolks of 3 hard-cooked eggs
12 slices well cooked bacon, broken in half
1 3 by 3-inch (8 by 8cm) square fresh coconut (see NOTE)
1½ cups seedless red or green grapes

2 medium red or green peppers (12 ounces total, 340g)
1 cup sweet-pickle slices, cut into ¼-inch (6mm) strips
1½ cups tiny peas, steamed
1 large avocado (8 ounces, 225g), cut into ½-inch (12mm) dice and tossed with 1 tablespoon fresh lemon juice

As each ingredient is processed, remove from work bowl and place in individual small dishes. Wipe out work bowl with paper towel as necessary between batches.

Metal Blade: Process peanuts by pulsing until coarsely chopped. Process egg whites by pulsing until coarsely chopped. Process yolks until finely chopped. Process bacon until finely chopped.

Fine Shredding Disc: Use firm pressure to shred coconut.

All Purpose Slicing Disc (4mm): Use light pressure to slice grapes.

Stand peppers on cutting board. Use sharp knife to cut 3 or 4 vertical slices, leaving only core and stem. Remove any membrane from slices.

Medium Slicing Disc (3mm): Stack pepper slices and stand them lengthwise in feed tube, wedging them in tightly to hold. Use light pressure to slice.

Line slices up on cutting board and use knife to cut into square dice.

All condiments, except peas and avocado, can be prepared 1 day in advance, wrapped airtight and refrigerated.

NOTE: To prepare fresh coconut, see page 60.

CHICKEN HASH WITH WILD RICE

The Larousse Gastronomique, *the bible of French cuisine, lists 29 different versions of hash — each of them ample proof that it's an ingenious and elegant way to present leftovers. This one is, too — a flavorful combination of moist poultry and nutty wild rice with bits of fresh vegetables and a smooth cheese-flavored sauce.*

Mornay Sauce

1 ounce (30g) imported Parmesan cheese, at room temperature
1 ounce (30g) mozzarella cheese
3 tablespoons unsalted butter
3 tablespoons flour
1 1/2 cups (360ml) milk
1/4 teaspoon salt
Freshly grated nutmeg
Freshly ground white pepper

Hash

1/2 cup loosely packed parsley leaves
6 large shallots (4 1/2 ounces total, 130g)
1 medium celery rib (2 ounces, 55g), strings removed with vegetable peeler, cut into 1-inch (2.5cm) pieces
2 tablespoons unsalted butter
1 medium tomato (6 ounces, 170g), halved, seeded and quartered
2 cups cooked wild rice
3 cups diced cooked chicken or turkey
1 teaspoon sugar
1 1/2 teaspoons dried oregano
1 teaspoon salt
Freshly ground pepper

Fifteen minutes before baking, place rack in center of oven and preheat to 500°F (260°C). Have 8 by 13-inch (20 by 33cm) oval gratin dish ready (7-cup, (1.7L) capacity).

Metal Blade: Process both cheeses until very fine.

Melt butter in 1-quart (1L) saucepan. Add flour and cook gently, stirring often, for 2 minutes. Add milk, salt, nutmeg and pepper and stir constantly until thick. Remove from heat and cool slightly. Stir in cheeses and adjust seasoning.

Makes 1 1/2 cups (360ml).

Metal Blade: Process parsley until minced; remove and reserve. Turn on machine, drop shallots and celery through feed tube and process until minced.

Melt butter in 10-inch (25cm) skillet over medium heat. Add shallots and celery and cook until very soft but not brown — about 8 minutes.

Metal Blade: Process tomato by pulsing until coarsely chopped.

Add to skillet with rice, chicken, sugar, oregano, salt, pepper and reserved parsley and cook just until heated through — about 2 minutes. Remove from heat and stir in 1 cup (240ml) of Mornay sauce. Transfer to gratin pan. Hash can be prepared to this point 1 day in advance. Bring to room temperature before baking. Bake for 20 minutes. Spoon remaining sauce over top and broil 6 inches (15cm) from heat until brown and bubbly. Serve immediately.

Makes 6 servings.

1 small onion (2 ounces, 55g), peeled
   and halved
2 slices firm white bread (2 ounces
   total, 55g), quartered
1 teaspoon curry powder
1 teaspoon salt
1/2 teaspoon Hungarian paprika
   Freshly ground white pepper
1/2 cup (120ml) whipping cream
3 tablespoons unsalted butter,
   softened
5 chicken thighs with skin, bones

and tendons removed, chilled and
cut into 1-inch (2.5cm) pieces (10
ounces meat, 285g)
3 boneless chicken-breast halves,
   with skin and tendons removed,
   chilled and cut into 1-inch (2.5cm)
   pieces (10 ounces meat, 285g)
4 tablespoons unsalted butter
4 tablespoons safflower oil
   Buttered Cucumbers (recipe
   follows)

CURRIED
CHICKEN
MEDALLIONS
WITH
BUTTERED
CUCUMBERS

*This recipe is a
lesson in economy,
cleverly disguised
by great taste and
style of
presentation. The
medallions are
patties of coarsely
ground white and
dark meat — a
combination that
is especially
tender and juicy.
And the food
processor, not a
meat grinder, does
the job. The curry
flavor is very
subtle, but if you
prefer, substitute
freshly grated
nutmeg or fresh
herbs.*

Metal Blade: Turn on machine, drop onion through feed tube and process until minced. Add bread, curry powder, salt, paprika, pepper, cream and butter and process for 5 seconds; remove and reserve. Put both dark and white meat in work bowl and pulse to chop coarsely. Return reserved mixture to work bowl and pulse just until combined — about 6 times. Do not overprocess; the meat should have some texture.

Transfer to bowl, cover and refrigerate for at least 6 hours or overnight.

With lightly floured hands, gently shape 1/4 cup of chicken mixture into 2 1/2-inch (6cm) round. Repeat with remaining chicken. The medallions can be wrapped individually and frozen. Thaw before sautéeing.

Gently heat 2 tablespoons each of butter and oil in two 10-inch (25cm) skillets. Sauté medallions, turning once, until lightly browned on both sides — about 9 minutes. Serve with Buttered Cucumbers.

Makes twelve 2 1/2-inch (6cm) patties, enough for 4 to 6 servings.

1/4 cup loosely packed parsley leaves
3 large cucumbers (2 1/4 pounds total,
   1kg), peeled, split, with seeds
   removed, cut into 2-inch (5cm)
   lengths

1 stick unsalted butter (4 ounces,
   115g), chilled
1/2 teaspoon salt
   Freshly grated nutmeg
   Freshly ground white pepper

Metal Blade: Process parsley until minced; remove and reserve.

Medium Shredding Disc: Lay cucumbers in feed tube and use light pressure to shred.

Melt 2 tablespoons of butter in 12-inch (30cm) skillet over high heat. Add cucumbers and cook until they are slightly wilted and most of their liquid has cooked away — about 15 minutes. Season with salt, nutmeg and pepper. Cut remaining butter into 5 pieces. Whisk in, one piece at a time, waiting until each piece is incorporated before adding another. When all butter is added, stir in parsley and adjust seasoning.

Makes 2 2/3 cups.

GLAZED CORNISH HENS STUFFED WITH FRUIT PILAF

These tender and juicy little birds are hybrids. Each one weighs from 1¹/₄ to 1¹/₂ pounds (570 to 680g) — perfect for an individual serving. For entertaining, they can be casual or elegant; they are always practical. When serving them at a formal dinner, I remove the backbone with kitchen shears to make them easier to eat. Most Cornish hens are sold frozen. If allowed to thaw slowly in the refrigerator and cooked at the high temperature indicated, they are excellent.

Hens

8 Cornish hens, thawed slowly in refrigerator if frozen
Salt or seasoning salt
Freshly ground pepper

2 tablespoons safflower oil
1 recipe Fruit, Rice and Wheat Berry Pilaf (see Index)

Glaze

²/₃ cup (160ml) apricot preserves

1 tablespoon water

Garnish

1 medium seedless orange, scored, cut flat at bottom, halved if necessary to fit feed tube

2 bunches watercress or parsley sprigs

Fifteen minutes before baking, place rack in center of oven and preheat to 450°F (230°C). Select roasting pan(s) large enough to hold hens without touching one another.

Wash hens and pat dry. Clip wing tips. Season cavities with salt and pepper. Brush skin with oil and sprinkle with salt and pepper.

Loosely fill cavities of hens with pilaf. Tie legs together, tuck in wings and transfer to roasting pan(s). Roast for 20 minutes, reduce temperature to 350OF (175OC) and roast for 20 minutes more.

Combine preserves and water in small saucepan and cook until melted; strain.

All Purpose Slicing Disc (4mm): Stand orange in feed tube and use firm pressure to slice.

Brush hens generously with glaze and continue roasting until deep bronze — about 5 to 10 minutes. Remove from oven and let rest for 10 minutes.

Center hens on large platter. Overlap orange slices along length of platter and garnish ends of platter with watercress or parsley.

Makes 8 servings.

3 heads garlic (7 ounces total, 200g), with cloves separated but unpeeled
¾ cup (180ml) safflower oil
1 tablespoon sugar
Salt
Freshly ground pepper
4 Cornish hens, thawed in refrigerator overnight if frozen
1 teaspoon Hungarian paprika

2 tablespoons Oriental sesame oil
1 cup (240ml) Chicken Stock (see Index) or chicken broth
1 tablespoon oyster sauce
2 tablespoons ruby Port
1 teaspoon cornstarch dissolved in 1 tablespoon cold Chicken Stock or broth

ROAST CORNISH HENS WITH CARAMELIZED GARLIC

This recipe with subtle Oriental flavors is from Jean Delaveyne, chef and owner of Le Camelia, located in a suburb of Paris. Despite the large amount of garlic, slow-cooking tames its pungency into delectable sweetness. The garlic will be soft enough to spread, so crusty French bread is a perfect accompaniment.

Put garlic in rapidly boiling water to cover for 30 seconds. Drain well and run under cold water until cool enough to handle. Peel. Transfer to 1-quart (1L) saucepan and add oil. Cook very gently for 25 minutes. *Do not allow to brown.* Drain oil and reserve 1½ tablespoons. (Remainder can be used for salad dressing, garlic mayonnaise, etc.) Transfer warm garlic cloves to mixing bowl and toss thoroughly with sugar, ½ teaspoon of salt and pepper.

Heat 1½ tablespoons of oil from garlic in heavy 8-inch skillet (20cm) over medium-high heat until very hot. Add garlic, increase heat to high, and shaking pan constantly, cook it until caramelized — about 3 minutes. Remove from heat and set aside.

Fifteen minutes before baking, place rack in center of oven and preheat to 450°F (230°C).

Season hens inside and out with salt, pepper and paprika. Add sesame oil to ovenproof skillet(s) large enough to hold hens without touching. Heat sesame oil until very hot. Place hens on their sides in skillet and sear quickly, turning with tongs to second side as soon as first side is brown. Do not place hens on breast or back. Transfer to oven and bake for 15 minutes, turning twice to alternating sides. *Reduce oven heat to 400°F (205°C)* and continue baking for 30 minutes, turning them after 15 minutes. Transfer hens to heated platter and keep warm while preparing sauce.

Drain any meat drippings into 1½-quart (1.5L) saucepan. Add stock or broth, oyster sauce and Port and blend well. Bring to boil over medium heat, then cook for 3 minutes. Stir in cornstarch mixture and whisk constantly until thickened. Taste and adjust seasonings with salt and pepper, if necessary.

To serve, arrange hens on platter and surround with mounds of garlic. Spoon sauce over hens and garlic. Garlic may be eaten with hens or spread on French bread.

Makes 4 servings.

ROAST CAPON WITH GREEN PEPPERCORNS AND LIME

Roasting the capon at high temperature yields juicy meat and crisp skin, a lesson I learned from Frédy Girardet. It also splatters the oven, but the results are worth it. Lime juice and green peppercorns create a slightly astringent sauce that underscores the richness of the meat. Girardet serves this on Sautéed Belgian Endive (see Index).

1 5- to 6-pound (2.3 to 2.7kg) capon
2 tablespoons safflower oil
  Salt
  Freshly ground pepper
³/₄ cup (180ml) ruby Port
1 cup (240ml) Chicken Stock (see Index), or chicken broth
3 tablespoons green peppercorns, drained (see NOTE on page 83)
2 tablespoons fresh lime juice
1 stick unsalted butter, chilled, cut into 8 pieces
  Zest of 1 lime, removed with zester

Fifteen minutes before baking, place rack in center of oven and preheat to 475°F (245°C). Lightly oil shallow roasting pan. Rub capon with oil and season with salt and pepper. Put in pan on its side and roast for 30 minutes. Reduce temperature to 425°F (220°C) and roast for 40 minutes more. During cooking, turn bird 3 times from one side to other with tongs or spatula, being careful not to tear skin. Do not place it on its back or breast.

Transfer to platter and discard fat from pan. Put pan on stove over high heat. When it is hot, add Port and loosen any particles from bottom of pan. Add stock or broth and cook until reduced to ²/₃ cup (160ml). Return capon to pan and cook over high heat, spooning juice over bird until it is richly glazed. Transfer capon to serving platter.

Strain sauce into small non-aluminum saucepan and add green peppercorns and lime juice. Bring to boil, then whisk in butter, 1 tablespoon at a time, waiting until each piece is incorporated before adding another. Adjust seasoning. Pour sauce over capon and garnish with lime zest. Serve immediately.

Makes 6 servings.

THANKSGIVING DINNER

Maple Glazed Pecans
Smoked Oyster Soup with Spinach and Watercress
Roast Turkey with Sausage and Chestnut Stuffing
Carrots and Rutabagas with Honey and Lemon
Brussels Sprouts with Cream and Garlic
Cranberry Chutney
Golden Harvest Rolls
Chilled Pumpkin Soufflé
French Apple Tart
Lemon Sherbet

Turkey Stock

Turkey heart, gizzard and neck
1 medium onion (5 ounces, 140g), peeled and halved
1 large carrot (4 ounces, 115g), cut into 2-inch (5cm) pieces
1 large celery stalk (3 ounces, 85g), including leafy top, cut into 2-inch (5cm) pieces
2 parsley sprigs
1/4 teaspoon salt
Water to cover

Turkey

1 16- to 18-pound (7.3 to 8kg) turkey, preferably fresh
2 tablespoons salt
1/2 teaspoon freshly ground pepper
3 tablespoons safflower oil
Sausage and Chestnut Stuffing (recipe follows)

Put turkey heart, gizzard, neck, onion, carrot, celery, parsley and salt in 3-quart (3L) saucepan and add water to cover. Cover and cook gently for 1 1/2 hours. Remove heart and neck meat and cut into 1/4-inch (6mm) dice for stuffing. Reserve gizzard for stuffing or gravy, if desired. Strain stock and discard vegetables.

Fifteen minutes before baking, place rack in center of oven and preheat to 475°F (245°C).

Rinse body and neck cavities of turkey, drain and pat dry. Mix salt and pepper and sprinkle 1 teaspoon into each cavity. Spoon stuffing loosely into each cavity; do not pack tightly since stuffing expands as it cooks. Place any extra stuffing in 1-quart (1L) casserole. Tie turkey legs together, tuck in wings and skewer to close. Blunt the points of skewers with several layers of foil. Brush with remaining oil and sprinkle with remaining seasoning.

Working on large, flat surface, cut three 3-foot (90cm) lengths of heavy-duty aluminum foil. Place them next to each other to make a sheet that measures 3 feet by 4 1/2 feet (90 by 135cm). Form one continuous piece of foil by double-folding edges where they meet. Make sure seams are tightly sealed; foil must be airtight. Carefully fit foil into pan and make sure seams are still sealed. Place turkey in pan and bring foil up over sides of turkey, leaving airspace on sides and top of turkey. Seal to form airtight package.

Bake in preheated oven for 2 1/2 hours. Open foil very carefully; there will be a lot of steam. Brush breast with remaining 1 tablespoon of oil. Fold foil down to protect leg and thigh area, but leave breast exposed. Continue to cook until breast is deep brown and internal temperature is 170°F (75°C) — about 20 or 30 more minutes. (To read temperature, insert an instant-reading thermometer into thigh meat right next to breast. Do not push it through to bone.) Remove bird from oven, bring foil up over it, and let it stand for 20 minutes before carving.

Makes 12 to 14 servings.

ROAST TURKEY

Encasing the turkey in foil for roasting is a recent discovery. I'm sure I'll never use another method because this one produces such juicy, succulent meat. Once it's in the oven, the turkey requires no basting or other attention until the last half hour. Piecing together the foil is something of a challenge, but once mastered, it's quite easy to do.

SAUSAGE AND CHESTNUT STUFFING

Like most of us, I'm a staunch traditionalist when it comes to stuffing a turkey. I've used Sausage and Chestnut Stuffing almost as long as I've been cooking Thanksgiving dinner.

3 medium onions (12 ounces total, 340g), peeled and quartered
Turkey liver, cut into $1/8$-inch (3mm) dice
1 pound (455g) bulk pork sausage, preferably "hot", crumbled
3 large celery stalks (9 ounces total, 255g), strings removed with vegetable peeler, cut into 2-inch (5cm) pieces
1 pound (455g) day-old French bread, including crust, cut into

$1/2$-inch (12mm) cubes (about 8 to 10 cups)
1 pound (455g) fresh chestnuts, peeled (see NOTE)
1 teaspoon crumbled dried sage
1 teaspoon ground thyme
1 cup (240ml) Turkey Stock (see previous recipe)
1 to $1 1/2$ cups (240 to 360ml) Half and Half or light cream
$1/2$ teaspoon salt, or to taste
Freshly ground pepper

Metal Blade: Process onions by pulsing to chop them coarsely.

Transfer to 10-inch (25cm) skillet with turkey liver and sausage. Cook gently for 25 minutes. Transfer to large mixing bowl.

Metal Blade: Process celery by pulsing to chop coarsely.

Add to mixing bowl along with bread, chestnuts, sage, thyme, heart and neck meat and combine. Add 1 cup (240ml) each of turkey stock and Half and Half and toss to combine. The stuffing should be moist, but not wet or soggy. If it is too dry, add remaining cream as necessary. Taste and adjust seasoning. The stuffing should be highly seasoned.

Makes enough for 18-pound (8kg) turkey.

NOTE: To peel chestnuts, slice $1/8$-inch (3mm) of shell from flat side of each one. Put in pan with cold water to cover and bring to boil. Cook for 1 minute. Use slotted spoon to remove several at a time and let them cool only until they can be easily handled. Then peel shells and inner skins; they are easier to peel while still warm.

TURKEY BREAST WITH FRESH ORANGE AND PORT SAUCE

The inspiration for this is a veal dish served at Michel Guérard's restaurant in Eugénie-les-Bains, France. It is very low in both calories and fat, an appealing characteristic of Guérard's "cuisine-minceur" cooking. You can use veal if you prefer, but for both flavor and value, turkey breast is excellent. Fresh turkey breasts are readily available. If you can't find one, ask your butcher to order it.

1 5- to 6-pound (2.3 to 2.7kg) fresh turkey breast
1 teaspoon salt
Freshly ground pepper
1 tablespoon safflower oil
1 tablespoon unsalted butter
2 large shallots (1 ounce total, 30g), peeled
1 teaspoon orange zest, removed with zester or grater
½ cup (120ml) Port wine
⅔ cup (160ml) fresh orange juice
1 cup (240ml) Chicken Stock (see Index), or chicken broth
1 medium orange, unpeeled, scored, cut flat at bottom, halved if necessary to fit feed tube
Watercress sprigs

Fifteen minutes before baking, place rack in center of oven and preheat to 450°F (230°C). Have 12-inch (30cm) ovenproof skillet ready.

Use boning knife to cut each breast half from bone in one piece. With butcher's cord, tie each piece into neat cylinder and season with salt and pepper. Melt butter and oil in skillet over high heat. When hot, quickly sear breast pieces, one at a time, and reserve. Discard fat.

Metal Blade: Turn on machine, drop shallots and orange zest through feed tube and process until minced. Add Port, orange juice, stock or broth, and pepper and process for 2 seconds.

Add mixture to skillet and bring to boil over high heat. Add turkey and bake until meat registers 170°F (75°C) on instant-reading thermometer, basting often with sauce — about 35 minutes. Transfer meat to platter and cover with tent of aluminum foil to keep warm while finishing sauce. Over medium-high heat, cook sauce in skillet until reduced to ⅔ cup (160ml) — about 15 minutes.

All Purpose Slicing Disc (4mm): Stand orange in feed tube and use firm pressure to slice.

Cut turkey into thin slices and arrange in overlapping slices on warm serving platter. Drizzle with sauce and garnish with watercress sprigs and orange slices. Serve immediately.

Makes 8 servings.

½ cup loosely packed parsley leaves
3 large garlic cloves, peeled
¾ cup (180ml) fresh lemon juice
½ cup (120ml) extra-virgin olive oil
2 teaspoons dried rosemary
1 teaspoon salt

Freshly ground pepper
1 5- to 6-pound (2.3 to 2.7kg) fresh turkey breast
6 tablespoons unsalted butter, chilled and cut into 6 pieces
3 tablespoons drained capers

Metal Blade: Put parsley in work bowl and turn on machine. Drop garlic through feed tube and process until minced. Add lemon juice, oil, rosemary, ½ teaspoon of salt and pepper and process for 3 seconds.

Transfer to large plastic bag and add turkey. Seal airtight and marinate for 4 hours at room temperature or refrigerate overnight. Bring to room temperature before proceeding.

Fifteen minutes before baking, place rack in center of oven and preheat to 400°F (205°C).

Remove turkey from marinade; reserve marinade. Pat turkey dry and season with remaining salt and pepper. Place turkey in roasting pan and bake for ½ hour. Baste periodically with marinade (reserving ⅔ cup, 160ml, for sauce) while cooking until thermometer registers 165°F (75°C) — about 1 hour longer. Let rest while finishing sauce.

Heat ⅔ cup (160ml) of marinade in 1-quart (1L) non-aluminum saucepan. When hot, whisk in butter one piece at a time, waiting until each piece melts before adding another. Stir in capers, heat through, but do not allow to boil. Adjust seasoning.

Serve turkey in thin slices, with Lemon Caper Sauce.

Makes 8 to 10 servings.

Talking Turkey

★ Once available only as a big bird, turkey can now be bought in parts. Not only legs, wings, thighs and breast sections, but even sliced cutlets from the breast, are in the butchers' display at many supermarkets. Turkey is moderately priced and it is suited to a wide variety of culinary treatments. Drumsticks, spread lavishly with barbecue sauce and grilled, are delicious and easy food for summer, while cutlets from the breast can be prepared in the same way as ultra-expensive veal scallops. The recipes on both these pages substitute turkey breast for veal roast.

MARINATED TURKEY BREAST WITH LEMON AND CAPER SAUCE

The first time I served this, I had trouble convincing my guests that it was turkey and not a ruinously expensive veal roast. That's how tender and succulent turkey is when marinated, and roasted at a high temperature. Part of the marinade is reserved and enriched with butter and capers for the sauce.

BREASTS OF DUCK WITH HONEY AND LEMON

This dish from Roger Vergé is unquestionably one of the most delicious ways to prepare duck. It's time-consuming, but well worth the effort for a special occasion. I've divided the preparation into steps so most of it can be done in advance. Vergé serves Corn Pancakes with the duck (see Abby Mandel's Cuisinart Classroom). The French Potato Cake (see Index) is also delicious with it.

Duck
3 ducks, 4½ to 5 pounds (2 to 2.3kg) each

1 tablespoon salt
Freshly ground pepper

Sauce
Duck carcasses
1 large onion (8 ounces, 225g), peeled and quartered
2 large carrots (8 ounces total, 225g), cut into 1-inch (2.5cm) pieces
4 medium celery ribs (8 ounces total, 225g), strings removed with vegetable peeler, cut into 1-inch (2.5cm) pieces
8 parsley sprigs
2 large garlic cloves, peeled and halved
1 bay leaf
2 teaspoons fresh thyme or ½

teaspoon dried
3 cups (720ml) light, fruity red wine, like Beaujolais
1 tablespoon tomato paste
3 cups (720ml) Veal Stock (see Index)
⅛ teaspoon cornstarch
1 teaspoon water
1 tablespoon honey
2 tablespoons strained fresh lemon juice
1 stick unsalted butter (4 ounces, 115g), chilled
Salt
Freshly ground pepper

Garnish
1 lemon
½ cup (120ml) water

6 tablespoons confectioners' sugar

Fifteen minutes before baking, place rack in center of oven and preheat to 500°F (260°C). Have large shallow baking pan(s) ready.

Remove gizzards and livers from ducks; they will not be used in this preparation. Save necks for sauce. Wash ducks and pat dry. Remove large pieces of fat from around cavities. Season with salt and pepper.

Put ducks, breast side up, in baking pan(s). (If necessary, use 2 pans so birds don't touch.) Bake for 12 minutes. Turn and bake for 13 minutes more. Remove from oven and let cool for 30 minutes. Discard fat, but do not wash pan.

Place ducks breast side up on cutting board. Cut along carcass with boning knife to remove thigh and leg in one piece. Cut breast meat from carcass in 1 piece. Discard skin and fat from breasts; reserve thighs and legs for another use; they will not be needed in this preparation. Ducks can be cooked 2 days in advance and refrigerated. Bring to room temperature before proceeding.

Fifteen minutes before cooking sauce, place rack in center of oven and preheat to 500°F (260°C).

Use kitchen shears to cut each carcass into 6 pieces. Put these pieces in roasting pan with necks and bake for 30 minutes, stirring every 10 minutes. Discard fat.

Metal Blade: Process onion, carrots and celery in 2 batches, pulsing until they are coarsely chopped.

Add to roasting pan along with parsley, garlic, bay leaf and thyme, and roast for 10 minutes more. Remove from oven and decrease temperature to 250°F (120°C).

Add wine and tomato paste to pan and boil, uncovered, on top of stove until reduced to ³/₄ cup (180ml) — about 18 minutes. Add stock, return pan to oven and bake for 30 minutes.

Discard bones. Place strainer lined with double thickness of cheesecloth over bowl. Strain vegetables, pressing out as much liquid as possible. You should have about 4 ¹/₂ cups (1L) of liquid. Refrigerate until fat solidifies, then remove and discard fat. Transfer liquid to 2-quart (2L) saucepan and boil until reduced to 1 ¹/₄ cups (300ml) — about 35 minutes. As liquid cooks, skim surface as necessary. Mix cornstarch with 1 teaspoon of water; add to sauce and cook for 2 minutes.

Cook honey in 1-quart (1L) saucepan over medium-high heat until deep gold, but not dark — about 3 minutes. Add lemon juice and cook, stirring often, for 2 minutes. Stir in reduced duck sauce. Sauce can be prepared up to 2 days in advance and refrigerated.

Use vegetable peeler to remove zest from lemon in long strips. Cut strips into long shreds about ¹/₁₆ inch (2mm) wide. Cook in small saucepan with water and sugar, stirring constantly, until syrup thickens enough to coat zest; do not let syrup brown. Garnish can be made up to 1 week in advance. Refrigerate zest in syrup and reheat gently at serving time.

To serve, gently reheat sauce. Cut 6 tablespoons of butter into 6 pieces. When sauce is hot, whisk in butter, 1 piece at a time, waiting until each piece is fully incorporated before adding another. Adjust seasoning and keep warm until serving time.

Melt remaining butter in 10-inch (25cm) skillet over high heat. When hot, decrease heat to medium-high, place duck breasts in pan and cook, turning once — about 2 minutes for rare. Cut each breast vertically into 7 or 8 diagonal slices. Reassemble each breast and spoon about 3 tablespoons of sauce over it. Garnish each with 4 or 5 strands of lemon zest and serve immediately.

Makes 6 servings.

NOTE: Legs and thighs can be reheated and used in salad of mixed greens with hot vinaigrette. Heat well flavored red-wine vinaigrette with splash of port and add duck gizzard and liver. Pour over greens and arrange legs and thighs over top.

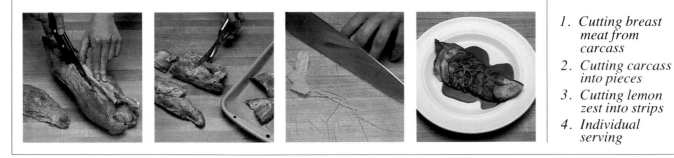

1. *Cutting breast meat from carcass*
2. *Cutting carcass into pieces*
3. *Cutting lemon zest into strips*
4. *Individual serving*

DUCK CURRY WITH CABBAGE AND APPLES

The duck is steamed in its skin to keep the meat juicy, but the skin and all the fat are then removed. Only the duck meat is used in the curry. Everything can be used in other dishes, however: the carcasses for duck stock, the rendered fat for frying potatoes, and the skin for crisp cracklings. Chicken can be substituted for the duck; just be careful not to overcook it. It will take less time. Serve with Spicy Eggplant with Yogurt, and Indian Bread Puffs (see Index).

Duck
- 2 ducks, about 5 pounds (2.3kg) each
- 2 cups (480ml) water
- 1/4 cup (60ml) cider vinegar
- 1 cinnamon stick
- 4 whole cloves
- 1 1/2 tablespoons unsalted butter
- 1 1/2 tablespoons safflower oil

Vegetables
- 1 3/4-inch (2cm) cube fresh ginger, peeled
- 2 medium onions (12 ounces total, 340g), peeled
- 2 tablespoons unsalted butter
- 1 pound (455g) green cabbage, cored and cut to fit feed tube
- 2 large Granny Smith apples (1 pound total, 455g), peeled, halved and cored
- 1 1/2 to 2 cups (360 to 480ml) Chicken Stock (see Index), or chicken broth
- 1/4 cup (60ml) tomato paste
- 1/4 cup (60ml) cider vinegar
- 1 tablespoon ground coriander
- 2 teaspoons salt
- 1 teaspoon crushed red pepper flakes
- 1/2 teaspoon cinnamon
- 1/4 teaspoon turmeric
- 1/4 cup snipped fresh chives

Cut legs and thighs from ducks. Carefully cut skin from breast area. With boning knife, cut along breastbone to remove each breast half in 1 piece.

Put water, vinegar, cinnamon and cloves in bottom of steamer pan. Insert steamer and add legs and thighs. If there is any exposed flesh, cut skin from carcass and drape it over. Cover and cook over medium heat until tender — about 25 minutes. When cool enough to handle, discard skin and cut meat into 1-inch (2.5cm) strips.

Melt butter and oil in 12-inch (30cm) skillet over medium-high heat. When hot, add breasts and cook, turning only once — about 1 1/2 minutes per side for rare. Cut horizontally into 1/3-inch (8mm) slices; reserve. Discard butter and oil and reserve skillet for vegetable preparation.

Metal Blade: Turn on machine, drop ginger through feed tube and process until minced; remove and reserve.

Thin Slicing Disc (2mm): Use firm pressure to slice onions.

Melt butter in skillet. Add onions and cook gently until soft but not brown — about 8 minutes.

Thin Slicing Disc (2mm): Use firm pressure to slice cabbage.

French Fry Disc: Use medium pressure to cut one apple. (If you do not have French Fry Disc, see page 229.)

Add cabbage, processed apple, ginger, 1 1/2 cups (360ml) of stock or broth, tomato paste, vinegar, coriander, salt, red pepper flakes, cinnamon and turmeric. Cover and cook over medium heat for 20 minutes.

French Fry Disc: Use medium pressure to cut remaining apple.

Add to skillet with thigh and leg meat and stir gently. The mixture should be very moist, but not fluid. Add more broth, if necessary. Cover and cook just until apple begins to soften — about 5 to 6 minutes. Add breast meat and cook only until hot. Do not overcook. Adjust seasoning and serve, sprinkled with chives. Can be prepared up to point of adding breast meat 1 day in advance, and refrigerated. Wrap cooked breast separately and reserve. To reheat, stir in additional $^1/_2$ to $^3/_4$ cup (120 to 180ml) chicken broth, as needed, and breast meat. Cook just until heated through.

Makes 6 to 8 servings.

Ginger-Beef Stir-Fry

185   *Poultry*

GINGER-BEEF STIR-FRY

Flank steak is ideal for quick cooking — it is lean, tender and tasty, and it slices perfectly in the food processor.

1¼ pounds (565g) flank steak, trimmed of fat
2 large garlic cloves, peeled
1 1 by ½-inch (2.5cm by 12mm) piece fresh ginger root, peeled
1 jalapeño pepper, seeded, if desired (see NOTE
4 large scallions (3½ ounces total, 100g), including green tops, cut into 1-inch (2.5cm) pieces
1 tablespoon light-brown sugar

1 teaspoon Oriental sesame oil
¾ teaspoon salt
1 medium red bell pepper (5 ounces, 140g)
30 medium snow peas (4 ounces total, 115g), with strings removed
8 large mushrooms (4 ounces total, 115g), quartered
3 tablespoons peanut oil
2 tablespoons oyster sauce

Cut meat to fit feed tube so grain will be perpendicular to slicing disc. Place on baking sheet lined with waxed paper and freeze until firm but not solid; you should be able to pierce it through with tip of sharp knife. (Meat can be frozen up to 2 months. When it is firm, wrap each piece individually and seal in airtight bag. When ready to use, thaw to firmness described above.)

Metal Blade: Turn on machine, drop garlic, ginger and pepper through feed tube and process until minced. Add scallions and process until minced. Add sugar, sesame oil and ½ teaspoon of salt and process until mixed — 5 seconds.

Extra Thick (8mm) or Thick (6mm) Slicing Disc: Stand meat in feed tube and use firm pressure to slice.

Transfer meat and marinade to large plastic food bag and marinate for at least 30 minutes at room temperature or up to 8 hours in refrigerator.

Stand red pepper on cutting board. Use sharp knife to cut off sides in 3 or 4 vertical slices, leaving only core and stem. Trim any membrane from slices.

All Purpose Slicing Disc (4mm): Stack slices and stand them lengthwise in feed tube wedging them in tightly to hold. Use light pressure to slice.

Heat 2 tablespoons of peanut oil in wok or 12-inch (30cm) skillet. Add meat and marinade and stir-fry just until partially cooked — about 3 minutes. Meat should still be pink in center. Remove and reserve.

Heat remaining oil in same pan and add snow peas, mushrooms and remaining salt. Stir fry over medium-high heat until vegetables begin to soften — about 2 minutes. Add red peppers and cook until they are tender but still crisp — about 1 more minute. Return meat, add oyster sauce, toss gently and cook just until heated through — 1 to 2 minutes. Adjust seasoning and serve immediately.

Makes 6 servings.

NOTE: It's best to wear rubber gloves when handling hot chiles like serranos and jalapeños. Oil in seeds and veins can irritate skin and eyes.

2 tablespoons safflower oil
2 tablespoons unsalted butter
2 pounds (910g) stewing beef, cut
   into 1-inch (2.5cm) cubes (see
   NOTE)
3/4 teaspoon salt
   Freshly ground pepper
2 large garlic cloves, peeled
2 medium onions (12 ounces total,
   340g), peeled

3/4 cup (180ml) dry red wine
3/4 cup (180ml) Beef Stock (see Index),
   or beef broth
2 tablespoons red-wine vinegar
1 tablespoon tomato paste
1 1/2 cups fresh cranberries (7 1/2 ounces,
   215g)
1/3 cup firmly packed light brown
   sugar (2 2/3 ounces, 75g)
2 tablespoons flour

BEEF STEW WITH CRANBERRIES

This is a homespun stew that's been given a new twist by the sweet and sour flavors of cranberries and brown sugar. Slow cooking makes the meat tender and the onions sweet. Like all stews, it's even better reheated; if possible, plan to make it at least a day before serving. Serve with buttered rice or noodles.

Heat 1 tablespoon each of oil and butter in 6-quart (6L) pot. When it is hot, add half the beef and brown it well on all sides; remove and reserve. Heat remaining oil and butter and brown remaining meat. Remove pot from heat, remove meat and discard fat. Return meat to pot and toss with 1/2 teaspoon of salt and freshly ground pepper.

Metal Blade: Turn on machine, drop garlic through feed tube and process until minced; add to pot.

Medium Shredding Disc: Use firm pressure to shred onions. Use slotted spoon to lift onions from their juice and add to pot. Discard juice.

Add wine, stock or broth, vinegar, tomato paste and remaining 1/4 teaspoon of salt to pot and bring to boil. Reduce to simmer, cover and cook until meat is tender — about 2 hours.

Metal Blade: Pulse to chop cranberries coarsely with brown sugar and flour.

Add to pot, stir well and cook for 10 minutes longer.

Can be served immediately, but best if made up to 4 days in advance and reheated.

Makes 6 servings.

NOTE: 2 pounds (910g) of pork or lamb, cut into 1-inch (2.5cm) cubes, can be substituted for beef.

RIO GRANDE TOSTADO CASSEROLE

The spicy flavors of Tex-Mex cooking are very well suited to this easy family-style casserole.

2 large garlic cloves, peeled
1 medium onion (5 ounces, 140g), peeled and quartered
1 pound (455g) lean beef chuck, cut into 1-inch (2.5cm) cubes
1/4 cup (60ml) tomato paste
1 1/4 teaspoons salt
1 teaspoon dried red chiles
1 teaspoon ground cumin
1 teaspoon dried oregano
6 ounces (170g) Monterey Jack cheese, cut into 6 pieces
6 ounces (170g) Colby Longhorn cheese, cut into 6 pieces
2 medium tomatoes (12 ounces total, 340g), halved, seeded and quartered

10 large scallions (8 ounces total, 225g), including green tops, cut into feed-tube lengths
2 firm, ripe avocados (1 pound total, 455g), peeled, pitted and cut flat at bottom
1 teaspoon fresh lemon juice
1 15-ounce (425g) can pinto beans, rinsed and well drained
1/4 cup cilantro, or fresh coriander, leaves
2 teaspoons red-wine vinegar
1 or 2 jalapeño or serrano peppers, cut in fine julienne
6 corn tortillas, quartered and fried until crisp
6 tablespoons sour cream

Fifteen minutes before baking, place rack in center of oven and preheat to 350°F (175°C). Butter 3-quart (3L) baking dish.

Metal Blade: Turn on machine, drop garlic through feed tube and process until minced. Add onion and beef and pulse 4 times, then process continuously until finely and uniformly chopped.

Transfer to 10-inch (25cm) skillet and cook over medium-high heat until well browned. Discard fat and stir in tomato paste, 1 teaspoon of salt, chiles, cumin and oregano.

Metal Blade: Process both cheeses together until finely chopped; remove and reserve. Pulse to chop tomatoes coarsely; transfer to strainer and let drain.

Medium (3mm) or All Purpose Slicing Disc (4mm): Stand scallions in feed tube and use light pressure to slice; remove and reserve.

Thick Slicing Disc (6mm): Stand avocados in feed tube and use very light pressure to slice. Remove, toss with lemon juice and reserve.

Metal Blade: Process beans, cilantro and vinegar with remaining 1/4 teaspoon of salt until smooth, stopping once to scrape work bowl.

Layer ingredients in baking dish in following sequence: meat, hot peppers, scallions, tomatoes, bean mixture, avocados and cheese. Can be prepared to this point 1 day in advance, covered airtight and refrigerated. Bring to room temperature before baking.

Bake, uncovered, until lightly browned — about 30 minutes. Remove from oven and cover with aluminum foil. Let stand for 10 minutes before serving with tortilla chips and sour cream.

Makes 6 servings.

2¼ pounds (1kg) boneless beef, like top or bottom round
6 medium onions (2¼ pounds total, 1kg), peeled
3 tablespoons safflower oil
1 tablespoon sugar
2½ tablespoons flour
1¼ cups (300ml) beer
1 cup (240ml) Beef Stock (see Index), or beef broth
1 teaspoon dried thyme
Bouquet garni (1 sprig parsley, leafy tops of 2 celery stalks and 1 whole bay leaf, wrapped in cheesecloth)
Salt to taste
Freshly ground pepper
1½ tablespoons red-wine vinegar

FLEMISH BEEF CARBONNADE

This classic recipe demonstrates the unique character of beer as a cooking ingredient. Any beer will work: flat or fresh, dark or light. Cooking the onions slowly emphasizes their natural sugar, making them very sweet and mellow, a good foil for the slightly bitter beer flavor. The Carbonnade is a great make-ahead recipe that freezes and reheats very well.

Have 3-quart (3L) casserole ready. Cut meat to fit feed tube with grain perpendicular to slicing disc. Place on baking sheet lined with waxed paper. Freeze until firm to touch, but not frozen solid; you should be able to pierce it through with tip of sharp knife.

Meat can be frozen up to 2 months. When it is firm, wrap each piece individually and seal in airtight bag. When ready to use, thaw to firmness described above.

Medium Slicing Disc (3mm): Stand onions in feed tube and use firm pressure to slice.

Heat oil in 10-inch (25cm) skillet over medium heat. Add onions, cover and cook until very soft — about 15 minutes. Add sugar, reduce heat and cook gently, uncovered, until onions are golden brown — about 40 minutes. Watch carefully so onions do not burn. Add flour and cook, stirring often, for 2 minutes. Add beer, stock or broth, thyme and bouquet garni and cook until slightly thickened — about 10 minutes.

Fifteen minutes before baking, place rack in center of oven and preheat to 350°F (175°C).

Thick Slicing Disc (6mm): Stand semi-frozen meat in feed tube and use firm pressure to slice.

Season sliced meat with salt and pepper. Spoon ⅓ of onions into casserole. Add ½ of sliced meat, then continue making layers of onions and meat, finishing with onions. Cover tightly and bake until meat is tender — about 2 to 2½ hours. Remove bouquet garni, add vinegar and stir gently. Adjust seasoning.

Makes 6 to 8 servings.

GINGER VARIATION: Peel 1 by ½-inch (2.5cm by 12mm) piece of fresh ginger and mince with metal blade. Add to onions after removing them from heat.

SLICED BEEF MIROTON

I developed this recipe for a food-processor demonstration at the Food Editors' Conference in 1976. My aim was to serve a traditional dish that followed contemporary taste and was also economical. The formula comes directly from a recipe printed in 1750, but the food processor preparation is definitely today's style.

$^1/_3$ slice white bread ($^1/_3$ ounce, 10g)
$^1/_4$ cup loosely packed parsley leaves
2 large garlic cloves, peeled
3 medium onions (1 pound total, 455g), peeled and cut to fit feed tube
5 tablespoons unsalted butter
1 tablespoon flour
2 to 3 cups (480 to 720ml) Beef Stock

(see Index), or beef broth
2 tablespoons red-wine vinegar
1 tablespoon tomato paste
$^1/_2$ teaspoon salt
Freshly ground pepper
$^1/_2$ teaspoon Dijon mustard
$1^1/_2$ pounds (680g) trimmed leftover pot roast or boiled beef, very well chilled

Fifteen minutes before baking, place rack in center of oven and preheat to 375°F (190°C). Have 14-inch (35cm) gratin pan ready. Bring 3 quarts (3L) of water to boil.

Metal Blade: Process bread and parsley until minced; remove and reserve. Turn on machine, drop garlic through feed tube and process until minced; remove and reserve.

Medium Shredding Disc: Use medium pressure to shred onions. Transfer to boiling water and cook for 5 minutes; drain well.

In 10-inch (25cm) skillet, melt 4 tablespoons of butter. Add onions and garlic and cook gently, uncovered, until lightly colored — about 15 minutes. Stir in flour and cook for 2 minutes. Add 2 cups (480ml) of stock or broth, vinegar, tomato paste, salt and pepper. Increase heat to medium and simmer for 20 minutes. Sauce should be consistency of whipping cream. If it is too thick, add additional stock or broth. Remove from heat and stir in mustard.

Cut meat to fit feed tube with grain perpendicular to slicing disc.

All Purpose Slicing Disc (4mm): Stand meat in feed tube and use firm pressure to slice.

Arrange in gratin pan, overlapping slices slightly, and pour sauce over. Melt remaining tablespoon of butter and combine with parsley and bread crumbs; sprinkle over meat.

Can be prepared to this point up to 1 day in advance and refrigerated or frozen up to 3 months. Bring to room temperature before baking. Cover and bake in preheated oven for 15 minutes. Uncover and cook until hot — about 15 minutes more. Serve immediately.

Makes 6 servings.

4 6-ounce (170g) fillets of beef
Salt
1 tablespoon green peppercorns,
  rinsed and patted dry (see NOTE
  on page 83)
4 tablespoons unsalted butter,
  softened
2 tablespoons safflower oil

2 large shallots (1 ounce total, 30g),
  peeled
1 cup (240ml) Veal Stock (see Index),
  or beef broth
¹/₄ cup (60ml) Cognac
1 tablespoon whipping cream
Freshly ground pepper

**FILLET OF
BEEF WITH
GREEN
PEPPERCORN
SAUCE**

*Pungent green
peppercorns
complement the
rich beef. The
recipe illustrates
the deglazing
technique. Liquid
— usually stock or
spirits, is added to
a sauté or roast
pan and simmered
to dissolve
coagulated juices.
The resulting
liquid is used as a
sauce base or
added to a sauce
base to enhance
flavor. The
technique and
recipe were taught
to me by Gérard
Boyer of
Restaurant Boyer
in Reims.*

Bring meat to room temperature, pat dry and lightly salt both sides. Put peppercorns in small dish and mash them with back of spoon. Add 1 tablespoon of butter and mix well. Spread mixture evenly on fillets, about ¹/₂ teaspoon per side.

Heat oil over medium-high heat in heavy 12-inch (30cm) skillet. When it is very hot, arrange fillets in pan, making sure they do not touch each other. Cook, turning only once, until meat is done as desired. Transfer to warm platter and cover with tent of aluminum foil.

Metal Blade: Turn on machine, drop shallots through feed tube and process until minced.

Discard fat from skillet and return it to medium-high heat. Add shallots and scrape up any particles from bottom of pan. Cook until soft — about 2 minutes. Add stock or broth and Cognac and cook until reduced to ²/₃ cup (160ml). Strain and return to skillet over medium heat. Cut remaining 3 tablespoons of butter into thirds. Whisk in one piece at a time, waiting until each is fully incorporated before adding another. When butter has been added, add cream and adjust seasoning. Do not allow to boil.

Spoon about 3 tablespoons of sauce over each piece of meat and serve immediately.

Makes 4 servings.

*Fillet of Beef with
Green Peppercorn*

SLICED CORNED BEEF WITH WHIPPED HORSERADISH CREAM

A friend persuaded me to try this traditional Irish favorite. I've prepared it for every St. Patrick's Day since, and at other times as well. The do-ahead cooking has several advantages. Not only is most of the work done before serving time, but much of the fat can easily be removed after the meat is refrigerated.

6 pounds (2.7kg) corned beef brisket
2 medium onions (8 ounces total, 225g), peeled and quartered
2 large garlic cloves, peeled
2 small leafy celery ribs (2 ounces total, 55g), cut into thirds
1 bay leaf
Whipped Horseradish Cream (recipe follows)

Put beef in 8-quart (8L) pot with onion, garlic, celery and bay leaf, add water to cover and simmer just until tender — from 4 to 5 hours. To ensure neat slices, do not overcook. Remove meat from cooking liquid. Cool, then wrap airtight and refrigerate overnight.

Fifteen minutes before baking, place rack in center of oven and preheat to 350°F (175°C).

Trim all fat from meat and cut to fit feed tube with grain perpendicular to slicing disc.

All Purpose Slicing Disc (4mm): Stand well chilled meat in feed tube and use medium pressure to slice.

Overlap slices on piece of aluminum foil. Cover with another piece of foil and crimp edges to seal. Bake until heated through — about 15 to 17 minutes. Serve with Whipped Horseradish Cream (recipe follows).

Makes 6 to 8 servings.

WHIPPED HORSERADISH CREAM

1 medium garlic clove, peeled
1 1½ by 1½-inch (4 by 4cm) piece fresh horseradish (1½ ounces, 45g)
1 cup (240ml) whipping cream, chilled
2 teaspoons red-wine vinegar
1 teaspoon Worcestershire sauce
3 drops Tabasco sauce
½ teaspoon salt

Metal Blade: Turn on machine, drop garlic and horseradish through feed tube and process until minced. With machine running, pour cream through feed tube and process until thick. Scrape work bowl, add vinegar, Worcestershire and Tabasco sauces and salt and process for 5 seconds.

Whipped Horseradish Cream can be refrigerated up to 2 days.

Makes about 1¼ cups (300ml).

2 pounds (910g) lean veal stew meat, trimmed and cut into 1½-inch (4cm) cubes
1 teaspoon dried basil
1 teaspoon salt
   Freshly ground pepper
1 tablespoon unsalted butter
1 tablespoon safflower oil
2 large garlic cloves, peeled
2 medium onions (10 ounces total, 285g), peeled and quartered
¼ cup (60ml) dry vermouth or dry white wine
½ cup (120ml) Veal Stock (see Index) or beef broth
1 1-pound (455g) can plum tomatoes, drained
1 pound (455g) mushrooms, trimmed, with 2 opposite sides cut flat
1 small leek (5 ounces, 140g) with coarse greens trimmed, cut into feed-tube lengths

This simple stew combines tender chunks of veal with mushrooms and leeks in a richly flavored tomato broth. Most of the mushrooms are added at the start, but a few are folded in toward the end of cooking so they keep their texture. If fresh chanterelles or shiitake mushrooms are available, add a quarter pound of them during the last 20 minutes instead of the white button mushrooms.

Fifteen minutes before baking, place rack in center of oven and preheat to 350°F (175°C). Have 3-quart (3L) stove-to-oven casserole ready.

Pat meat dry and season with basil, salt and pepper. Melt butter and oil in casserole. Cook meat, in 3 batches, until well browned on all sides. Set all meat aside and discard all but 1 tablespoon of fat from casserole.

Metal Blade: Turn on machine, drop garlic through feed tube and process until minced. Add onions and pulse until they are finely chopped.

Return casserole to medium-high heat and add contents of work bowl. Cook, stirring often, until vegetables begin to soften. Add vermouth and stir well, loosening any particles from pan. Add stock or broth.

Metal Blade: Add tomatoes and pulse until they are coarsely chopped. Add to casserole.

Thick Slicing Disc (6mm): Stand mushrooms in feed tube flat side down and use light pressure to slice.

Add ⅔ of mushrooms, mushroom trimmings and all of meat to casserole and stir thoroughly. Cover and bake for 1¼ hours.

Thick Slicing Disc (6mm): Stand leek in feed tube and use medium pressure to slice.

Add to casserole along with remaining mushrooms and continue baking until meat is tender, about 15 to 20 minutes longer.

Can be served immediately, refrigerated up to 3 days or frozen up to 4 months. To reheat, bring to room temperature, then bake in preheated 350°F (175°C) oven until hot, about 30 minutes.

Makes 6 servings.

NAVARIN OF LAMB WITH SPRING VEGETABLES

Traditionally, a navarin was a treat limited to spring, since that was the only season when tender, young lamb was available. Now, such lamb is in the market all year. Deliciously crisp vegetables complete the fresh taste of the stew. Vary them according to what is available; just be sure not to overcook them. Add vegetables that cook quickly, like green beans, peas, asparagus or zucchini, toward the end of the cooking.

1¹/₂ pounds (680g) lean lamb shoulder, cut into 1¹/₂-inch (4cm) cubes
1 teaspoon salt
Freshly ground pepper
2 tablespoons unsalted butter
2 tablespoons safflower oil
¹/₂ cup loosely packed parsley leaves
2 large garlic cloves, peeled
1 6-ounce (170g) can tomato paste
1 cup (240ml) dry red wine
1 cup (240ml) Lamb or Chicken Stock (see Index), or chicken broth
6 ounces (170g) fresh green beans, cooked until tender but still crisp, cut into feed-tube lengths

3 medium onions (14 ounces total, 395g), peeled and cut to fit feed tube
4 medium parsnips (10 ounces total, 285g), peeled and cut into feed-tube lengths
4 medium carrots (10 ounces total, 285g), peeled and cut into feed-tube lengths
4 celery stalks (8 ounces total, 225g), strings removed with vegetable peeler, cut into feed-tube lengths
1 bay leaf
1¹/₂ teaspoons dried thyme

Fifteen minutes before baking, place rack in center of oven and preheat to 350°F (175°C). Have 4-quart (4L) stove-to-oven baking dish ready.

Pat lamb dry and season with salt and pepper. Heat butter and oil in baking dish. When hot, cook meat in 2 batches until well browned on all sides. Remove from pan and reserve. Discard fat from pan.

Metal Blade: Process parsley until minced; remove and reserve. Turn on machine, drop garlic through feed tube and process until minced. Add tomato paste and wine and process for 2 seconds.

Return casserole to high heat. When very hot, add contents of work bowl and stock or broth. Stir over high heat, loosening any particles from bottom of pan. Remove from heat and add meat.

Thick Slicing Disc (6mm): Stand green beans in feed tube and use light pressure to slice; wrap airtight and refrigerate. Stand onions, parsnips and carrots in feed tube and use firm pressure to slice. Stand celery in feed tube and use medium pressure to slice.

Add bay leaf, thyme and all vegetables, except green beans, to casserole. Stir gently and press vegetables into liquid. Cover tightly and bake for 1 hour. (Can be prepared to this point 3 days in advance and refrigerated.)

Continue to cook for 45 minutes. Stir in green beans, cover and cook for 15 minutes more. Garnish with reserved parsley.

Makes 6 servings.

1 8- to 9-pound (3.5 to 4kg) leg of
   lamb, boned
2 tablespoons safflower oil
   Salt
   Freshly ground pepper
3 large garlic cloves, peeled

1 stick unsalted butter (4 ounces,
   115g), chilled
1/2 cup (120ml) ruby Port
1/3 cup (80ml) Veal Stock (see Index),
   or beef broth
   Juices from cooked meat
   Watercress for garnish

ROAST LAMB WITH PORT WINE-AND-GARLIC SAUCE

This classic recipe of Frédy Girardet is unbelievably simple. Roasting the lamb quickly at an extremely high temperature yields juicy, tender meat. You may be tempted to roast it longer than 25 minutes, but believe me — and your meat thermometer — it will be perfectly cooked in that time, sumptuously rare as served at Girardet's restaurant. The paper-thin slices of garlic sweeten as they cook, and add an interesting, decorative touch to the sauce.

Fifteen minutes before baking, place rack in center of oven and preheat to 500°F (260°C). Have shallow roasting pan ready.

Cut lamb to remove 2 large muscles from upper leg in 2 pieces. These are top and bottom rounds; they should weigh 3 1/2 to 4 pounds total (1.5 to 1.8kg). Reserve 2 side flaps for Shish Kebab, lamb patties or stew. Pat meat dry with paper towels. Rub with oil and generously season with salt and pepper. Place in pan and bake until instant-reading thermometer reads 120°F (50°C) for rare, about 25 minutes. Cover with tent of aluminum foil and let rest for 20 minutes. Meanwhile, prepare sauce.

Ultra Thin Slicing Disc (1mm): Use light pressure to slice garlic.

In 1-quart (1L) saucepan, gently cook garlic in 2 tablespoons of butter until soft but not brown — about 10 minutes. Add Port, stock or broth and cook until reduced to 2/3 cup (160ml).

When meat is removed from oven, add any accumulated juice to saucepan and cook until reduced to 2/3 cup (160ml). Cut remaining 6 tablespoons of butter into 6 pieces. Over medium-high heat, whisk in butter, one piece at a time, waiting until each piece is incorporated before adding another. Taste and adjust seasoning.

Cut meat at slight angle in thin slices and arrange on platter. Spread with 3 tablespoons of sauce and several slices of garlic. Garnish with watercress and pass remaining sauce.

Makes 6 to 8 servings.

Roast Lamb with Port Wine-and-Garlic Sauce

MIDDLE EASTERN SKEWERED LAMB WITH LEEKS, BEANS AND TOMATOES

This colorful and delicious recipe is a creation of Varouj Vartanian of The Casbah restaurant in Chicago. Cooking the lamb separately from the sauce ensures that it stays tender, juicy and rare. The sauce does not reheat well so plan to make it just before serving. It's a simple preparation taking no more than 20 minutes.

Marinade

1/3 cup (80ml) red-wine vinegar
1/2 cup (120ml) safflower oil
1/4 cup (60ml) olive oil
2 tablespoons tomato paste

1/2 teaspoon salt
1/2 teaspoon Hungarian paprika
1 3/4 pounds (795g) boneless leg of lamb, cut into 1 1/2-inch (4cm) cubes

Sauce

1 cup loosely packed parsley leaves
1/4 cup loosely packed cilantro or fresh coriander leaves
2 large garlic cloves, peeled
1 medium leek (8 ounces, 225g), with coarse greens trimmed, cleaned and cut into feed-tube lengths
3 tablespoons unsalted butter
1 tablespoon flour
1 cup (240ml) Lamb or Chicken Stock (see Index), or chicken broth
2 teaspoons fresh lemon juice

1/2 teaspoon salt
1/2 teaspoon Hungarian paprika
1/4 teaspoon dried oregano
1/4 teaspoon turmeric
Freshly ground pepper
1 medium tomato (5 ounces, 140g), peeled, seeded and quartered (see page 217)
1/2 cup canned Great Northern or navy beans, rinsed and drained

Combine marinade ingredients in large food storage bag and add lamb. Seal and toss to coat meat with marinade. Refrigerate for 4 hours or overnight, turning several times.

Metal Blade: Process parsley and cilantro until minced; remove and reserve. Turn on machine, drop garlic through feed tube and process until minced.

Thick (6mm) or All Purpose Slicing Disc (4mm): Stand leek in feed tube and use medium pressure to slice.

Melt butter in 8-inch (20cm) skillet over medium heat. Add garlic and leeks, cover and cook until soft — about 6 minutes. Stir in flour and cook for 1 more minute. Add stock or broth, lemon juice, salt, paprika, oregano, turmeric and pepper. Bring to boil over high heat, then cook, stirring often, until thick — about 3 to 4 minutes.

Metal Blade: Pulse to chop tomato finely. Add to skillet with beans. Cook until heated through — about 3 minutes. Keep sauce warm while meat is broiling. Add reserved parsley and cilantro when ready to serve.

Fifteen minutes before broiling, place rack 6 inches (15cm) from heat; preheat broiler. Remove lamb from marinade and pat dry. Put 6 pieces of lamb on each of 4 skewers and season with salt and pepper. Broil for 4 minutes, turning once, for rare meat; 1 to 2 minutes longer for medium. Remove lamb from each skewer onto dinner plate and top with 1/2 cup (120ml) of sauce. Serve immediately.

Makes 4 servings.

Lamb

1 9-pound (4kg) leg of lamb, boned
Salt
Freshly ground pepper

1¹/₂ tablespoons unsalted butter
1¹/₂ tablespoons safflower oil

Sauce

²/₃ cup (160ml) Lamb Stock (see Index) or ¹/₂ cup (120ml) beef broth

3 large shallots (2 ounces total, 55g), peeled

6 medium mushrooms (2 ounces total, 55g)

2 tablespoons sherry vinegar

¹/₃ cup (80ml) dry white wine or dry vermouth

3 tablespoons unsalted butter, chilled and cut into thirds

Salt to taste

Freshly ground pepper

LAMB MEDALLIONS WITH SHERRY VINEGAR

This simple preparation is from the 2-star Crillon Hotel in Paris. I've substituted a leg of lamb for the saddle that was used in the original recipe, since the saddle is difficult to obtain and very expensive. Serve the lamb with Zucchini Flans with Zucchini and Tomato Garnish (see Index) as they do at the Crillon.

Separate meat along seams and trim away fat and gristle. Cut 2 large muscles into ¹/₂-inch (12mm) slices, allowing 6 ounces (170g) per serving. Remaining meat can be frozen and used for Shish Kebab, patties, curry, casseroles, etc. Pat dry with paper towels and lightly season one side with salt and pepper.

Heat butter and oil in 10-inch (25cm) skillet over high heat. When sizzling, quickly sear meat in batches, seasoned side down. Lightly season top, turn with tongs and sear until cooked to taste — preferably rare or medium rare. As each batch is cooked, transfer slices to warm plate and cover with tent of aluminum foil to keep them warm. When all meat is cooked, discard fat and keep skillet hot.

If you are using Lamb Stock, boil in small saucepan until reduced to ¹/₃ cup (80ml). Do not reduce beef broth.

Metal Blade: Turn on machine, drop shallots through feed tube and process until minced. Add mushrooms and pulse to chop coarsely.

Add shallots and mushrooms to hot skillet and cook over high heat for 2 minutes, stirring to loosen brown bits from bottom of pan. Add vinegar, cook for 1 minute, then add reduced lamb stock or beef broth and wine. Simmer for 3 minutes. Strain mixture and return it to skillet. When hot, whisk in butter, one piece at a time, waiting until each piece is incorporated before adding another. Adjust seasoning and keep warm.

Fan several slices of meat on lower half of each of 6 dinner plates. Spoon about 2 tablespoons of sauce over meat and serve immediately.

Makes 6 servings.

MARINATED LAMB WITH PROVENCAL BEANS

Marinating the meat for two days allows a full transfer of flavor from the marinade to the meat; besides, the tenderizing effects are remarkable. When the meat is removed, the marinade is used to flavor the beans. The marinade is delicious with beef also, especially tenderloin.

4 large garlic cloves, peeled
1/2 cup (120ml) dry red wine
1/4 cup (60ml) plus 1 tablespoon sherry vinegar
1/4 cup (60ml) plus 2 tablespoons extra-virgin olive oil
1 tablespoon Dijon mustard
1 teaspoon dried oregano
1 tablespoon salt
  Freshly ground pepper
  Sirloin end of leg of lamb, boned (about 3 1/2 pounds, 1.5kg, after boning)
1 pound (455g) navy beans, soaked overnight in cold water
2 medium onions (8 ounces, 225g), peeled and quartered
1 1/2 cups loosely packed parsley leaves
  Marinade from meat (see NOTE)
3/4 to 1 cup (180 to 240ml) Lamb or Beef Stock (see Index), or beef broth
1/2 cup (120ml) tomato paste
1 1/2 teaspoons dried basil
1/2 teaspoon ground cumin
2 large tomatoes (15 ounces total, 425g), halved

Metal Blade: Turn on machine, drop 2 garlic cloves through feed tube and process until minced. Add wine, 1/4 cup (60ml) each of vinegar and oil, mustard, oregano, 1 teaspoon of salt and pepper and process for 3 seconds.

Transfer to large plastic bag and add lamb. Seal airtight and refrigerate for 12 to 48 hours, turning bag occasionally.

Drain beans and put in 6-quart (6L) pan with 1 onion and cold water to cover. Bring to boil, then cover. Reduce heat and simmer gently until beans are just tender — about 50 minutes. Do not overcook. Drain beans and discard onion. Beans can be cooked a day in advance and refrigerated.

Fifteen minutes before baking, place rack in center of oven and preheat to 500°F (260°C). Have shallow roasting pan ready.

Drain meat, reserve marinade and let meat come to room temperature. Pat dry and season with 1 teaspoon of salt and pepper. Place in pan and bake until instant-reading thermometer inserted into thickest part registers 125°F (50°C) for rare — about 24 minutes. Remove from oven, cover with tent of aluminum foil and let rest for 20 minutes before slicing. While meat is cooking, finish beans.

Metal Blade: Process parsley until minced; remove and reserve. Turn on machine, drop remaining garlic and onion through feed tube and process until minced.

In 10-inch (25cm) sauté pan, gently cook garlic and onion in 2 tablespoons of olive oil, stirring often, until soft but not brown — about 12 minutes. Add reserved marinade, 3/4 cup (180ml) of stock or broth, tomato paste, 1 tablespoon of vinegar, 1 teaspoon of salt, basil, cumin and pepper and bring to boil. Simmer gently for 5 minutes, stirring often. Add beans and continue to cook for 10 minutes longer.

French Fry Disc: Use light pressure to cut tomatoes. Use slotted spoon to lift tomato pieces from juice and seeds and add to beans. (If you do not have French Fry Disc, see page 229.)

Cook just until heated through. Add reserved parsley and adjust seasoning. Serve immediately.

Makes 8 servings.

NOTES: Beans can be prepared early in day they are to be served. Make sure meat has marinated for at least 12 hours before removing from marinade. Reheat beans gently at serving time, adding stock or broth if they are dry.

To prepare without lamb, substitute following ingredients from lamb marinade:

2 garlic cloves　　　　　　　　　　1/4 cup (60ml) extra-virgin olive oil
1/4 cup (60ml) sherry vinegar　　　　1/2 teaspoon salt

Marinated Lamb with Provençal Beans

BONELESS LEG OF LAMB WITH PEPPERCORN MUSTARD CRUST

This is an excellent recipe for entertaining since much of the cooking can be done in advance. It's equally good hot or at room temperature, so it does well on a buffet table. The charcoal flavor that infuses the meat provides a delicious counterpoint to the piquant mustard crust. And the peppercorns add a note that is sharp but not overpowering.

4 teaspoons black peppercorns
4 teaspoons dried green peppercorns
4 teaspoons white peppercorns
1 boned leg of lamb (5 to 5¹/₂ pounds, 2.3 to 2.5kg)
2 large garlic cloves, peeled and halved
²/₃ cup (160ml) dry red wine
2¹/₂ tablespoons olive oil

1 tablespoon dried, crushed rosemary
1 teaspoon salt
¹/₂ cup (120ml) Dijon mustard
³/₄ teaspoon dried basil
¹/₄ teaspoon dried tarragon
¹/₄ teaspoon sugar
Fresh rosemary for garnish (optional)

Crush peppercorns coarsely in coffee grinder or with mortar and pestle or rolling pin. Put half into large plastic food bag and add meat, garlic, wine, oil, 2¹/₂ teaspoons of rosemary and salt. Seal securely and refrigerate for at least 8 hours, or overnight, turning bag occasionally. Remove from refrigerator about 1 hour before cooking.

Fifteen minutes before broiling, place rack 4 to 6 inches (10 to 15cm) from heat and preheat broiler, or prepare hot fire on outdoor grill.

Remove lamb from marinade and pat dry. Sear on all sides — about 4 to 6 minutes. Let cool. Meat can be seared 1 day in advance and refrigerated. Bring to room temperature before proceeding.

Fifteen minutes before baking, place rack in center of oven and preheat to 500°F (260°C). Place wire rack in roasting pan and put 1 inch (2.5cm) of water into bottom of pan.

Starting at short side, roll meat into tight cylinder. Tie securely at 1-inch (2.5cm) intervals, then tie once lengthwise.

Combine mustard, basil, tarragon, sugar and remaining rosemary and spread evenly over meat. Press remaining crushed peppercorns into surface. Put meat, seam side down, on wire rack and bake until instant-reading thermometer registers 120°F (50°C) for rare — about 30 to 35 minutes.

Let stand at least 10 minutes before carving. Slice thinly and arrange on serving platter. Garnish with sprigs of rosemary if desired. Serve warm or at room temperature.

Makes 10 servings.

3 pounds (1.4kg) pork tenderloin,
    trimmed and cut into 1-inch
    (2.5cm) cubes
1 teaspoon salt
    Freshly ground pepper
2 tablespoons safflower oil
2 large garlic cloves, peeled
1 medium onion (5 ounces, 140g),
    peeled and quartered
1/2 cup (120ml) plus 2 tablespoons dry
    white wine
1/2 cup (120ml) Chicken Stock (see
    Index), or chicken broth

1 1/2 teaspoons dried thyme
1 large leek (12 ounces, 340g), with
    coarse greens trimmed, cut into
    feed-tube lengths
1 medium fennel bulb (12 ounces,
    340g), with feathery greens
    trimmed, cut into feed-tube
    lengths (see NOTE)
2 tablespoons flour
10 tiny new red potatoes (8 ounces
    total, 225g), unpeeled, cooked
    until just tender
3 tablespoons snipped fresh chives

*This casserole of
tender cubes of
pork loin mixed
with garden
vegetables makes
a complete meal.
The delicate anise
flavor of fennel
complements the
mild flavor of
pork. The dish has
the appeal of all
casseroles: it can
be made several
days in advance
and reheated. Add
the potatoes, leeks
and fennel on
reheating, so they
stay fresh and
crisp.*

Fifteen minutes before baking, place rack in center of oven and preheat to 350°F (175°C). Have 4-quart (4L) stove-to-oven casserole ready.

Pat meat dry and season with salt and pepper. Heat oil in casserole over high heat. When hot, brown meat in several batches, removing each batch as cooked. For uniform browning, do not overcrowd. When all meat is browned, discard fat.

Metal Blade: Turn on machine, drop garlic and onion through feed tube and process until minced.

Transfer to casserole and stir over medium-high heat, loosening brown bits from bottom of pan. Add 1/2 cup (120ml) of wine, stock or broth, thyme and meat. Cover and bake for 1 1/2 hours.

All Purpose Slicing Disc (4mm): Stand leek and fennel in feed tube and use medium pressure to slice.

After 1 1/2 hours of baking, mix flour and remaining 2 tablespoons of wine until smooth; stir into casserole along with leeks, fennel and potatoes. Cover and bake for 30 minutes more. Adjust seasoning and garnish with snipped chives.

Makes 6 to 8 servings.

NOTE: If fresh fennel is not available, substitute equal weight of celery and 2 teaspoons fennel seeds.

SAVORY STUFFED CABBAGE

A delicious and hearty blend of pork, beet greens, prunes and cabbage is tucked into cabbage leaves, then baked in broth to succulent perfection. It is arranged to look like a perfectly shaped dome of cabbage. Serve plain or with Tomato or Red Pepper Marmalade (see Index).

1 large head green cabbage (2¹/₂ pounds, 1.2kg)
3 large garlic cloves, peeled
2 medium onions (12 ounces total, 340g), peeled and quartered
3 tablespoons unsalted butter
1 cup parsley leaves
2 slices white bread (3 ounces total, 85g), broken into pieces
1¹/₂ pounds (680g) boneless pork loin,

cut into 1¹/₂-inch (4cm) cubes
8 ounces (225g) beet greens, with stems and center veins removed
12 pitted prunes (4 ounces total, 115g)
2 large eggs
2¹/₂ teaspoons salt
2 teaspoons Dijon mustard
¹/₂ teaspoon ground allspice
Freshly ground pepper

Cooking Liquid

3 cups (720ml) Chicken Stock (see Index) or chicken broth
1 cup (240ml) water
1 small carrot (2 ounces, 55g), cut into 1-inch (2.5cm) pieces

1 medium onion (4 ounces, 115g), quartered
2 garlic cloves, peeled
4 sprigs parsley
2 bay leaves
2 whole allspice berries

Fifteen minutes before baking, place rack in center of oven and preheat to 350°F (175°C). You will need 4-quart (4L) covered casserole, 3- or 4-quart (3 or 4L) mixing bowl and double thickness of cheesecloth to line mixing bowl.

Cut "X" about ¹/₂-inch (12mm) deep into core of cabbage. Cook in 4 quarts (4L) of boiling, salted water for 10 minutes; drain and cool. Remove large outer leaves and cut out thick veins. Cabbage heart (about 10 to 12 ounces, 285 to 340g) will be chopped; it is not necessary to separate its leaves.

Metal Blade: Turn on machine, drop garlic through feed tube and process until minced. Add onions and pulse until finely chopped.

Melt butter in 8-inch (20cm) skillet and add contents of work bowl. Cook gently until soft — about 5 minutes. Transfer to large mixing bowl. As you process each of the following ingredients, add it to mixing bowl.

Metal Blade: Process parsley and bread until minced. In 2 batches, process pork until uniformly and finely ground. In 2 batches, process beet greens until minced. Pulse to process prunes to size of raisins. Quarter cabbage heart and pulse until finely chopped.

Add eggs, salt, mustard, allspice and pepper to bowl and mix to combine. Line mixing bowl with double thickness of cheesecloth, allowing generous overlap. Arrange large cabbage leaves in bowl, round end down, overlapping as necessary to cover surface. Add ¹/₃ of meat mixture in even layer. Cover with cabbage leaves and repeat layers 2 more times.

Bring ends of cheesecloth up and twist tightly to make round, compact ball. Tie with string and trim away excess cheesecloth. Transfer to casserole and add cooking liquid. Cover and bake for 2 hours. Remove cabbage from broth and let rest for 15 minutes.

Untie cheesecloth. Invert cabbage onto serving platter, unwrap and discard cheesecloth. To serve, cut into wedges.

Can be made up to 3 days in advance and refrigerated. Cook as directed and refrigerate wrapped cabbage in cooking liquid. Serve at room temperature or reheat. To reheat, cover and bake in preheated 350°F (175°C) oven for 1 1/2 hours.

Makes 6 to 8 servings.

Carl Sontheimer, President of Cuisinarts, coached me on sausage-making, generously sharing his tried and true ratio of lean meat to fat. I've observed it ever since, with great success. Serve these sausages with bread and mustard. And be adventuresome about the mustard — try a tangy Dusseldorf or Bavarian type.

1 1/2 cups loosely packed parsley leaves
2 large garlic cloves, peeled
3 large shallots, (1 1/2 ounces total, 45g), peeled
2 slices white bread (2 ounces total, 55g), broken into 6 pieces
2 tablespoons instant nonfat dry-milk powder
1 tablespoon Seasoning Salt (recipe follows)
3/4 teaspoon coarsely ground pepper
1 1/4 pounds (570g) lean pork loin, well chilled, cut into 1-inch (2.5cm) cubes

12 ounces (340g) pork fat, well chilled, cut into 1-inch (2.5cm) cubes
1 large carrot (6 ounces, 170g), scrubbed and cut into thirds
1 medium onion (5 ounces, 140g), peeled and stuck with 2 whole cloves
2 bay leaves
8 sprigs parsley
1/2 teaspoon dried thyme
5 quarts (5L) water

Metal Blade: Put parsley in work bowl and turn on machine. Drop garlic and shallots through feed tube and process until minced. Add bread, milk powder, Seasoning Salt and pepper and process until bread is finely crumbed — about 10 seconds. Remove 1/2 of mixture and reserve. Add 1/2 of pork loin and 1/2 of fat to crumb mixture in work bowl. Pulse 4 times, then process continuously until very finely chopped — about 30 seconds; remove and reserve. Process remaining crumb mixture, pork loin and fat.

Shape mixture into cylinders 4 inches (10cm) long and 1 1/4 inches (3cm) thick. Wrap in double thickness of fine-mesh cheesecloth and tie ends with string.

Put carrot, onion, bay leaves, parsley, thyme and water in 8-quart (8L) pot and bring to boil. Add sausages and simmer gently until temperature is 160°F (70°C) — about 25 minutes. Remove with slotted spoon, unwrap and serve warm or at room temperature.

Makes 9 sausages.

1. *Loin and fat in work bowl*
2. *Shaping into cylinders*
3. *Wrapping in cheesecloth*
4. *Tying ends*

SEASONING SALT

For pâtés, sausages and terrines. It can be refrigerated indefinitely in an airtight container.

2 tablespoons salt
1 teaspoon dried tarragon
1 teaspoon ground allspice
1 teaspoon Hungarian paprika
1 teaspoon ground coriander

$^1/_2$ teaspoon cinnamon
$^1/_2$ teaspoon freshly grated nutmeg
$^1/_4$ teaspoon dried marjoram
$^1/_8$ teaspoon ground cloves

Combine all ingredients in small covered container.

Makes about $^1/_4$ cup.

MCINTOSH BREAKFAST SAUSAGE

I love breakfast sausage, but had eliminated it from my menus because of concern about fat and additives. Now, with a food processor, I control the kind of meat, the amount of fat and the seasonings; I'm glad to serve it again. These unusual sausages are great with pancakes.

1 large shallot ($^1/_2$ ounce, 15g), peeled
1$^1/_2$ pounds (680g) pork butt, trimmed and cut into 1-inch (2.5cm) cubes
$^1/_2$ large McIntosh apple (3 ounces, 85g)
1 large egg
2 tablespoons pure maple syrup
Dash of Tabasco sauce
1$^1/_4$ teaspoons salt

$^1/_2$ teaspoon freshly ground pepper
$^1/_2$ teaspoon freshly grated nutmeg
$^1/_4$ teaspoon ground ginger
$^1/_4$ teaspoon ground allspice
$^1/_4$ teaspoon sage leaves
2 tablespoons flour, for shaping patties
Unsalted butter and safflower oil, for frying

Metal Blade: Turn on machine, drop shallot through feed tube and process until minced. Add $^1/_2$ of pork, and apple, egg, syrup, Tabasco sauce, salt, pepper, nutmeg, ginger, allspice and sage. Pulse 4 times, then process continuously until finely and uniformly chopped, stopping once to scrape work bowl. Transfer to large mixing bowl. Process remaining pork in same manner.

Add to mixing bowl and combine. Divide mixture in half and put each piece on plastic wrap. Working through plastic, form each piece into 5 by 2$^1/_2$-inch (13 by 6cm) cylinder. Can be prepared to this point 1 day in advance.

Cut each cylinder into 8 equal slices. With lightly floured hands, shape each slice into patty $^1/_2$-inch (12mm) thick. Heat $^1/_2$ teaspoon each of butter and oil in 12-inch (30cm) skillet or griddle over medium-high heat. When hot, cook sausages over heat sufficiently high to brown patties quickly — about 3$^1/_2$ minutes per side. Drain on paper towels. Continue cooking in batches, adding more butter and oil as necessary. Serve immediately.

Makes 16 patties.

ALL-BEEF VARIATION: Substitute equal amount of lean beef chuck, cut into 1-inch (2.5cm) cubes, for pork.

2 tablespoons chili powder, or to
  taste
1 teaspoon dried oregano
3/4 teaspoon salt
1/2 teaspoon ground cumin
2 pounds (910g) lean pork loin,
  trimmed, cut in 1-inch (2.5cm)
  cubes
2 tablespoons safflower oil
2 tablespoons unsalted butter
3 large garlic cloves, peeled
1 medium onion (5 ounces, 140g),
  peeled

1/2 cup (120ml) Beef Stock (see Index)
  or beef broth
1 tablespoon dark-brown sugar
1 jalapeño pepper, seeded if desired
  to handle hot peppers, see page 186
6 medium scallions (3 ounces total,
  85g), including green tops, cut into
  1-inch (2.5cm) pieces
3 medium tomatoes (1 pound total,
  455g), seeded and quartered
1 14 1/2 ounce (410g) can white
  hominy, drained (see NOTE)
2/3 cup (160ml) sour cream
  Lime wedges

CHILI PORK STEW

An agreeably spicy blend of fork-tender chunks of meat, crunchy fresh vegetables and hominy. Serve a basket of warm flour tortillas with it and icy cold beer to wash down the hot peppers. Beef stew meat works just as well as pork in this recipe. I use them interchangeably, depending on market prices.

Fifteen minutes before baking, place rack in center of oven and preheat to 350°F (175°C). Put chili powder, oregano, salt, cumin and meat in large bowl and toss together.

Heat 1 tablespoon each of oil and butter in 3-quart (3L) stove-to-oven casserole over medium-high heat. When hot, brown 1/3 of pork cubes on all sides. Set aside and cook remaining pork in 2 batches, adding oil and butter if necessary. Do not allow to burn.

Metal Blade: Turn on machine, drop garlic through feed tube and process until minced. Add onion and pulse to chop coarsely.

Add vegetables to casserole and stir over high heat, loosening any particles from bottom of pan. Add meat, stock or broth and brown sugar and stir well. Cover, place in oven and bake until meat is tender — about 1 1/2 hours. Can be made in advance up to this point. Refrigerate up to 2 days or freeze up to 3 months. Bring to room temperature before proceeding.

Metal Blade: Turn on machine, drop pepper through feed tube and process until minced. Add scallions and tomatoes and pulse to chop coarsely.

Add vegetables to casserole along with hominy and stir well. Bake until heated through, about 20 minutes.

Serve immediately with sour cream and lime wedges.

Makes 4 to 6 servings.

NOTE: Hominy is a variety of white corn that is specially treated to plump it and remove its seed germs. One cup of cooked sweet corn may be substituted.

FRESH CRANBERRY CHUTNEY

Tart cranberries make a spectacular chutney. This mildly spicy version is both sweet and tangy. It's delicious with pork and poultry, especially turkey. I've even served it instead of more traditional cranberry relishes at Thanksgiving. It dresses up leftover turkey, too, in a salad or on a sandwich.

2 medium garlic cloves, peeled
1 medium onion (6 ounces, 170g), peeled and quartered
4 cups fresh cranberries (14 ounces, 395g)
³/₄ cup firmly packed light brown sugar (6 ounces, 170g)
¹/₃ cup (80ml) cider vinegar
¹/₄ teaspoon dry mustard
¹/₄ teaspoon ground ginger
¹/₄ teaspoon ground allspice
¹/₄ teaspoon ground cardamom
¹/₄ teaspoon ground cloves
¹/₄ teaspoon crushed red pepper flakes
1 large ripe pear (8 ounces, 225g), peeled and quartered

Metal Blade: Turn on machine, drop garlic through feed tube and process until minced. Add onion and pulse to chop coarsely.

Transfer mixture to 2-quart (2L) non-aluminum saucepan and add cranberries, ¹/₂ cup sugar (4 ounces, 115g), vinegar, mustard, ginger, allspice, cardamom, cloves and pepper flakes. Bring to boil over high heat, then reduce heat and cook gently, uncovered, stirring often, until very thick — about 40 minutes.

Metal Blade: Pulse to chop pear coarsely and add to pan. Cook 10 minutes longer and remove from heat. Stir in remaining sugar.

Serve hot, cold or at room temperature. Can be made in advance and refrigerated up to 4 weeks.

Makes about 2¹/₂ cups.

ONION COMPOTE

Michel Guérard serves this condiment at his restaurant in Eugénie-les-Bains, France. Mildly sweet onions are offset by the tang of wine vinegar. It's delicious with simple roasted or grilled meats.

8 medium sweet onions (3 pounds total, 1.4kg), peeled
2 tablespoons unsalted butter
¹/₄ cup (60ml) red-wine vinegar
1 teaspoon grenadine syrup
1¹/₄ teaspoons salt
Freshly ground pepper
4 tablespoons unsalted butter, quartered (optional)

Thin Slicing Disc (2mm) or Medium Slicing Disc (3mm): Stand onions in feed tube and use firm pressure to slice.

Melt 2 tablespoons of butter in 4-quart (4L) pan. Add onions, cover and cook gently for 1¹/₂ hours. Uncover and cook over medium heat, stirring occasionally, until liquid has evaporated — about 30 minutes. Add vinegar, grenadine syrup, salt and pepper and cook for 10 minutes longer over medium-high heat, stirring often. Do not allow to burn. If desired, whisk in 4 tablespoons of butter, 1 tablespoon at a time, waiting until each piece is incorporated before adding another.

Can be prepared a week in advance and gently reheated at serving time.

Makes 3 cups (720ml).

1 by ¹/₂-inch (2.5cm by 12mm) piece fresh ginger root (¹/₄ ounce, 10g), peeled
1 pound (455g) mushrooms, stems trimmed, with 2 opposite sides cut flat

1¹/₂ teaspoons salt
1 tablespoon unsalted butter
1¹/₂ teaspoons fresh lemon juice
2¹/₄ cups sugar (1 pound, 455g)
¹/₄ teaspoon pure vanilla extract
3 ounces (90 ml) liquid fruit pectin

Metal Blade: Turn on machine, drop ginger through feed tube and process until minced; remove and reserve.

All Purpose Slicing Disc (4mm): Stand mushrooms in feed tube flat side down and use light pressure to slice.

Transfer mushrooms to plastic bag and add salt. Seal bag and shake gently to distribute salt. Refrigerate for 12 hours or overnight, turning bag occasionally. Place strainer over 2-cup (480ml) measuring cup and drain mushrooms, pressing gently to extract at least ³/₄ cup (180ml) of liquid. Transfer liquid to a 1¹/₂-quart (1.5L) saucepan. Cook over medium-high heat until reduced to 1 tablespoon.

Meanwhile, melt butter in 10-inch (25cm) skillet with lemon juice. Add mushroom slices and cook gently until all moisture has evaporated, about 10 minutes. Do not allow to brown. Add mushrooms, sugar and reserved ginger root to mushroom liquid in saucepan. Cook over medium-high heat, tossing gently with wooden spoon until sugar begins to melt and mixture becomes liquid. Bring to rolling boil and boil over high heat for 1 minute, stirring several times. Remove from heat and immediately stir in vanilla and pectin. Cool, then refrigerate up to 1 month. Serve at room temperature.

Makes 2¹/₂ cups (600ml).

MUSHROOM MARMALADE SAUCE

Jean Delaveyne of Le Camelia in the Parisian suburb of Bougival created this brilliant recipe. It's intensely flavored, exotic and a treat for mushroom lovers. Serve as a relish with beef or lamb, on sandwiches or on toasted bread rounds for canapés.

Condiments for Meats and Poultry

HONEY MUSTARD SAUCE

Serve with cold meats like beef, ham and chicken. It's also good mixed with mayonnaise and added to chicken or turkey salad.

2 tablespoons mustard seeds
1/4 cup (60ml) Dijon mustard
1 large egg yolk
2 tablespoons honey
1 teaspoon white-wine vinegar
1/2 teaspoon salt
1/4 teaspoon ground allspice
1/2 cup (120ml) safflower oil

Metal Blade: Put mustard seeds, mustard, egg yolk, honey, vinegar, salt and allspice in work bowl and turn on machine. Pour oil through feed tube in thin, steady stream. Adjust seasoning. Can be covered airtight and refrigerated up to 2 weeks.

Makes 1 cup (240ml).

TARRAGON-SHALLOT MAYONNAISE

A cold version of Béarnaise sauce that's delicious on beef, lamb or chicken. It also elevates a simple egg salad to star status.

6 tablespoons fresh tarragon or 3 tablespoons dried
3 large shallots (1 1/2 ounces total, 45g), peeled
1 large egg
1 tablespoon white-wine vinegar
1 teaspoon Dijon mustard
3/4 teaspoon salt
Freshly ground black pepper
1 1/2 cups (360ml) safflower oil

Metal Blade: Put tarragon in work bowl and turn on machine. Drop shallots through feed tube and process until minced. Add egg, vinegar, mustard, salt, pepper and 3 tablespoons of oil and process for 1 minute. With machine running, drizzle remaining oil through feed tube in thin, steady stream. Once mixture has thickened, oil can be added more quickly. Can be covered airtight and refrigerated up to 10 days.

Makes 1 3/4 cups (420ml).

APPLE RAISIN CHUTNEY

An intriguing blend of spices, sugar and cider vinegar transforms tart apples and sweet raisins into a delicious sweet and sour chutney. In the summer months, an equal weight of unpeeled peaches or nectarines can replace the apples, but decrease the sugar to 1 cup (7 ounces, 200g).

3 medium garlic cloves, peeled
1 by 1/2-inch (2.5 by 12mm) piece fresh ginger root (1/4 ounce, 10g), peeled
2 medium onions (12 ounces total, 340g), peeled and quartered
4 large Granny Smith apples (2 pounds total, 910g), peeled and quartered
1 1/4 cups firmly packed light-brown sugar (10 ounces, 285g)
1 cup (240ml) cider vinegar
1/2 cup golden raisins (2 1/2 ounces, 70g)
2 tablespoons mustard seeds
1/2 teaspoon dry mustard
1/2 teaspoon ground allspice
1/4 teaspoon ground cardamom
1/4 teaspoon ground cloves
3/4 teaspoon crushed red pepper flakes

Metal Blade: Turn on machine, drop garlic and ginger through feed tube and process until minced. Add onion and pulse to chop coarsely. Transfer onions to 3-quart (3L) non-aluminum saucepan. Add apples to work bowl, in two batches, and pulse until they are finely chopped. Add to saucepan with remaining ingredients. Bring to boil over high heat, then reduce heat and cook gently, stirring often, until very thick — about 50 minutes. Serve hot, cold or at room temperature. Can be refrigerated up to 4 weeks.

Makes about 3 cups (720ml).

2 large garlic cloves, peeled
1 medium carrot (4 ounces, 115g),
  peeled and cut into 1-inch (2.5cm)
  pieces
1 medium celery stalk (4 ounces,
  115g), cut into 1-inch (2.5cm)
  pieces
1 medium onion (5 ounces, 140g),
  peeled and quartered
1 large tomato (8 ounces, 225g),
  quartered and seeded

1 12-ounce (340g) can tomato paste
1½ cups (360ml) water
¼ cup (60ml) cider vinegar
¼ cup (60ml) molasses
¼ cup firmly packed dark brown
  sugar (2 ounces, 55g)
¼ cup (60ml) Worcestershire sauce
¼ cup (60ml) light corn syrup
1½ teaspoons salt
1 teaspoon crushed red pepper flakes

CHUNKY TEXAS-STYLE BARBECUE SAUCE

A mahogany-red sauce that's easy and versatile. Its spicy flavor goes well with chicken, ribs, pork sandwiches and beef brisket.

Metal Blade: Turn on machine, drop garlic through feed tube and process until minced. Add carrot, celery and onion and process until finely chopped. Add tomato and pulse until coarsely chopped.

Transfer contents of work bowl to 3-quart (3L) non-aluminum saucepan along with remaining ingredients. Bring to boil, then simmer gently, uncovered, until thickened — about 40 minutes.

Use immediately or refrigerate up to 3 weeks.

Makes 1 quart (1L).

FISH & SHELLFISH

When I began to teach in 1974, fish cookery was a mystery to many of my students. Now, fish is often the meal of choice. Contemporary cooks like its nutritive value; low-calorie and cholesterol count, and quick preparation. Fish is not only healthful and practical, a near-perfect food — it's delicious and versatile too! Grilled Prawns and Mussels are appropriate for an outdoor barbecue, rich Shellfish Stew is right for a party, and Steamed Scrod with Herbed Scallion Pasta makes fine fare for friends or family.

Thanks to modern air transport, fresh fish is available almost everywhere in the United States. Flash-frozen fish can also be of good quality; by all means use it when fresh fish isn't available. Whether you poach, grill, steam, sauté, fry or bake fish, one rule always applies. Do not overcook it. The oft repeated guideline to cook fish until it flakes is wrong. If it flakes, it's overcooked. Cook fish just until it turns opaque and feels firm to the touch, not one second longer.

FISH AND SHELLFISH

FISH

Fish Packets with Ginger
Marinated Baked Salmon
Steamed Scrod with Herbed Scallion
*   Pasta and Tomato Sauce*
Fish with Brown Butter and Capers
Fish Fillets with Celery Root and White
*   Port Sauce*
Monkfish with Saffron-Scented Vegetables
Baked Fish Fillets with Vegetables and
*   Butter Sauce*
Fish Fillets with Leeks and Chives
Fish Fillets with Sautéed Fennel and
*   Lemon Dill Sauce*
Brook Trout with Spiced Onions

SHELLFISH

Steamed Mussels in Basil Butter
Shrimp and Vegetable Tempura
Shellfish Stew
Shrimp Escabeche
Scallop Packets with Fresh Sorrel and
*   Tomato*
Lemon Shrimp with Garlic and Oregano
Grilled Prawns and Mussels with Two
*   Sauces*

For additional recipes, see these chapters

FIRST COURSES

Scotch Salmon Salad
Lobster Salad with Port Vinaigrette
Salad of Scallops and Julienned
*   Vegetables*
Chilled Mussels with Saffron Mayonnaise
Oysters with Curry and Carrot
Broiled Scallops on Shells
Steamed Scallop Seviche
Shrimp Wrapped in Cabbage Leaves with
*   Caviar Butter*
Fish and Leek Mousseline with Red-Wine
*   Sauce*
Seafood Sausage with Tomato Cream
*   Sauce*
Fish Terrine

SOUPS

Fish and Vegetables in Broth with
*   Cilantro*
Mussels in Their Own Broth

PASTA, RICE AND BEANS

Pasta Rolls with Scallops and Tomato
*   Cream Sauce*

SALADS AND SALAD DRESSINGS

Cold Curried Chicken and Shrimp Salad

TALKING ITALIAN

Antipasti:
Lemon Shrimp with Garlic
and Oregano
Eggplant Relish with
Tomatoes and Red Onions
Red Peppers and Anchovies
Zucchini with Cheese and
Pine Nuts
Julienned Carrot Salad
with Capers and Lemon
Italian Flat Bread
Frozen Flourless Chocolate
Cake with Brandied Cream

Roast Chicken with
Garden Vegetables
previous pages

1 ¹/₂-inch (12mm) square fresh
ginger root, peeled
2 large garlic cloves, peeled
¹/₄ cup (60ml) safflower oil
2 tablespoons soy sauce
2 tablespoons Oriental sesame oil
1 tablespoon dark-brown sugar
4 medium scallions (2 ounces, 55g),
including green tops, cut in
feed-tube widths
1 large carrot (4 ounces, 115g)
peeled, cut into feed-tube widths
6 6-ounce (180g) scrod fillets or
salmon or halibut fillets or steaks,
of equal thickness

Metal Blade: Turn on machine, drop ginger and garlic through feed tube and process until minced. Add both oils, soy sauce and sugar and process for 20 seconds, stopping once to scrape work bowl; remove and reserve.

Thin Slicing Disc (2mm): Lay scallions in feed tube and use light pressure to slice into slivers.

3mm Julienne Disc or Medium Shredding Disc: Lay carrot in feed tube and use firm pressure to process.

Cut six 12-inch (25cm) squares of parchment paper or aluminum foil. Place 1 fillet in center of each piece of parchment or foil. Divide marinade among fillets and brush over fish. Measure fish at thickest part; width will determine cooking time. Divide vegetables evenly among fillets. Fold parchment or foil over fish and tightly seal all edges with double fold. Refrigerate at least 30 minutes or up to 8 hours.

Fifteen minutes before baking, place rack in center of oven and preheat to 500°F (260°C). Place packets on baking sheet and bake in preheated oven, allowing 10 minutes for each inch of thickness of fish. (If fish is 1 ¹/₂ inches at its thickest part, for example, cook it for 15 minutes.)

Carefully open packets and transfer to serving plate. Serve immediately.

Makes 6 servings.

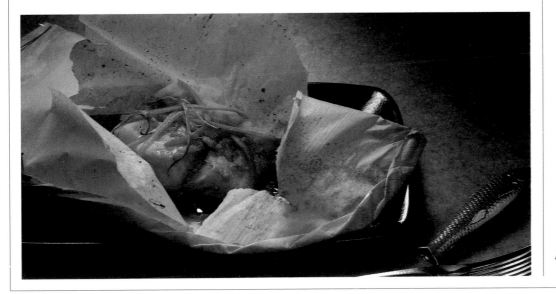

*Fish Packets
with Ginger*

MARINATED BAKED SALMON

This recipe comes from Chef Jean Pierre Bonin of the dining room of the Crillon Hotel in Paris, which has been awarded 2 stars in the Michelin Guide. Few hotel restaurants have achieved such status; it's clear that the Crillon has earned the distinction. For proof, try this simple recipe. A delicious marinade adds flavor to fresh salmon, which is sliced so thin that it cooks in 2 minutes.

2¹/₄ pounds (1kg) salmon fillets, skinned
¹/₄ cup (60ml) extra-virgin olive oil
¹/₄ cup (60ml) grapeseed oil
¹/₄ cup (60ml) fresh lemon juice

¹/₄ cup (60ml) dry white wine or dry vermouth
1¹/₄ teaspoons salt
¹/₄ teaspoon freshly ground white pepper

Garnish
2 tablespoons extra-virgin olive oil
1 large tomato (8 ounces, 225g), peeled, seeded and diced (to peel tomatoes, see page 217)

¹/₄ teaspoon salt
Pinch of sugar
Freshly ground pepper

Arrange salmon on baking sheet lined with waxed paper. Place in freezer until firm but not frozen — about 15 minutes. Cut on diagonal into slices as thin as possible, about ¹/₁₆-inch (2mm).

Combine both oils, lemon juice, wine or vermouth, 1 teaspoon of salt and pepper in large food storage bag and add salmon. Seal tightly and marinate for 30 minutes at room temperature, turning bag over several times. Prepare garnish while salmon marinates.

Heat oil in small skillet. Add tomato, salt, sugar and pepper and cook gently until heated through. Keep warm as salmon cooks or reheat at serving time.

Fifteen minutes before baking salmon, place rack in center of oven and preheat to 550°F (290°C).

Line jelly-roll pan with aluminum foil. Lightly butter foil and sprinkle with remaining ¹/₄ teaspoon of salt and pepper.

Remove salmon from marinade and blot to remove excess liquid. Arrange in single layer on jelly-roll pan and bake just until surface of fish lightens in color — about 2 minutes. Divide among 6 warm plates. Garnish with about 1 tablespoon of tomato and serve immediately.

Makes 6 servings.

NOTE: At the Crillon, individual servings are baked on ovenproof dinner plates. I have tested it this way and it works very well. Most china can withstand the high oven temperature for the short baking time. However, I won't guarantee anyone's china but my own, so I suggest using a jelly-roll pan.

½ lemon, cut into wedges
2 teaspoons dried basil
2 bay leaves

6 6-ounce (170g) scrod fillets
Herbed Scallion Pasta (see Index)
Fresh Tomato Pasta Sauce (see Index)

Strands of green pasta topped with pure white fish and a dash of vibrant red tomato sauce combine to make a most attractive dish that is low in calories and fat.

Cut 6 pieces of parchment paper or aluminum foil slightly larger than fillets.

Add lemon, basil and bay leaves to water in bottom of steamer. Bring to boil and add steamer insert; water should not touch bottom of insert. Place each fillet on piece of parchment or foil and fit in steamer in single layer. Cover tightly and cook just until fish turns opaque, but does not flake. Depending on thickness of fillet, this will take from 6 to 8 minutes; do not overcook. Use paper or foil to lift each piece when cooked.

Arrange bed of Herbed Scallion Pasta on each of 6 plates. Top with fillet and spoon over ½ cup (120ml) of Fresh Tomato Pasta Sauce. Serve immediately.

Makes 6 servings.

1 stick unsalted butter (4 ounces, 115g)
2 tablespoons white-wine vinegar
2 tablespoons drained capers
2 cups (480ml) Court Bouillon (see Index)

¼ teaspoon salt
4 6-ounce (170g) West Coast snapper or sea bass fillets

FISH WITH BROWN BUTTER AND CAPERS

The marvelously talented Gilbert Le Coze makes fine use of simple ingredients. The vinegar and capers provide an astringency that cuts the richness of the butter and the sweetness of the fish. For this recipe, Le Coze uses ray fish, rarely found in America. I suggest available fish that work as well.

Gently melt butter in small saucepan. Skim foam from top and transfer remainder to clear glass. Rinse and dry pan. Let butter stand for 10 minutes, then spoon clear liquid from glass into pan, leaving behind white sediment that has settled at bottom. (The clear liquid is clarified butter.) Cook gently until butter is light golden brown — about 5 minutes. Add vinegar, capers, 1 tablespoon of Court Bouillon and salt. Keep warm while cooking fish.

Put remaining Court Bouillon in 10-inch (25cm) sauté pan and add fillets. Cook over medium heat just until opaque. Depending on thickness of fillets, this will take 6 to 8 minutes; do not overcook. Use slotted spatula to lift fillets from pan; drain and blot dry.

Transfer each fillet to warm dinner plate and spoon sauce over. Serve immediately.

Makes 4 servings.

FISH FILLETS WITH CELERY ROOT AND WHITE PORT SAUCE

This unusual recipe comes from Gerard Boyer of Restaurant Boyer in Reims. It's the only recipe I know that pairs celery root with fish, and it works remarkably well. Boyer steams the fish over fish stock, which flavors it very lightly. You can, of course, use water.

1 large celery root (18 ounces, 510g), peeled

1 1/2 cups (360ml) safflower oil

Sauce

4 large shallots (2 ounces total, 55g), peeled

1 stick plus 2 tablespoons unsalted butter (5 ounces total, 140g)

1/3 cup (80ml) champagne vinegar or

white-wine vinegar

1 cup (240ml) white Port

2/3 cup (160ml) whipping cream

Salt to taste

Freshly ground white pepper

Fish

3 to 6 cups (720ml to 1.5L) Fish Stock (see Index) or water

3/4 teaspoon salt

Freshly ground white pepper

6 6- to 7-ounce (170 to 200g) fillets of grouper, monkfish or red snapper

Cut celery root into 1/4-inch (6mm) dice. Heat oil to 375°F (190°C) in 2 1/2-quart (2.5L) saucepan. Fry celery root in small batches until golden and transfer to paper towels to drain. (Let oil return to 375°F (190°C) before frying additional batches.) Can be prepared several hours in advance and held at room temperature.

Metal Blade: Turn on machine, drop shallots through feed tube and process until minced.

Cook shallots in 6 tablespoons of butter in 10-inch (25cm) skillet over medium-high heat, stirring often, until soft but not brown — about 5 minutes. Stir in vinegar and turn heat to high. Add Port and bring to simmer. Remove pan from stove and very carefully ignite Port with long match. Shake pan gently until flame subsides. Add cream and simmer gently for 10 minutes. Place fine strainer over bowl and strain sauce; return to skillet. Keep warm while cooking fish. Sauce can be prepared to this point 1 day in advance and refrigerated. Before continuing, heat to simmer. Whisk remaining 4 tablespoons of butter into sauce, 1 tablespoon at a time; wait until each piece is incorporated before adding another. Season to taste with salt and pepper. Keep sauce warm while cooking fish.

Add stock or water to steamer. Bring to boil and add steamer insert; stock should not touch bottom of insert.

Cut 6 pieces of parchment paper or aluminum foil slightly larger than fillets. Season fish with salt and pepper and place on parchment paper. Add fish to steamer in single layer, cover and cook until fish feels firm and turns opaque — about 7 to 9 minutes. Do not overcook. Using paper or foil to lift, remove fish as it is cooked. Blot to remove any excess liquid.

Cook celery root in 8-inch (20cm) sauté pan over medium-high heat until heated through. Add salt to taste.

Spread 2 1/2 tablespoons of sauce onto 6 individual serving plates and top with fish fillet. Divide celery root among plates and serve immediately.

Makes 6 servings.

2 large garlic cloves, peeled
2 medium carrots (7 ounces total, 200g), peeled and cut into 1-inch (2.5cm) pieces
2 large tomatoes (14 ounces total, 395g), peeled, quartered and seeded (see NOTE)
$^1/_4$ cup (60ml) plus 2 tablespoons

Court Bouillon (see Index)
$^1/_2$ teaspoon salt
$^1/_4$ teaspoon ground saffron
Freshly ground pepper
4 6-ounce (170g) monkfish fillets
1 cup (240g) Crème Fraîche (see Index)

MONKFISH WITH SAFFRON-SCENTED VEGETABLES

Gilbert Le Coze, chef and owner of the restaurant Le Bernardin in Paris, has a particular talent for preparing fish. Here, he uses saffron-scented vegetables as a flavorful base for baked escalopes of monkfish. The juice captured from the fish enriches the sauce.

Metal Blade: Turn on machine, drop garlic through feed tube and process until minced. Add carrots and process until minced. Add tomatoes; pulse 8 times to chop.

Transfer to 2-quart (2L) saucepan and add $^1/_4$ cup (60ml) of Court Bouillon, $^1/_4$ teaspoon of salt, saffron and pepper. Cover and cook gently for 1 hour.

Fifteen minutes before baking, place rack in center of oven and preheat to 500°F (260°C).

Hold long, thin knife at slight angle to fillets and cut them on diagonal into scallops $^1/_3$ inch (8mm) thick.

Spread vegetable mixture evenly in 12$^1/_2$-inch (31cm) stove-to-oven gratin pan. Arrange fish on top, fitting pieces closely together and overlapping them as little as possible. Spoon remaining 2 tablespoons of Court Bouillon over them, and season with remaining $^1/_4$ teaspoon of salt and pepper. Bake just until opaque — 7 to 10 minutes; do not overcook. Use slotted spatula to transfer fish to warm plate; cover and keep warm while finishing sauce.

Drain any juice from fish and add it with Crème Fraîche to vegetables in gratin pan. Boil, stirring constantly, until sauce thickly coats vegetables — about 7 minutes. Adjust seasoning.

Arrange fish on 4 dinner plates and spoon generous $^1/_3$ cup (80ml) of sauce over each portion. Serve immediately.

Makes 4 servings.

To peel tomatoes

★ Immerse them in boiling water for 15 to 20 seconds, depending on their ripeness. Lift out with a slotted spoon and hold under cold water until cool. Use a paring knife to core them and remove the skins, which should slip off easily.

BAKED FISH FILLETS WITH VEGETABLES AND BUTTER SAUCE

This recipe is from Roger Vergé's 3-star restaurant Le Moulin de Mougins, just outside of Cannes. The dish is most striking in appearance, with stripes of colorful fresh vegetables decorating each fillet.

Fish

6 6- to 7-ounce (170 to 200g) turbot, lake trout or sea bass fillets
Salt
Freshly ground pepper
1 small cucumber (8 ounces, 225g), peeled, split lengthwise, seeded and cut into feed-tube lengths
8 large mushrooms (6 ounces total, 170g), trimmed, with 2 opposite sides cut flat
1 large tomato (8 ounces, 225g), peeled and halved (to seed tomatoes, see page 217)
2 tablespoons unsalted butter
1 teaspoon fresh lemon juice
¹/₃ cup (80ml) dry white wine

Sauce

8 large shallots (4 ounces total, 115g), peeled
1 medium leek (7 ounces, 200g), with coarse green leaves trimmed away, well washed, split lengthwise and cut into feed-tube lengths
1 stick plus 2 tablespoons unsalted butter (5 ounces total, 140g), chilled, in 2 parts
¹/₄ cup (60ml) dry vermouth
1 cup (240ml) dry white wine
2 tablespoons whipping cream
Salt
Freshly ground white pepper

Fifteen minutes before baking, place rack in center of oven and preheat to 425°F (220°C). Butter 9 by 13-inch (23 by 33cm) baking dish. Season both sides of fish with salt and pepper and arrange fillets in single layer in dish.

All-Purpose Slicing Disc (4mm): Stand cucumber in feed tube and use medium pressure to slice; remove and reserve. Place mushrooms in feed tube flat side down and use light pressure to slice; remove and reserve. Stand tomato in feed tube and use light pressure to slice.

Melt 1 tablespoon of butter in 10-inch (25cm) skillet. Gently cook cucumber until just heated through — about 4 minutes. Remove from skillet and reserve. Melt remaining 1 tablespoon of butter in same skillet and add mushrooms and lemon juice. Cook until mushrooms begin to soften — about 3 minutes.

Place horizontal row of tomato, cucumber and mushroom on each fillet, placing them in that order. Season lightly with salt and pepper. Pour any accumulated juice from skillet and reserve for sauce.

Metal Blade: Turn on machine, drop shallots through feed tube and process until minced. Leave in work bowl.

Medium Slicing Disc (3mm): Stand leek in feed tube; use medium pressure to slice.

Melt 2 tablespoons of butter in skillet. Add shallots and leek and cook gently, stirring often, until soft — about 5 minutes. Add vermouth, 1 cup (240ml) of wine and reserved juice. Bring to boil, then let simmer, uncovered, for 15 minutes. Place strainer over bowl and strain mixture. Return liquid to skillet. May be prepared to this point several hours in advance. Cover and refrigerate fish; hold sauce at room temperature.

To finish recipe, add $^1/_3$ cup (80ml) of wine to fish in baking pan. Bake in preheated oven just until flesh is firm and opaque — about 8 to 9 minutes; do not overcook.

While fish is baking, finish sauce. Add cream and bring to simmer. Whisk in remaining butter, 1 tablespoon at a time; wait until each piece is incorporated before adding another. Adjust seasoning. Use slotted spatula to transfer fillets to individual serving plates and spoon sauce over. Serve immediately.

Makes 6 servings.

BAKED FISH FILLETS WITH VEGETABLES AND BUTTER SAUCE

1 large leek (12 ounces), with coarse green leaves removed, cleaned and cut into feed-tube lengths
2$^1/_4$ cups (540ml) Court Bouillon (see Index)
2 sticks unsalted butter (8 ounces, 225g), chilled and cut

into 16 pieces
3 tablespoons snipped fresh chives
$^1/_2$ teaspoon salt
   Freshly ground pepper
6 6-ounce (170g) black or striped bass fillets (see NOTE)

FISH FILLETS WITH LEEKS AND CHIVES

This recipe, from Gilbert Le Coze of Le Bernardin in Paris, is best in spring and summer when leeks are young and tender, and chives abundant.

Medium Slicing Disc (3mm): Stand leek in feed tube and use medium pressure to slice.

In 12-inch (30cm) skillet, cook leek in $^1/_4$ cup (60ml) of Court Bouillon over medium-high heat just until heated through — about 2 minutes. Whisk in butter, 2 pieces at a time; wait until each piece is incorporated before adding another. Add chives, salt and pepper.

Bring remaining 2 cups (480ml) of Court Bouillon to simmer in 10-inch (25cm) sauté pan. Cook fish in 3 batches until firm but not hard — about 6 to 8 minutes. Remove fish with slotted spatula, drain and cover with tent of aluminum foil to keep warm while remaining batches cook.

Arrange fish on platter or individual dinner plates and top with leeks and chives. Serve immediately.

Makes 6 servings.

NOTES: Le Coze cuts the fish into 1 by 1$^1/_4$-inch (2.5 by 3cm) strips. I prefer to use whole fillets.

Equal parts of clam juice and water can be substituted for Court Bouillon in both vegetable and fish preparation.

FISH FILLETS WITH SAUTEED FENNEL AND LEMON DILL SAUCE

Unassuming as this dish may look, its taste is memorable. The fennel is just barely cooked and it has a crisp texture that contrasts perfectly with the fish. It's another brilliant creation of Frédy Girardet, whose restaurant in Crissier, Switzerland, is widely considered one of the best in the world.

2 medium fennel bulbs (1¼ pounds total, 570g), with feathery greens trimmed, cut to fit feed tube
6 tablespoons unsalted butter
1 cup (240ml) extra-virgin olive oil
1¼ teaspoons salt
Freshly ground white pepper

3 tablespoons plus 1½ teaspoons fresh dill, or 1 tablespoon plus ½ teaspoon dried dillweed
3 tablespoons fresh lemon juice
6 6-ounce (170g) sole fillets
Fresh dill for garnish (optional)

Fifteen minutes before broiling, place rack 8 inches (20cm) from heat source and preheat broiler. Line broiler pan with aluminum foil.

Thick Slicing Disc (6mm): Stand fennel in feed tube and use medium pressure to slice.

Heat 2 tablespoons each of butter and oil in 10-inch (25cm) skillet. Add fennel, 1 teaspoon of salt, and pepper and cook until tender but still crisp — about 5 minutes. Add 1½ teaspoons of fresh dill or ½ teaspoon of dried dillweed. Remove from heat and reserve.

Put lemon juice, remaining 4 tablespoons of butter, remaining dill, salt, pepper and all but 1 tablespoon of remaining oil in 1-quart (1L) saucepan and bring to simmer.

Brush both sides of fillets with remaining oil and arrange on prepared broiler pan. Broil, watching them closely, until just firm to touch. Depending on thickness, this will take 6 to 8 minutes; do not overcook.

Place fennel on platter or individual plates and top with fish. Spoon warm sauce over and garnish with fresh dill, if available.

Makes 6 servings.

NOTE: If fennel is not available, substitute an equal weight of celery and 1 teaspoon fennel seeds.

DINNER INSPIRED BY FRÉDY GIRARDET
....
Mussels in their Own Broth
Fish Fillets with Sauteed Fennel and Lemon-Dill Sauce
Green Bean and Parsnip Purée
Cauliflower, Radishes and Pea Pods with Romaine Lettuce
Fresh Lemon Custard Tart

1 cup walnuts (4 ounces, 115g)
3 medium onions (12 ounces total, 340g), peeled and cut to fit feed tube
1/4 cup (60ml) olive oil
1/2 teaspoon salt
1/2 teaspoon ground turmeric
1/2 teaspoon ground cumin
1/4 teaspoon cinnamon
4 whole boneless brook trout (2 pounds total, 910g)
1/2 to 3/4 cup (120 to 180ml) safflower oil
1 lime, scored and cut flat at bottom

This unusual and slightly exotic recipe comes from the Middle East via Chicago. I learned it from Varouj Vartanian, a native Jordanian who traded a career in chemistry for The Casbah restaurant in Chicago. He calls the dish Mashkule and features it when trout are too good to pass by at the market.

Metal Blade: Pulse to chop walnuts coarsely; remove and reserve.

French Fry Disc: Stand onions in feed tube and use medium pressure to cut. (If you do not have French Fry Disc, see page 229.)

Heat olive oil over medium heat in 1-quart (1L) saucepan and add onions. Cook gently until very soft but not brown — about 14 minutes. Remove from heat and add walnuts, salt, turmeric, cumin and cinnamon.

Onions can be refrigerated up to 4 days. Reheat gently before stuffing fish.

Rinse fish under cold running water and carefully pat dry. Heat safflower oil over medium-high heat in 10-inch (25cm) skillet. Add 2 fish and cook, turning once, until golden brown — about 5 minutes per side. Transfer to warm plate and keep warm. Add more oil to pan if necessary and cook remaining fish.

Thin (2mm) or Medium Slicing Disc (3mm): Stand lime in feed tube and use firm pressure to slice.

Fill cavity of each fish with about 1/4 cup of spiced onions and gently press closed. Garnish with sliced lime and serve with remaining onions.

Makes 4 servings.

Brook Trout with Spiced Onions

STEAMED MUSSELS IN BASIL BUTTER

When everything else seems high-priced at the fish market, mussels always come through as a fantastic bargain. Here, they're prepared simply in a Provençal style with fresh tomatoes and a touch of garlic in a basil-scented butter. I love them as a light main course or a first course.

36 medium mussels (3 pounds total, 1.4kg)
¼ cup loosely packed parsley leaves
6 large shallots (3 ounces total, 85g), peeled
1 large garlic clove, peeled
6 tablespoons unsalted butter

2 medium tomatoes (10 ounces total, 285g), peeled, seeded and quartered (to peel tomatoes, see page 217)
2 tablespoons finely snipped fresh basil or 1 teaspoon dried
2 tablespoons Cognac or brandy

Scrub mussels and remove beards. Discard any open mussels that do not close when tapped on counter. Transfer to 6-quart (6L) pot, add 1 teaspoon of salt and cover with cold water. Let soak for 30 minutes. Wash several times to remove grit, then drain well. Rinse grit from pot.

Metal Blade: Process parsley until minced; remove and reserve. Turn on machine, drop shallots and garlic through feed tube and process until minced.

In same pot used for mussels, cook shallots and garlic in 2 tablespoons of butter until soft but not brown — about 4 minutes.

Metal Blade: Add tomatoes and pulse until coarsely chopped.

Add tomatoes, mussels and basil to pot and cook, covered, over medium-high heat until shells open — about 8 minutes. Discard any that do not open.

Remove mussels with slotted spoon, shaking them to drain any liquid from shells. Transfer mussels, in their shells, to large serving platter. Add Cognac or brandy to liquid in pot and cook over high heat until reduced by half. Line strainer with 4 thicknesses of cheesecloth and strain liquid into large bowl. Rinse grit from pan. Return liquid to pan and bring to simmer. Cut remaining 4 tablespoons of butter into 4 pieces and whisk in one piece at a time; wait until each piece is incorporated before adding another. Pour over mussels and garnish with reserved parsley. Serve immediately.

Makes 4 servings.

FIRESIDE SUPPER
Steamed Mussels in Basil Butter
Navarin of Lamb with Spring Vegetables
Bell Pepper Pasta
Mixed Greens with Walnut Vinaigrette
Pear Kuchen

Choose a mixture of ingredients that will appeal to you and your guests. Plan on about 6 ounces (170g) of shellfish and several vegetable selections per person. And by all means, use parsley. You'll love its delicate look and taste.

The Tempura batter is ethereally light if it's made just before using and kept well chilled.

Large mushrooms, with two opposite sides cut flat
Zucchini, cut into feed-tube lengths
Eggplant, preferably Japanese, unpeeled and cut to fit feed tube
Yams, unpeeled and cut to fit feed tube
Daikon or Japanese radish, peeled

and cut to fit feed tube
Scallions, white ends only
Broccoli flowerets
Parsley sprigs
Large or extra large shrimp, shelled and butterflied
Sea scallops, halved horizontally
3 cups (720ml) peanut oil
2 tablespoons Oriental sesame oil

Batter
1 cup cake flour (4 ounces, 115g)
2 tablespoons cornstarch
2 teaspoons baking powder

2 large egg whites
3/4 cup (180ml) ice water
Dipping Sauce (recipe follows)

Extra Thick (8mm) or Thick Slicing Disc (6mm): Stand mushrooms in feed tube flat side down and use light pressure to slice. Stand zucchini and eggplant in feed tube and use light pressure to slice. Stand yams and daikon in feed tube and use firm pressure to slice.

Arrange rows of shellfish and vegetables on large serving platter. Cover with plastic wrap and refrigerate for 1 to 4 hours.

Heat both oils in wok or 2-quart (2L) saucepan to 400°F (205°C). As they heat, prepare batter.

Metal Blade: Process flour, cornstarch and baking powder for 2 seconds. Add egg whites and water and pulse just until flour disappears, about 4 or 5 times. There will be small lumps in batter.

Transfer to small mixing bowl and set in larger bowl filled with ice. To ensure light, crisp coating, batter must be kept cold.

When oil reaches 400°F (205°C), remove shellfish and vegetables from refrigerator. Use paper towel to blot any moisture. Divide ingredients into serving portions. Fry each portion in batches to prevent overcrowding. Fry until golden — 1 to 2 minutes — removing each ingredient as it is cooked. Skim oil to remove particles and reheat to 400°F (205°C) before frying additional batches.

Serve immediately with Dipping Sauce.

SHRIMP AND VEGETABLE TEMPURA

When I serve Tempura, I plan an informal do-it-yourself party, where guests dip and cook their own selections. Since even a five-minute wait is too long for the crisp, batter-fried ingredients, this plan really works. It's also fun and it lets the host or hostess avoid a lot of last-minute work.

<table>
<tr><td>DIPPING
SAUCE</td><td>1 cup (240ml) chicken broth
1/2 cup (120ml) cream sherry
2 tablespoons nuoc nam (see NOTE)</td><td>1 1/2 teaspoons soy sauce
1 teaspoon sugar
1/2 teaspoon ground ginger</td></tr>
</table>

Put all ingredients in 1-quart (1L) saucepan and bring to boil. Sauce can be refrigerated up to 2 weeks.

Makes about 1 1/2 cups (360ml).

NOTE: *Nuoc nam* is a Vietnamese fish sauce, available in many Oriental markets. If it is not available, substitute 1/4 teaspoon of salt.

SHELLFISH STEW

This recipe is an adaptation of Gilbert Le Coze's signature dish at Le Bernardin in Paris. He uses as many as ten different kinds of shellfish, and even includes a spiny sea urchin when it's available. It's a superb dish, both to look at and to savor. This version uses readily available American shellfish. Follow Le Coze's iron-clad rule of using only the freshest seafood, and the stew will always be delicious.

3 pounds (1.4kg) mussels, preferably small
2 cups loosely packed parsley leaves
1 large garlic clove, peeled
2 medium shallots (1 ounce total, 30g), peeled
6 tablespoons unsalted butter
3 medium tomatoes (15 ounces total, 425g), peeled, seeded and quartered (see page 217)
3/4 cup (180ml) Crème Fraîche (see Index)
Freshly ground pepper
1/2 pound (225g) sea scallops, halved horizontally
4 oysters, opened, on half-shell

Scrub mussels and remove beards. Discard any open mussels that do not close when tapped on counter. Transfer to 6-quart (6L) pot with 1 teaspoon of salt and cover with cold water. Let soak for 30 minutes, wash several times to remove grit, then drain well. Return to pot with only water that clings to them. Cover and cook over high heat just until shells open — about 6 to 7 minutes. Discard any that do not open. Remove mussels with slotted spoon, shaking them to drain liquid from shells. Divide mussels, in shell, among 4 shallow serving dishes. Cover and keep warm while finishing stew. Line strainer with 4 thicknesses of cheesecloth and strain mussel liquor into bowl; reserve. Rinse grit from pot.

Metal Blade: Process parsley until minced; remove and reserve. Turn on machine, drop garlic and shallots through feed tube and process until minced.

In same pot used for mussels, cook garlic and shallots in butter until soft but not brown — about 2 minutes.

Metal Blade: Add tomatoes and pulse until finely chopped.

Add tomatoes, Crème Fraîche, 1/2 cup (120ml) of strained mussel liquor, pepper and all but 2 tablespoons of minced parsley to pot. Bring to boil, then cook for 5 minutes, stirring occasionally. Add scallops and cook just until opaque — about 2 minutes. Use slotted spoon to divide scallops among dishes holding mussels and top each with oyster. Spoon 1 tablespoon of hot sauce over each oyster, and divide remaining sauce evenly among dishes. Garnish with remaining parsley and serve immediately.

Makes 4 servings.

24 jumbo shrimp in shells (about 1¹/₄ pounds total, 570g), unthawed if frozen

¹/₄ cup loosely packed parsley leaves

2 large garlic cloves, peeled

1 medium onion (4 ounces, 115g), peeled and quartered

2 tablespoons olive oil

1 bay leaf

Freshly ground pepper

¹/₂ cup (120ml) dry vermouth

3 tablespoons Cognac

3 large tomatoes (1 pound total, 455g), peeled, seeded and quartered (to peel tomatoes, see page 217)

1 tablespoon fresh tarragon or 1 teaspoon dried

2 teaspoons fresh chervil or ¹/₂ teaspoon dried

3 tablespoons snipped fresh chives

¹/₂ teaspoon salt

(to peel tomatoes, see page 217)

Use kitchen shears to snip shell along back of shrimp, but do not remove shell. Remove black vein under running water; pat dry.

Metal Blade: Process parsley until minced; remove and reserve. Turn on machine, drop garlic through feed tube and process until minced. Add onion and pulse to chop coarsely.

Heat oil in 10-inch (25cm) skillet. Add garlic, onion, bay leaf and pepper and cook gently, stirring often, until onion is very soft but not brown — about 10 minutes. Increase heat to medium-high and cook shrimp in 3 batches, turning once, until opaque — about 2 minutes per side; do not overcook. Transfer to platter and cook remaining shrimp. When all shrimp are cooked, add vermouth and Cognac to skillet. Cook over high heat, loosening particles from bottom of pan. Cook, uncovered, until reduced to ¹/₄ cup (60ml). Discard bay leaf.

Metal Blade: Add tomatoes in 2 batches and pulse until coarsely chopped.

Add to reduced liquid with tarragon and chervil and cook for 5 minutes. Return shrimp in shells and cook gently until heated through — about 5 minutes. Add chives, salt and reserved parsley and serve immediately.

Makes 4 servings.

SHRIMP ESCABECHE

I learned this low-calorie recipe while working with Michel Guérard in the kitchen of his famed restaurant and spa Les Sources et Les Près d'Eugénie in southwest France. The kitchen there is divided in half: one side devoted to "cuisine minceur," the other to "cuisine gourmande." The Shrimp Escabeche comes from the "cuisine minceur" side, yet it is so delicious and fresh tasting that one is hardly aware it is diet food. Guérard serves the shrimp with the shells on, which makes a stunning presentation. For easier eating, you can peel them after cooking, but leave the tail intact.

SPA DINNER INSPIRED BY MICHEL GUÉRARD

Shrimp Escabeche
Turkey Breast with Fresh Orange and Port Sauce
Onion Compote
Purée of Zucchini in their Shells
Strawberry Sherbet

SCALLOP PACKETS WITH FRESH SORREL AND TOMATO

Baking seafood in airtight foil packets is a quick and effective way to prepare it. No juices or natural flavors are lost or wasted; instead, they're incorporated into the sauce. Prepared as written here, the dish is exactly as served at Le Bernardin in Paris. Decrease the amount of butter or omit it completely for a delicious, low-calorie version.

1 tablespoon unsalted butter, melted
1 large ripe tomato (8 ounces, 225g - see NOTE), peeled, seeded and quartered (to peel tomatoes, see page 217)
42 sea scallops (2¼ pounds total, 1kg)
1 teaspoon salt

Freshly ground pepper
10 medium sorrel leaves (1 ounce total, 30g), with stems removed (see NOTE)
1½ sticks unsalted butter (6 ounces total, 170g), chilled and cut into 12 pieces

Fifteen minutes before baking, place rack in center of oven and preheat to 500°F (260°C). Cut six 15-inch (38cm) squares of heavy duty aluminum foil. Brush one side of each with melted butter. Have jelly-roll pan ready.

Metal Blade: Add tomato and pulse to chop coarsely.

Toss scallops with salt and pepper and divide them evenly among pieces of foil. Add 2 tablespoons of chopped tomato to each. Stack sorrel leaves, roll them up tightly, and cut them crosswise into ⅛-inch (3mm) strips. Divide evenly among packets. Gently toss ingredients, being careful not to tear foil. Fold up sides of foil and crimp closed to form airtight packets.

Packets can be prepared several hours in advance and refrigerated. Bring to room temperature before baking.

Place packets on jelly-roll pan and bake in preheated oven for 5 minutes. Remove from oven and open carefully, leaving sides folded up. Add 2 pieces of butter to each and put pan on top of stove over 2 burners. Cook over high heat, shaking pan occasionally, until butter melts. Invert foil packets onto individual serving plates and serve immediately.

Makes 6 servings.

Scallop Packets with Fresh Sorrel and Tomato

NOTES: If vine-ripened tomatoes are not available, substitute canned tomatoes. (I prefer Del Monte tomato wedges.) Drain and chop coarsely with metal blade. You will need $^3/_4$ cup of chopped tomato.

If sorrel is not available, substitute 10 spinach leaves and add 2 teaspoons of fresh lemon juice to each foil packet.

36 medium shrimp (1$^1/_2$ pounds total, 680g), in shells, thawed if frozen
$^1/_4$ cup loosely packed parsley leaves
1 small onion (2 ounces, 55g), peeled and quartered
1 small garlic clove, peeled
$^1/_2$ cup (120ml) Balsamic Vinaigrette
(see Index)
1 lemon, scored and cut flat at bottom
1 teaspoon dried oregano
$^1/_2$ teaspoon crushed red pepper flakes
$^3/_4$ teaspoon salt
Freshly ground pepper

LEMON SHRIMP WITH GARLIC AND OREGANO

This is a simple recipe, but it is delicious and versatile. I often use it as the anchor of a large selection of antipasti, making a feast out of an array of marinated salads.

Use kitchen shears to snip shell along back of shrimp, but do not remove shell. Rinse shrimp and remove black vein; pat dry.

Metal Blade: Process parsley until minced; remove and reserve. Turn on machine, drop onion and garlic through feed tube and process until minced.

Heat Balsamic Vinaigrette with onion and garlic in 10-inch (25cm) skillet. Add $^1/_3$ of shrimp and cook over medium-high heat, turning once, until opaque — about 5 minutes. Repeat with remaining shrimp. Let cool slightly. Peel shrimp, leaving tail intact.

All-Purpose Slicing Disc (4mm): Use firm pressure to slice lemon.

Toss shrimp, lemon, reserved parsley, oregano, pepper flakes, salt and pepper in large mixing bowl and serve immediately. Can be made 1 day in advance. Toss all ingredients except lemon, cover and refrigerate overnight, turning shrimp occasionally to coat with marinade. About 3 hours before serving, add lemon.

Serve garnished with lemon slices.

Makes 6 servings.

1. Snipping shell   2. Removing vein   3. Peeling shrimp   4. Individual dish

GRILLED MUSSELS AND GRILLED PRAWNS WITH TWO SAUCES

Summer cooking should be easy, which is why I favor a grill. Here, a small amount of mesquite wood is used to delicately flavor meaty prawns and fresh mussels. The sauces are delicious accompaniments and easily prepared in advance.

36 to 42 small mussels (1 1/2 to 2 pounds total, 680 to 910g)
18 jumbo prawns (2 1/4 pounds total, 1kg) see NOTE
Extra-virgin olive oil

Garlic Lemon Sauce (recipe follows)
Sesame Mustard Sauce (recipe follows)

Scrub mussels and remove beards. Discard any open mussels that do not close when tapped on counter. Transfer to 6-quart (6L) pot, add 1 teaspoon of salt and cover with cold water. Let soak for 30 minutes. Wash several times to remove grit, then drain mussels well.

Use kitchen shears to snip shell along back of prawns, but do not remove shell. Hold prawns under running water, and remove black vein. Pat dry and brush lightly with oil.

Place prawns about 6 inches (170g) above hot charcoal mixed with 1 1/2 cups of mesquite wood chips. Cover grill and cook for about 3 minutes. Turn prawns, add mussels and continue cooking just until done; do not overcook. Prawns will become opaque in about 6 minutes. Mussel shells will open in about 3 minutes; discard any that do not open.

Serve Garlic Lemon Sauce with mussels and Sesame Mustard Sauce with prawns.

Makes 6 servings.

NOTE: Large (16 to 18 per pound) or jumbo (12 to 14 per pound) shrimp in shells can be substituted for prawns. They will cook more quickly.

GARLIC LEMON SAUCE

Zest of 1/2 lemon, removed with zester or grater
2 large garlic cloves, peeled
2 tablespoons fresh lemon juice
1 large egg yolk

1/2 teaspoon salt
1/16 teaspoon cayenne pepper
1/2 cup (120ml) extra-virgin olive oil
1 to 3 tablespoons milk (if necessary)

Metal Blade: Put zest in work bowl and turn on machine. Drop garlic through feed tube and process until minced. Add lemon juice, egg yolk, salt and cayenne and process for 30 seconds. With machine running, slowly drizzle oil through feed tube; mixture will thicken to the consistency of thin mayonnaise. If it is too thick, add milk, 1 tablespoon at a time. Adjust seasoning.

Sauce can be refrigerated up to one week.

Makes 2/3 cup (160ml).

¹/₃ cup (80ml) Dijon mustard
2 tablespoons honey
2 tablespoons sesame tahini
2 teaspoons white-wine vinegar

2 teaspoons Oriental sesame oil
¹/₂ teaspoon salt
1 large egg yolk
¹/₂ cup (120ml) safflower oil

Metal Blade: Process mustard, honey, tahini, vinegar, sesame oil, salt and egg yolk for 30 seconds. With machine running, slowly drizzle oil through feed tube. Once mixture thickens to consistency of mayonnaise, oil can be added more quickly.

Sauce can be refrigerated up to one week.

Makes about 1 cup (240ml).

If you do not have a Julienne Disc

★ Use this "double-slicing" technique. Cut ingredient into largest size that fits feed tube. Slice with 2 or 3 mm Slicing Disc. Stack slices perpendicular to Slicing Disc, fitting them in snugly to hold. Slice again, to make matchstick strips. Other slicing discs can be used, depending on the thickness you prefer.

If you do not have a French Fry Disc

★ The French Fry Disc is used to "dice" some ingredients, and to cut others into long strips.

To "dice" onions or tomatoes, chop them coarsely in small batches with the Metal Blade, or cut them with a knife on a cutting board. Tomatoes should be peeled and seeded first. To "dice" avocados, cut them with a knife into ¹/₄-inch (6mm) cubes.

To cut long strips of apples, carrots, potatoes or zucchini, "double-slice" them as follows: Cut into largest size that fits feed tube. Slice with All-Purpose (4mm) or Thick (6mm) Slicing Disc. Stack slices perpendicular to slicing disc, fitting them in snugly to hold. Slice again, to make matchstick strips. You can also use a knife on a cutting board.

SHELLFISH BARBECUE
Vegetable Basket with
Fresh Herb Dipping Sauce
Dill Cheese Crisps
Grilled Prawns and
Mussels with Two Sauces
Vegetable Packets with
Tarragon Butter
Frozen Chocolate
Supremes

Lamb Medallions with Sherry, 197